The Citizens' Ledger

Robert C. Hockett

The Citizens' Ledger

Digitizing Our Money, Democratizing Our Finance

palgrave
macmillan

Robert C. Hockett
Cornell University
Ithaca, NY, USA

ISBN 978-3-030-99565-2 ISBN 978-3-030-99566-9 (eBook)
https://doi.org/10.1007/978-3-030-99566-9

Cover illustration: RetroClipArt/shutterstock.com

This Palgrave Macmillan imprint is published by the registered company Springer Nature Switzerland AG
The registered company address is: Gewerbestrasse 11, 6330 Cham, Switzerland

Prologue: Money Without "Middlemen"

Imagine that you wish to make a payment to a friend or a house-sitter who's looked after your home while you've been traveling, or to a retail store where you're purchasing clothing or groceries, or to a parking meter while out or a tax authority at tax time, or to firm or other productive unit in which you wish to invest. Imagine further that you're owed a refund on your recent tax payment, or are awaiting a paycheck or some public benefit, or are borrowing from a bank or community development financial institution ("CDFI") to start-up a business or grow a business you already operate.

Presently these multiple transactions will likely occur over multiple "platforms" or "networks," and will require multiple "payment media" to proceed. You might pay the house-sitter in paper currency or over Venmo, say, then use a chip card or strip card at the store, slip coins into a parking meter, and send a check to a broker or tax authority. Your tax refund, in turn, might itself come as a check or direct deposit into a bank account you maintain, your wage or salary as paper, and your loan or other investment proceeds as a cashier's check or a new account opened for you by a commercial or investment bank.

These "polyglot" means of paying and being paid complicate your life in various ways. For one thing, you must carry multiple objects around with you, and keep in mind multiple passwords and PIN numbers. For another thing, the security—and privacy—afforded by some of these payment media will differ significantly from what's offered by others. And, perhaps worst of all, in some of these cases your payments won't "clear" until some appreciable time after they "post"—"settlement" of your transactions will often be lagged, that's to say, not occurring "in real time."

But these are just the most obvious worries or inconveniences thrown up by our "Babel" of multiple parallel payment systems. In many jurisdictions, the U.S. conspicuous among them, most payments other than those in cash require the maintenance of bank transaction accounts—the accounts with which chip cards and strip cards, not to mention most payment platforms like Zelle, Venmo and PayPal, are typically associated. Yet such accounts can be difficult to maintain, particularly for those who aren't wealthy and can't afford fees of the kinds banks and payment platform companies charge us.

The result is that some 25% of the citizenry in the wealthiest country in the world, for example—the United States ("U.S.")—are "unbanked" or "underbanked." Small businesses fare little better—the "interchange" and related fees they must pay to facilitate electronic payments are prohibitive for many. That's a bit odd in a "commercial republic" like that which the U.S. purports to be, let alone any "monetary exchange economy" like that of most if not all "developed" countries. In such republics and their economies, value-transfer and-storage platforms—that is, payment and savings modalities—surely amount to essential commercial and financial infrastructures, public goods that by definition ought to be freely available to all.

Yet that is not all. Thanks to the intimate link between money and payment systems drawn out in this book, modern republics must modulate *transaction activity*—that is, "money supplies" and "money velocity"—in order to manage "price stability" and "financial stability"—that is, "inflation" and "deflation," "bubbles" and "busts." Where the payments system makes use of intermediaries—banks, payment platform companies, and the like—the authorities charged with this form of maintenance must work through "middleman" institutions—commercial banks, "dealer" banks, and the like. This brings much leakage to credit and monetary policy, diminishing its efficacy in both inflationary booms and deflationary busts. In effect, public action is hostage to private interest. For public infrastructure is captive to private toll-takers.

Now imagine a simpler, more elegant, more streamlined value-storage and -transfer architecture… Your iPhone or other "smart device" holds a digital wallet networked horizontally to all other citizens' and businesses' wallets and vertically to the republic's fiscal and/or monetary authorities—its finance ministry ("FM") and/or its central bank ("CB"). To make payments to friends, employees, businesses, tax authorities, materials suppliers, or anyone else in their personal or professional capacities, you simply credit their wallets while debiting yours. Payments to you or your business take the same form—creditings of your wallet and corresponding debitings of your payors' wallets, all "in real time."

Your wallet also serves as a value-storage device—a personal and/or professional digital "savings account." The fiscal or monetary authority might also pay interest on our wallet accounts—as central banks do now on private sector banks' "reserve accounts," and as finance ministries do on the sovereign debt instruments—treasury "bonds," "bills," and "notes"—that so many of their citizens (perhaps you yourself) purchase as safe savings vehicles. These rates then can be raised or lowered to encourage more or less saving accordingly as the republic's monetary and fiscal agencies must encourage slower spending to lower inflation or accelerated spending to counteract deflation (a.k.a. "recession" or "depression"). Et voila, leak-proof monetary policy.

But there is more. Because smart device ownership is far more universal than bank account ownership—in the U.S., for example, only 5%, not 25%, of the population is "unphoned"—the problem of the "unbanked" and "underbanked" is all but eliminated. Payment network fees paid by businesses, meanwhile, disappear. In presently "developing" countries, relatedly, a full banking and payments system can be had without trudging through the decades of slow steps the "developed" world had to traverse to establish full national "brick and mortar" banking and investment systems.

Further, communities that find that various forms of presently unremunerated "care work" contribute to aggregate wealth and hence public revenue over time—a secondary schooler tutoring primary schoolers, for example, or a young person giving home care to an older person—can incentivize more such work by remunerating it over smart devices. The "proof of work" ("POW") protocols that new digital payment technologies enable can for their part ensure real services—value adding services—are performed for these remunerations.

These same technologies also afford means of cryptographically protecting individuals' and businesses' digital identities and transactional privacy. The payment architecture can be programmed to replicate the privacy advantages now offered only by cash, while capturing the security advantages offered only by electronic networking. Digitization, in other words, can be made "all good," with no offsetting "bad with the good" disadvantages or "tradeoffs."

In effect, what we're imagining now is a *digital infrastructure* that isomorphically mirrors the underlying *credit and debit*, the *asset and liability*, structures of all modern productive commercial societies. Legally and institutionally speaking, all modern economies amount to massive social balance sheets, on which comprehensive "double-entry book-keeping" would include every public and private unit's debts and entitlements, all interlinked liability and asset structures. No actually tabulated balance sheet quite does this, of course (though we'll find that central bank records quite nearly do it), but this is nevertheless the legal, monetary, and financial structure of all commercial societies—including most of the societies of modern Africa, Asia, Europe, Oceania, and the Americas—established since the late medieval or early modern eras.

Present-day payment and value-accounting practices obscure this shared underlying structure, and in so doing enable all manner of inefficiency and rent-extraction, as multiple for-profit entities purport to offer—for a price—bits and pieces of a dismembered commercial and financial infrastructure that should be—and can be—made freely available to all. The upshot is intolerable injustice and massively scandalous waste.

It doesn't have to be this way. While our present value-accounting, value-storage, and value-transfer systems are understandable outgrowths of an earlier time when the state of technology simply didn't allow for comprehensive account-keeping across whole economies, that earlier time is now past. New modes of data-compiling, -storing, and -collating enable the construction of literal physical ledgers (in electronic digital form) that replicate the de facto ledgers that are all of our modern commercial and financial economies' fund-stocks ("savings") and fund-flows ("payments").

Something much like this compiling and tracking is done by our central banks worldwide already, for it's the only way they can fulfill their public money-management mandates not "in the dark," but transparently, with full knowledge, "in the full light of day." But what our public instrumentalities—our central banks and finance ministries—benefit by we the citizens should benefit by too. Since *they*, our public *agents*, "keep" economy-wide macro ledgers, *we*, their principals, ought to be able to *use* them—to save and to spend, to invest and be invested in, through them.

Happily, the new savings and payments technologies discussed in this book will enable just that. They will enable our savings and payments, and hence also our investment, modalities to catch up with our computing and communications modalities. That will effectively convey the productivity and efficiency gains wrought by the latter to our practices and infrastructures that make up the former.

We must act quickly, however. For the rent-taking middleman institutions that have benefitted by the old regime see the threats posed to their oligopoly by the emerging regime. They are accordingly acting quite swiftly to ensure that the public efficiencies offered by new technology remain restricted, for-profit, and thus expensive. Too many central banks, in turn, seem to be willing to listen to these interests as they now upgrade their national payments systems with the aforementioned technologies.

When you hear references to "central bank digital currencies" or "CBDC," as we're all apt to hear now, this is what's being referenced. It is the task of this book to show you both why to keep paying attention, and how to weigh-in. It's about what to demand as a citizen—a citizen of a free and productive commercial republic.

Praise for *The Citizens' Ledger*

"Computer scientists, financiers, and even some economists seem often to overlook the ways money, finance and accounting on the one hand, and money, banking, and central banks on the other hand all interact. One result is that treatments of central bank-issued digital currencies ('CBDCs') tend to lose sight of the full range of critical consequences – and opportunities! – that flow from alternative possible digital currency arrangements.

After Hockett's treatise, no such unsystematic or incomplete 'siloed' thinking will be possible. In highly accessible prose supplemented by simple intuitive diagrams, Hockett shows how the trillions of commercial and financial transactions that occur in our economies each day can be modeled as single national account books of millions of interlocking personal and institutional balance sheets – full 'Citizens' Ledgers' that digital technology is now able to replicate.

The potential this opens is far more interesting – and far more exciting – than most current discussions of CBDC appear to appreciate. As Hockett demonstrates, the future now available to us includes transactional privacy and free banking services for all households and businesses, leak-proof monetary policy for all central banks, and a transformed financial system that is once again geared toward production instead of mere speculation."

—U.S. Congressman Ro Khanna, *Professor of Economics and author of* Dignity in a Digital Age (2022) *and* Entrepreneurial Nation (2012)

"With the inclusive vision and bold energy that have become hallmarks of Robert Hockett's work, *The Citizens' Ledger: Digitizing Our Money, Democratizing Our Finance* does not disappoint. In it, Hockett challenges readers to imagine – and then operationalize – a universal public savings and payments infrastructure for people he calls American 'citizens of the contemporary commercial republic.' Fans and foes alike of digital financial technologies will revel in the breadth and sheer exhilaration of Hockett's ambitious and sweeping proposal to reimagine the US financial system, and to dare policymakers to reply to the question 'why not?'"

—Sarah Bloom Raskin, *Colin W. Brown Distinguished Professor of Law, Duke University Law School; former Deputy Secretary of the Treasury, 2013–2017; former Governor, Federal Reserve Board, 2010–2013*

"In this exciting book, the uniquely imaginative legal and financial scholar, Robert Hockett, proposes a streamlined way to make our newly electronic 'Babel' of cash payment methods far more equitable and efficient. New digital technologies make it possible, he envisions, to reduce the complexity of these payments to a single electronic wallet for every citizen. This new universal savings and payments platform, administered by the Treasury or the Federal Reserve System, would sharply reduce costs, speculative excesses, and opportunities to defraud, while also eliminating the problems of financial exclusion and the unbanked with a single stroke. Hockett comes full circle from an earlier, simpler but less opportunistic age to reduce the current digital cacophony and excess profit exploitation to a productive minimum. It's the first book of its kind, and likely to be the definitive word on its subjects."

—Jeff Madrick, New York Times *economics columnist; Editor,* Challenge *magazine; author of* Invisible Americans, Seven Bad Ideas, The Age of Greed, The End of Affluence, Taking America, *and other books*

"For far too long, our financial system and its apologists have conditioned consumers and savers to believe that banking and monetary services are best handled by private sector intermediaries alone. As America's foremost architect of democratic financial systems, Bob Hockett has given policymakers at every level of government the blueprint to bank the unbanked and streamline our savings, payments, and monetary policy infrastructures without exploiting or extracting value from people or business firms.

Instead of blindly ushering predatory fintech products and wasteful cryptocurrency exchanges into their communities, all lawmakers at every level of government in the US and abroad must read this book to learn how to democratize finance and rebuild public capital."

—Ronald Tae Sok Kim, *New York State Assemblyman for the 40th District*

"This book starts from the novel premise that 'all modern economies amount to massive social balance sheets' and draws transformative conclusions from that starting point. In so doing it gives the reader a fresh perspective to understand how all modern economies, and the financial systems attached to them, have developed. It expertly outlines how our vast networks of payment and accounting practices and institutions have evolved, but also rightly impresses upon us the urgency of developing savings and payments technologies that will now allow us to streamline, simplify, and benefit from this evolving space.

Currently, our existing institutions and protocols are failing to keep up, and more troubling, rent-taking middlemen that have benefited from the old regime are moving quickly to thwart the adoption of a framework that would ensure public efficiencies offered by new technology. This book presents a clear-eyed vision for how financial systems can evolve to reflect more just and equitable access to the public, and not just to private, profit-seeking institutions and entities that seek to keep this realm obscure. It is essential reading for anyone interested in digital currency, financial systems, monetary policy, payments regimes, and the democratization of finance."

—Amara Enyia, *Advisory Board, Public Banking Institute; and Board of Directors, Chicago Community Loan Fund*

"Breathtaking. Visionary. The ideas developed in this book unlock new frontiers for civic technical solutions to many persistent challenges."

—Michael Warner, *San Francisco, Project Manager, Multiple Central Bank Digital Currency Initiatives*

Contents

List of Figures

1

Introduction: Money, Finance, and Production in Contemporary Commercial Republics

Many of the world's citizens, Americans included, pride themselves both on their innovative cultures and the associated dynamisms of their productive economies. Many likewise celebrate their modern polities' foundings as democratic republics—*res publicae* ("public things") inclusively constituted and managed by more or less materially independent and freely associating citizens, households, and firms (*personae privata*).[1]

This modern ideal of the "commonwealth" or "good society," traceable in large measure to seventeenth-century English Oppositionist, eighteenth-century French and Scottish Enlightenment, and nineteenth-century German Romantic updatings of Renaissance Italian and Roman Republican antecedents, often travels together with two related conceptions—those of a "commercial republic" and the "exchange economy" that serves as any such republic's material substrate.[2] The structures named by these terms in turn open the door to often-puzzling or -troubling forms of hybridity in the realms of production and finance in such societies—including all contemporary commercial republics.

R. C. Hockett, *The Citizens' Ledger*,
https://doi.org/10.1007/978-3-030-99566-9_1

1.1 Money and Production, Public and Private: The Two-by-Two Matrix of Commercial Republican Economies

Key to the formation and healthy maintenance of any commercial society and associated economy are their forms of *money* and *finance*—the means by which current resources find productive deployment in the creation of future resources, or "wealth."[3] Virtually by definition in any such society and associated economy, these forms themselves will involve at least some degree of private sector project-planning and associated "private ordering."[4]

Finance being a matter of channeling today's resources to the production of tomorrow's resources, and such "channeling" in any exchange economy being at least partly a matter of contractual transfer, *financial* modalities and the forms of money they use will make at least some use of *commercial* modalities.[5] They will employ modes of payment—forms of money—through which productive units can purchase access to productive "inputs" that they do not already have—that is, finance their productive operations—in producing the "outputs" that constitute their material wealth.[6]

This reliance of monetary and financial modalities on commercial modalities in any exchange economy on the one hand, and the aforementioned "mixed" public/private character of any republic, including a commercial republic, on the other hand, confront the citizens of any such republic with a critical foundational choice. That is the choice of what roles the "public" and "private" sectors will play in *supplying* the indispensible value-transfer ("payment"), value-storage ("saving"), and other commercial and financial infrastructures used by productive units on the one hand, and what associated roles public and private should play in governing productive financial *flows* via those structures on the other hand.[7]

Should production itself be a private sector affair while financing production is made a public sector affair, for example? Should the reverse be the case? Or should *both* finance and production be mainly public or mainly private affairs?

In most modern commercial republics, citizens have more or less definitively answered, to their own satisfaction at least, the "who does production" question—at least from the late eighteenth century to the present-day: they have thus far elected to leave production primarily, though not of course solely, "in private hands." We modern republican citizens don't have extensive networks of "public sector industry" and "state-owned enterprises," for example, even though we do have many "government corporations" and "government-sponsored enterprises" ("GSEs").[8]

Where the *financing* of production is concerned, by contrast, modern commercial republics have been decidedly more ambivalent throughout their histories—and this, we shall see, is at least partly attributable to technological factors.

On the one hand, they have founded and operated national and supranational development banks—the First and Second Banks of the U.S. and the Landesbanken and Sparkassen system of Germany, for example. These helped oversee and finance national economic development in the late eighteenth and nineteenth centuries.[9] Meanwhile the U.S.'s War.

Finance Corporation ("WFC") and Reconstruction Finance Corporation ("RFC"), to note two more recent examples, presided over national war mobilization and productive revitalization during the first half of the twentieth century while the world's post-war regional development banks—the European Bank for Reconstruction and Development ("EBRD"), the World Bank ("IBRD"), the Asian Development Bank ("ADB"), the Inter-American Development Bank ("IADB"), the European Investment Bank ("EIB"), etc., of the second half of the same century—did much the same for the wider world.[10].

On the other hand, our commercial republics—especially but not solely the Anglophone ones—have also allowed nominally private sector "financial services industries" both to flourish and to grow into ever-larger parts of their GDP-measured macroeconomies, especially over the past 50 years.[11] And we frequently tell ourselves to this day that this industry is the primary driver—indeed both the coordinator and the "fuel"-supplier—of our national production processes themselves.[12]

The fact of the matter, then, is that while the modern commercial republic's productive processes both are and have always to this point been by and large privately ordered, our financial systems are and have always been *hybrid* in character. They have been mixes of combined public and private sector credit allocation on the one hand, and variably successful public credit modulation on the other hand—success and failure in turn fluctuating with changing degrees of public sector appreciation that credit allocation on the one hand, and modulation on the other, cannot ultimately be kept separate.[13]

It is this problem—that of fluctuating success and failure in the mixed public/private financing of private sector production—which we'll address, even solve, through the new savings and payment technologies addressed in this book. I aim to do that by showing how new monetary technologies give us the means to end ever-more dysfunctional financial hybridity itself, by separating our monetary and financial systems into distinct public and private sector components along lines that make good institutional sense as a matter of both democratic republican justice and commercial republican productive efficiency.

But specifying in detail what this entails requires more specificity both about the nature of our distinctly contemporary *species* of financial hybridity on the one hand, and about what susceptibilities to disease are encoded in the DNA, so to speak, of those species on the other hand.

Explicating what parts or portion of our financial systems should be made forthrightly part of "the commons" in our "commonwealths," in other words, requires that we carefully explicate what parts of it already are.[14]

1.2 Ills of Financial Hybridity—And Their Possible Money-Tech Cure

For the past 150 to 200 years, modern financial systems have operated not only as *generically* hybrid arrangements, but more specifically as public–private *franchise* arrangements.[15] At the core of our finance franchises lie sovereign publics (the "publics" of our "republics") and their money-modulators—the issuers and managers of their monetized full faith and credit, their "money"—on the one hand, and the private sector financial institutions and markets that are publicly licensed to allocate most of the resultant "credit-money" used in these republics on the other hand.[16]

The U.S. provides an instructive example. For the half-century following the mid-1860s, its public money-modulator was the Office of the Comptroller of the Currency ("OCC"), a regulator whose name is suggestive but whose role grew progressively more obscure to the public once its original mandate was transferred, in principal part, to the newly established, largely German-inspired, Federal Reserve System ("FRS," "Fed") circa 1913.[17] Since the latter date, and especially since the U.S. banking reforms of the Depression-era 1930s, the Fed has served as the American republic's primary money-modulator, while private sector financial institutions have continued to act as its primary, though not as its sole, money-allocators.[18]

Over the last decade, developments in several distinct "spaces" or "spheres" have prompted what is in effect, even if not yet in name, a broad reassessment of both American and other hybrid financial arrangements in commercial republics worldwide. One such development has been the global financial debacle of just over a decade ago, as followed by its debt- deflationary sequel—a still-lingering malady that proximately originated in American financial dysfunction and ultimately culminated in global economic devastation.[19]

These events and their extended aftermath have led some to propose elimination or curtailment of the mandate of the public member of our public–private finance franchises—"end[ing] the Fed," as one familiar cry heard in America has it[20]—or binding its hands by removing the public credit element from public credit-money through reinstating some variant of the antiquated practice of "pegging" currencies to exogenously given stocks of glittering metals.[21] The same developments have prompted others to propose elimination or curtailment of the mandate of the *private* members of our public–private finance franchise arrangements—that is, to eliminate or dramatically reduce our banking institutions' credit-disseminating role through "100% money" (also known as "narrow banking"), or, somewhat more modestly, what I will call "40% money" proposals.[22] These calls have been common not only in the U.S., but across multiple contemporary commercial republics.

A second, related development prompting a rethink of our contemporary model of public–private hybrid finance has been a growing awareness, on the part of many observers, that substantial sectors of the developed economies' citizenries not only are disproportionately harmed by finance-associated productive dysfunction, but also are denied access both to essential savings and payment infrastructures and, therefore, to the very financial systems that too often generates financial and, with it, productive breakdown in the first place.[23] This recognition, the modern manifestations of which first began to appear in the late 1980s and 1990s, has prompted calls for publicly facilitated microlending or microfinance, for an "Occupy Bank," for public banking, for strengthened Community Reinvestment Acts and cognate legislation, and for sundry forms of publicly facilitated financial inclusion or "banking [of] the poor."[24] Although proponents do not always seem fully cognizant of it, these proposals link up quite intimately with the first class of proposals via an underappreciated yet quite consequential common denominator—the role that widening wealth and income inequality plays in underwriting both commercial-cum-financial exclusion *and* financial-cum-macroeconomic fragility.[25]

Finally, a third development prompting a rethink of our hybrid contemporary forms of public–private finance has been the spread of the new technologies of trade and payment—in effect, new commercial infrastructures—that are the subject of this book.[26] These have led some to prognosticate, in some cases breathlessly, that sovereign currencies are destined to be pushed aside and replaced by privately issued cryptocurrencies, digital assets, and other forms or outgrowths of "fintech."[27] Advocates of this crypto-utopian (I will call it "cryptopian") persuasion sometimes sound rather like "metalists" of the sort mentioned above, inasmuch as they tout cryptocurrencies' contrived scarcity as a characteristic that renders them something like twenty-first-century "digital gold."[28]

Other, in my view more careful, observers also see promise in blockchain, other distributed ledger ("DLT"), and cognate computing and coding technologies of the kind that now underwrite crypto-assets, but see promise of a much different sort.[29] They see the prospect of a safer, faster, and more secure value-storage and -transfer system—a payments system that, depending on who deploys and administers it, can make for more just and efficient central banking and finance too.[30]

1.3 Digitized Citizen Ledger Finance as Our Newly Available Cure

As previously noted, this book will show how to end our dysfunctional forms of financial hybridity and address the aforementioned "what part of our commonwealth's financial system should be part of the commons" question by developing and substantiating the case for the latter view—the view that sees qualified promise in public deployment of digital technology in the realms of both commerce and finance.[31] Just as importantly, and in the same cause, I make a new case for the "pro-public" camps in respect of the other two recent developments just noted—critique of the private financier's role in our commercial republics' hybrid financial systems, and advocacy of more unambiguously *public* forms of banking and finance in our productive republics.[32]

The book will do all of this with a single far-reaching proposal that finds its most intuitively tractable schematic expression on both the asset and the liability sides of present-day central bank and national treasury balance sheets—effectively our public ledgers, or what I'll call "Citizens' Ledgers." And I'll make my case on grounds of both political justice and productive efficiency on the one hand, and the "developed" world's shared commercial and financial history on the other—a history that manifests a distinct teleological trajectory.[33]

The proposal, which I call digitized "Citizen-Ledger Finance," is in a way simple and long overdue, even while bearing many attractively transformative ramifications that appear to have escaped notice till now. It is that our republics' monetary and fiscal authorities—our central banks and finance ministries—cease conducting their money-modulating and implicit capital-allocating operations primarily *indirectly*, via the media of private sector bank reserve accounts, associated private sector bank and capital market lending, and central bank open market operations in generic sovereign debt securities on private sector financial markets, and instead do so *directly*—by (a) channeling digitally monetized public full faith and credit primarily through both new and existing *public investment institutions* rather than mainly through allocatively unsupervised private sector depository institutions and "shadow banks" as they do now, on the asset side of the balance sheet; and (b) new national payments platforms and associated systems of what I call digital Citizen and Resident Wallets, on the liability side of the digital balance sheet.[34]

The public investment institutions, all species of which I have discussed elsewhere,[35] will channel digitized finance capital primarily to productive and socially desirable infrastructural and productive primary goods and service market investments, not to speculative secondary and tertiary securities and derivative market churn.[36] They will thereby take the central banks and finance ministries out of the business of financing or otherwise abetting mere betting in securities and derivative markets, and move them instead into the publicly critical work, essential in any commercial republic or exchange economy where productive units engage in private ordering, of financing inclusively productive activity and public goods provision on the asset side of the public balance sheet.

The corresponding digital Citizen and Resident Wallets on the liability side of the balance sheet will for their part be dividend-yielding or interest-bearing, much as are present-day private sector bank reserve accounts held with central banks and individual demand deposits held at depository institutions or money market funds. But now the returns will effectively convey stakes in our republics' productive accumulation—their sustainable "economic growth"—to the citizenries and business enterprises operating in salutary sectors of the "real" economy, rather than rents paid to publicly privileged, privately owned speculative financial institutions.

Returns on Citizen and Resident Wallets will be raiseable when it proves necessary, during bubbles or unsustainable booms, collectively to scale back aggregate credit-money generation and associated spending.[37] They will likewise be lowerable, even to negative rates or their functional ("helicopter money") equivalent, when it proves necessary to boost credit generation or debt-free spending during busts or recessions.[38]

Citizen and Resident Wallets in this sense will lend themselves— pun only partly intended—to digital "QE for the People" and central bank "helicopter drops" directly to citizens and their productive enterprises, rather than to commercial banks and other favored financial institutions, during times of acute financial or economic distress calling for extraordinary expansion measures like those pioneered by the Bank of Japan ("BOJ"), the U.S. Fed, and the European Central Bank ("ECB") earlier in the present century.[39] This will in turn make for far more direct— and, I shall argue, more inclusive and distributively just—monetary and even fiscal policy than do present arrangements. It will also make for much greater and more equitable productive, commercial, and financial participation on the part of our citizenries, as well as a fit use for new fintech technologies as these now develop and proliferate.[40]

In effect, then, what I propose is to reclaim those public utility functions that our hybrid finance franchise arrangements now outsource to private sector franchisee institutions, and to return them "in house" to our sovereign republican franchisor institutions.[41]

There will still be, of course, privately accumulated wealth, privately offered financial services for wealth-accumulators, and private sector investments of many a familiar kind. But there will no longer be indefinitely extended, monetized public full faith and credit flowing (or hemorrhaging) toward artfully inflated secondary and tertiary financial and derivatives markets as our present arrangements enable and, all too often, all but assure.[42] Instead digitized public full faith and credit will flow only toward primary markets and such secondary or tertiary markets—like those for home mortgage, higher education, small business, family farm, and public utility loans—as legitimately require, for reasons sounding in justice or systemic market failure, sovereign assistance.[43]

Private investors will likely increase their primary market investment activity, as distinguished from secondary and tertiary market speculative activity, as well under the new digital arrangements designed in this book's pages. That will be thanks to the impetus—and the collectively underwritten stability—that sustained public investment in those primary and other markets affords: an impetus and stability whose absence at present denies, in classic "market failure" fashion, productive investment opportunities to yield-requiring "patient capital."[44]

Meanwhile, secondary and tertiary markets, which with public credit-money are now larger by orders of magnitude than any bona fide liquidity or hedging need ever could justify, will become mainly private affairs—and much smaller on that account.[45] Indeed, they will become what they have long falsely claimed that they are—sites of "one-to-one" credit-*intermediation* rather than "one-to-many" credit-*multiplication* and "none- to-many" credit-*generation.*[46]

And while fintech is not strictly *necessary* to make all of this possible—indeed the U.S., for example, could, and probably should, have put in place some rudimentary version of Citizen Ledger Finance during the New Deal if not indeed earlier, when Fedwire was introduced back in 1918[47]—it certainly makes things both easier and more urgent today than they would have looked yesterday. That is particularly so now, as central banks worldwide look to upgrade their national payments infrastructures even while private sector financial conglomerates look to commandeer crypto and fintech development to their own, hardly pro bono purposes.[48]

The book's full proposal and justifying argument proceed as follows. Chapter 2 first fixes a few critical terms of art and the relations among the things these terms name. This is to aid understanding of the claims, arguments, and proposals the book makes—claims that implicate fields that anyone can understand once those fields' "economese" and "financialese" jargons are rendered intelligible.

Chapter 3 then briefly rehearses the constitutive elements and transactional relations—the agents and structure and "flows"—of that hybrid franchise arrangement which now characterizes most contemporary financial systems.[49] It describes how the flows of credit-money throughout our financial systems are essentially flows of monetized public full faith and credit from central banks, through private sector banks, financial markets, and "shadow banks," to primarily speculative borrowers.[50] It also reminds readers of why this form of credit-generation and –dissemination is far more unproductive and indeed even destructive than mere "intermediation" would be.

Chapter 4 then briefly recounts the political, economic, and monetary circumstances that prompted and partly justified public/private financial hybridity when our combined money and payments, banking, and financial systems were first instituted, ad hoc and in stages, over a century ago.[51] This is important not just for reasons of contextualization and associated intelligibility, but also in order to show how the logic of recent financial and monetary history has been carrying us toward the digitized Citizen Ledger Finance that I advocate all along.

Chapter 5 then lays out the ways in which matters have changed since the first days of our contemporary hybrid financial arrangements— ways that now render the full franchise arrangement no longer necessary or, it now seems, even tenable. In effect, it verifies in the present the teleology that Chapter 4 finds in the past.

Chapter 6 commences the process of mapping my digitized public "finance-reclamation" proposal—again, digital "Citizen Ledger Finance"— in detail, addressing at each stage what failures in the present arrangement the proposed new arrangement will rectify.[52] In so doing it traces the ramifications of my proposed digital changes throughout the financial system, as well as its implications for familiar but no longer sensible distinctions we draw between public fiscal and monetary operations.

Chapter 7 maps out specific logistics in detail, and highlights the senses in which digitized Citizen Ledger Finance again can be seen as an end-state toward which our contemporary commercial, monetary, and financial evolution across the "developed" world has been trending or groping for at least a century and a half, if not longer.[53]

In effect, I show, we are now reaching a stage of development at which consolidated "public ledger finance," which is inherently more stably productive and equitable but for centuries was less feasible than "token finance" once societies grew too large and far-flung to keep plenary citizen "account books," is once again possible. This is the real promise of digital fintech—the promise of consolidating money, payments, and finance into something that is publicly guided, productive, and sustainable again.

Chapter 8 makes clear how new digital technologies make both implementation and operation of Citizen Ledger Finance both much easier and more necessary than would otherwise have been the case, even while they are not, strictly speaking, necessary to do what I believe now needs doing. In this connection it also discusses specific technical options for the Democratic Digitization component of digitized Citizen Ledger Finance, including the options now being explored by forward-looking central banks worldwide.

Chapter 9 addresses anticipated objections and alternatives to digitized Citizen Ledger Finance, demonstrating along the way the superiority of what I here advocate to competing suggestions that I suspect likely critics will favor.[54] I then conclude and look forward.

Notes

1. *Cf.* ROBERT HOCKETT, A REPUBLIC OF OWNERS (forthcoming Yale University Press, 2022). Also Robert Hockett, *The Capital Commons* (Cornell Law Sch., Research Paper No. 8-20-2020), available at https://scholarship.law.cornell.edu/cgi/viewcontent.cgi?article=1127&context=clsops_papers https://scholarship.law.cornell.edu/cgi/viewcontent.cgi?article=1127&context=clsops_pape; and Robert Hockett, *The Wealth of Our Commonwealth* (Cornell Law Sch., Research Paper No. 9-20-2020), https://papers.ssrn.com/sol3/papers.cfm?abstract_id=3808790.
2. *Id. See also* Robert Hockett, *A Jeffersonian Republic Through Hamiltonian Means: Values, Constraints, and Finance in an American 'Ownership Society'*,

79 S. Cal. L. Rev. 45 (2006) [hereinafter *Jeffersonian Republic*]; Robert Hockett, *Materializing Citizenship: Finance in a Producers' Republic*, 63 EMORY L. J. 55 (2014) [hereinafter *Materializing Citizenship*]; and Robert Hockett, *Pre-liberal Autonomy & Post-liberal Finance*, 77 L. & Contemp. Prob. 105, 126 (2014) [hereinafter *Pre-liberal Autonomy*].

3. *See* sources cited *id*. *See also* Robert Hockett, *Rousseauvian Money* (Cornell Law Sch., Research Paper No. 18-48), https://papers.ssrn.com/sol3/papers.cfm?abstract_id=3278408 [hereinafter *Rousseauvian Money*]; and Robert Hockett & Aaron James, Money from Nothing (2020).
4. *See id*.
5. *Id. See also* Robert Hockett, *The Democratic Digital Dollar: A Digital Savings and Payment Payments Platform for Fully Inclusive State, Local, and National Money and Banking Systems*, 10 Harv. Bus. L. Rev. 1, 2 (2020) ("Because a money is simply what counts for purposes of accounting, accumulating, and transferring value within a given value-storage and -payments system,1 supplying a universally accessible architecture of the kind here designed is equivalent to supplying a universal (1) currency, (2) trade and payments, and (3) retail banking platform to all who participate.").
6. *Id.*
7. *Id.*
8. *See infra*, Chapters 3 and 4.
9. *Id.*
10. *Id.*
11. *Id.*
12. *Id.*
13. *See infra*, Chapter 3. The modulation versus allocation distinction, and the ultimate practical inseparability of the two, is introduced in Robert Hockett, *A Fixer-Upper for Finance*, 87 Wash. U. L. Rev. 1213 (2010) [hereinafter *Fixer-Upper*]. It also figures prominently in the work cited *infra*, note 18.
14. For more on the notions of "commons," "commonwealths," "republics," and "commercial republics," see Hockett, sources cited *supra*, notes 1, 2, and 3.
15. *See* Robert Hockett, *Finance Without Financiers in* Democratizing Finance 5–6 (Erik Olin Wright ed., Verso Press, 2022 [2015]) [hereinafter *Finance without Financiers*]; Robert C. Hockett & Saule T. Omarova, *The Finance Franchise*, 102 Cornell L. Rev. 1143, 1147 (2017); *see also infra* Chapter 3.
16. *Finance Without Financiers*, *id.*, at 9–11. For more on money, credit-money, modulation, and allocation *see supra*, note 13, and *infra* Chapters 3–6.
17. *See* Robert C. Hockett, *Money's Past Is Fintech's Future: Wildcat Crypto, the Digital Dollar, and Citizen Central Banking*, 2 Stanford J. Blockchain L. & Pol'y 1, 8 (2019) [hereinafter *Money's Past*] ("The Federal Reserve Act ('FRA') of 1913 established the Fed that we all know today, and transferred de facto and de jure administration of the national money supply from the Comptroller to this new entity.").

18. *See, e.g.,* ROBERT HOCKETT, FINANCING *the* GREEN NEW DEAL: A PLAN of ACTION AND RENEWAL (Palgrave Economics 2020) (discussing the modulatory and allocative tasks); *Fixer-Upper, supra* note 13 at 142 (introducing the idea of financial "regulation as modulation"); Robert Hockett, *The Macroprudential Turn: From Institutional 'Safety and Soundness' to Systemic 'Financial Stability' in Financial Supervision,* 9 VA. L. & BUS. REV. 201, 229 (2014) [hereinafter *Macroprudential Turn*] (notig that the reason the central bank is suited to regulate finance macroprudentially is because the central authority already is a money-modulator and that money underlies finance).
19. *See, e.g., Bretton Woods 1.0, supra* note 4, at 452 ("Scarce wonder, then, that the IMF reported, in 2009, the first worldwide economic contraction since the 1940s. Was the Fed asleep at the switch?"); *Fixer-Upper, supra* note 4, at 1218 (discussing the real estate crash of 2008 as an event that caused both an American and global financial downturn).
20. *See, e.g.,* RON PAUL, END THE FED 141 (2009) ("The Federal Reserve should be abolished because it is immoral, unconstitutional, impractical, promotes bad economics, and undermines liberty.").
21. *Compare* DAVID A. STOCKMAN, THE GREAT DEFORMATION: THE CORRUPTION OF CAPITALISM in AMERICA 706–712 (2013) (setting out thirteen different way in which the Fed and its policies could be reformed), and JAMES RICKARDS, CURRENCY WARS: THE MAKING OF THE NEXT GLOBAL CRISIS 255–258 (2012) (explaining various ways that the Fed's policies can be improved to have a better currency) with Robert C. Hockett, *Don't Catch His Eye,* SALON (April 4, 2013, 9:08 PM), https://www.salon.com/2013/04/04/don%E2%80%99t_catch_his_eye_david_stockman%E2%80%99s_alien_abduction_partner/ [https://perma.cc/VX8N-KANQ] (concluding that the solution is not to restrict the Fed, but rather to exercise good judgment ourselves).
22. For more on these proposals, *see infra* Chapter 7.
23. *See, e.g.,* Michael S. Barr & Rebecca M. Blank, *Savings, Assets, and Banking among Low-Income Households: Introduction and Overview,* in INSUFFICIENT FUNDS 1–22, 3 (Rebecca M. Blank and Michael S. Barr eds., 2009) (explaining the concept of financial inclusion in including financial services for the poor); ELLEN BROWN, THE PUBLIC BANK SOLUTION: FROM AUSTERITY TO PROSPERITY 397 (2013) [hereinafter PUBLIC BANK SOLUTION] (explains the public banking solutions at the federal level); ELLEN BROWN, WEB OF DEBT 342 (2012) [hereinafter WEB OF DEBT] (citing community banking as an example of public banking); BUILDING INCLUSIVE FINANCIAL SYSTEMS: A FRAMEWORK FOR FINANCIAL ACCESS (Michael S. Barr et al., eds. 2007) [hereinafter BUILDING INCLUSIVE FINANCIAL SYSTEMS] (discussing the current state of microfinance and ideas to increase access to financial services); ORGANIZING ACCESS TO CAPITAL: ADVOCACY AND THE DEMOCRATIZATION OF FINANCIAL INSTITUTIONS 10–13 (Gregory D. Squires ed., 2003) (detailing the benefits of the

Community Reinvestment Act as a reason for strengthening it); JULIA ANN PARZEN & MICHAEL HALL KIESCHNICK, CREDIT WHERE IT'S DUE: DEVELOPMENT BANKING FOR COMMUNITIES (1992) (discussing development banks and their role in expanding financial access); MICHAEL SHERRADEN, ASSETS AND THE POOR: NEW AMERICAN WELFARE POLICY 305–308 (1991) (explaining policy innovations that can result in greater asset building for the poor); MICHAEL SHERRADEN, *Asset-Building Policy and Programs for the Poor*, in ASSETS FOR THE POOR: THE BENEFITS OF SPREADING ASSET OWNERSHIP 302 (Thomas M. Shapiro & Edward N. Wolff eds., 2001) (discussing how the poor are unlikely to benefit from asset-based policies due to lack of participation and highly regressive tax benefits); LISA SERVON, THE UNBANKING OF AMERICA: HOW THE NEW MIDDLE CLASS SURVIVES 170 (2017) (arguing for more government involvement in the financial sector, and in banking, focus the banks on serving the public); MICHAEL A. STEGMAN, SAVINGS FOR THE POOR: THE HIDDEN BENEFITS OF ELECTRONIC BANKING (1999) (arguing electronic banking will expand financial access to the poor); MUHAMMAD YUNUS, A WORLD OF THREE ZEROS: THE NEW ECONOMICS OF ZERO POVERTY, ZERO UNEMPLOYMENT, and ZERO NET CARBON EMISSIONS 248 (2018) (explaining the creation and concept of social business funds to help the public); Michael S. Barr, *Banking the Poor*, 21 YALE J. REG. 121, 128 (2004) (explaining the importance of strengthening the community reinvestment act). For sympathetic but sober critiques, *see Pre-Liberal Autonomy*, supra note 2 at 126 (outlining the importance of public community reinvestment alternatives, among them microlending); *Materializing Citizenship*, supra note 2 at 68 ("Small-scale community reinvestment, development banking, and microlending, as well as reenlisting the Postal Service as a savings outlet for the financially humble, are all very good ideas—particularly the latter, in my view"). On the Occupy Money Cooperative, of which the author is a founding Board Member, *see The Occupy Money Card*, POPULAR RESISTANCE.ORG (July 22, 2013), https://popularresistance.org/the-occupy-card/ [https://perma.cc/XUR3-WHKS] (calling for using the occupy card to pay, and each transaction being a form of protest with every purchase against the financial institutions); *see also* Quentin Fottrell, *Is Occupy Debit Card Bad for the 99%?*, MARKETWATCH (October 8, 2013, 9:29 AM), https://www.marketwatch.com/story/is-occupy-debit-card-bad-for-the-99-2013-10-02 [https://perma.cc/HXL4-A8ZZ] (examining the consequences of the occupy card movement and its effects on financial markets).

24. *See, e.g.*, Margot Adler, *Occupy Groups Reimagine the Bank*, NPR (March 27, 2002), https://www.npr.org/2012/03/27/149443425/alternative-banking-groups-aid-occupy [https://perma.cc/CW5J-NFVF] (explaining the Occupy Bank Working Group's hopes of a democratic or national bank to better serve the underbanked community); Eillie Anzilotti, *The One Strategy*

That Could Finance the Whole Green New Deal, FAST COMPANY (June 26, 2019), https://www.fastcompany.com/90364616/public-banking-can-finance-the-green-new-deal [https://perma.cc/GVN5-VZNV] (discussing the rise of the public banking idea, the operation of public banks, and how they can aid in the Green New Deal); Marguerite S. Robinson, *The Microfinance Revolution: Sustainable Finance for the Poor*, THE WORLD BANK (2001), http://documents.worldbank.org/curated/en/226941468049448875/sustainable-finance-for-the-poor [https://perma.cc/YF8Z-YU9Z] (discussing the need for and benefits of microfinance).

25. *See* Robert Hockett, *Income Inequality and Financial Fragility*, 77 VANDERBILT L. REV. *EN BANC* 119, 120 (2018) (showing how significant wealth and income inequality is linked to market fragility); Robert Hockett & Daniel Dillon, *Income Inequality and Market Fragility: Some Empirics in the Political Economy of Finance*, Parts 1 & 2, 63 CHALLANGE 1 (2019), available at https://papers.ssrn.com/sol3/papers.cfm?abstract_id=2204710.
26. *See infra* Chapter 7. For a comprehensive overview, as attentive to perils as to opportunities, *see Finance Without Financiers*, *supra* note 15, at 25 (discussing new technologies in the modern shadow banking markets).
27. These claims are now far too numerous to cite comprehensively, and grow increasingly difficult to read without laughter, though I engage with them *below*. For a few recent examples typical of the genre, *see*, *e.g.*, Frank Holmes, *Bitcoin Could Replace Cash in 10 Years*, BUS. INSIDER (May 1, 2018, 6:44 PM), https://www.businessinsider.com/bitcoin-might-replace-cash-10-years-2018-5 (discussing the maturation and growth of digital currency and claiming cryptocurrency is a contender to replace cash in the future); Paul Schrodt, *Cryptocurrency Will Replace National Currencies by 2030, According to This Futurist*, MONEY (March 1, 2018), http://time.com/money/5178814/the-future-of-cryptocurrency/ [https://perma.cc/UF4N-FEA5] (explaining that cryptocurrencies are positioned to replace fiat currencies in the next 10 years); Aman Swami, *Cryptocurrency Will Replace Fiat Currency in the Future Says Famous Venture Capitalist*, DOLLAR DESTRUCTION (May 19, 2018), https://dollardestruction.com/5441/ [https://perma.cc/T5EP-C9F8] (discussing Tim Draper's view that cryptocurrency will replace fiat currencies completely).
28. *See, e.g.*, NATHANIEL POPPER, DIGITAL GOLD: BITCOIN AND THE INSIDE STORY OF THE MISFITS AND MILLIONAIRES TRYING TO REINVENT MONEY X (2015) (stating that in designing bitcoin, the "Cypherpunks" decided it should be scarce, a characteristic of successful coinage).
29. *See Money's Past*, *supra* note 3, at 10.

30. *See infra* Chapter 7, Section B; *see also Money's Past, supra* note 3, at 10; Robert Hockett, *Betting on Betacoin*, FORBES (December 17, 2017, 5:59 PM) https://www.forbes.com/sites/rhockett/2017/12/17/betting-on-beta-coin/#1661e5124670 [https://perma.cc/D456-LA4P] [hereinafter *Betting on Betacoin*].
31. My earlier, more tentative endorsements include, *e.g.*, *Finance without Financiers, supra* note 15, at 28–29 (discussing the Fed's relationship to repo technologies); *Money's Past, supra* note 3, at 1–2 (discussing growing public interest in cryptocurrencies); *Betting on Betacoin, supra* note 17.
32. In *Finance Without Financiers, supra* note 15, the prospect remained open that the public-private franchise arrangement could remain viable if the franchisor and its designated agents—in particular the Congress, the White House, the Fed and the Treasury—could remain mindful of the franchisor's critical role in the division of labor. *Finance without Financiers*, at 14–19. I still believe this, but am now more pessimistic about the likelihood of continuous cognizance, across differing political eras, of that that role. As I argue below, I think the proposal that I make here will effectively "institutionalize" that cognizance in a manner that renders it more robust and enduring.
33. *See infra* Chapters 6 and 7 (referencing Citizen Ledger Finance-related proposals).
34. There is some overlap between my proposal and (a) my more limited "Inclusive Value Ledger" legislation now proposed in the State of New York; (b) those of a number of central banks worldwide, discussed infra, Chapter 8; and (c) a number of friends and colleagues with whom I have discussed these and related matters for some five or six years now. *See, e.g.*, Robert Hockett, *The New York Inclusive Value Ledger: A Peer-to-Peer Savings and Payments Platform for an All-Embracing and Dynamic State Economy* (white paper, 2019) https://ronkimnewyork.com/downloads/The-New-York-Inclusive-Value-Ledger-Sept-2019.pdf (last visited February 7, 2022); JONATHAN MCMILLAN, THE END OF BANKING 159–161 (2014) (describing how ending private banking would lead to redefining the public sector's role in the financial system, particularly with respect to digital money); Morgan Ricks, John Crawford, & Lev Menand, *A Public Option for Bank Accounts (or Central Banking for All)* (Vanderbilt Law Research Paper 18–33, 2018), https://papers.ssrn.com/sol3/papers.cfm?abstract_id=3192162; David Andolfatto, *Fedcoin: On the Desirability of a Government Cryptocurrency*, MACROMANIA (February 3, 2015), http://andolfatto.blogspot.com/2015/02/fedcoin-on-desirability-of-government.html [https://perma.cc/4P2W-W6P2] (addressing Koning's proposal and proposing a "Fedwire for All," which would allow for any digital cash users to access closed centralized ledgers);

Central Banks Should Consider Offering Accounts to Everyone, ECONOMIST (May 26, 2018), https://www.economist.com/finance-and-economics/2018/05/26/central-banks-should-consider-offering-accounts-to-everyone (arguing that accounts with central banks should be widely-available); Nicholas Gruen, *Central Banking for All: A Modest Proposal for Radical Change*, NESTA, 6–8 (March 17, 2014), https://www.nesta.org.uk/report/central-banking-for-all-a-modest-case-for-radical-reform/ [https://perma.cc/Q6BH-5MUD] (supporting retail branches for central banking services and connecting government- sponsored banking accounts to more bank payment systems); J.P. Koning, *Fedcoin*, MONEYNESS (October 19, 2014), http://jpkoning.blogspot.com/2014/10/fedcoin.html [https://perma.cc/Q82Y-EX32] (advocating for the creation of "Fedcoin" and allowing users to remain anonymous by using accounting benefits available through the Fed); Dirk Niepelt, *Reserves for Everyone—Towards a New Monetary Regime?*, VOX, CEPR POLICY PORTAL (January 21, 2015), https://voxeu.org/article/keep-cash-let-public-hold-central-bank-reserves [https://perma.cc/W233-4RL5] (arguing that the public should have access to central bank accounts but that cash should not be phased out); Robert Sams, *Which Fedcoin?*, CRYPTONOMICS (February 5, 2015), https://cryptonomics.org/2015/02/05/which-fedcoin/ [https://perma.cc/QSY2-W52L] (analyzing Koning's and Andolfatto's arguments while also questioning why accounts with the Federal Reserve do not exist). More on these proposals *infra*, Chapter 9.

35. *See, e.g.*, sources cited *supra* note 4 (listing some of the author's scholarship on public investment institutions).
36. By "primary" market I mean the market for funds used to finance non-financial production. By "secondary" market I mean the market for re-sale of claims generated by primary market financing. And by "tertiary" market I mean the market for derivative claims referencing—that is, "bets" placed upon secondary market price movements among—claims traded on secondary markets. See infra, Chapter 2; and Hockett, *Wealth of Our Commonwealth*, *supra* note 1.
37. *See* Koning, *supra* note 21; Andolfatto, *supra* note 21; Sams, *supra* note 21; Ricks, Crawford, & Menand, *supra* note 21, at 22–23 (discussing how central banks could choose to raise rates when necessary).
38. These are in my view critically important features of the plan, for reasons sounding in the modulatory and allocative tasks mentioned in *supra* note 21. *See id*.
39. *See* Timothy A. Canova, *The Role of Central Banks in Global Austerity*, 22 IND. J. GLOBAL LEGAL STUD. 665, 689–693 (2015) (advancing the view that the Fed's approach to quantitative easing, which favored Wall Street financial institutions over Main Street businesses, was inadequate at bolstering broad sections of the economy after the 2008 financial crisis).

40. More on these features, too, *infra* Chapters 6 and 7 (addressing "Citizen Ledger Finance" and how it will both benefit new fintech and promote financial inclusion).
41. The importance of these matters is discussed thoroughly *infra* Chapters 3–7. They are also my primary concerns in, *e.g.*, *Finance without Financiers*, *supra* note 1; FINANCING THE GREEN NEW DEAL, *supra* note 18.
42. *Infra* Chapters 6 and 7.
43. *Id.* On some of those public secondary and tertiary market-making activities, *see, e.g.*, Robert Hockett, *Open Labor Market Operations*, 62 CHALLANGE 113, 121 (2019) [hereinafter *Open Labor*]; Robert Hockett, *Republican Home-Owning*, FEDERAL RESERVE BANK OF ST. LOUIS 15–16 (2018), https://www.stlouisfed.org/~/media/files/pdfs/hfs/assets/2018/tipping-points/hockett_tipping_points_paper_2018_12.pdf?la=en[https://perma.cc/SV42-E7RW] [hereinafter *Republican Home-Owning*] (discussing Fannie Mae's involvement in secondary market in mortgage instruments); *Jeffersonian Republic*, supra note 2 at 135–137 (addressing Fannie Mae's involvement in secondary market-making).
44. More on this impetus *infra* Chapter 6. *See also* Hockett, FINANCING THE GREEN NEW DEAL, *supra* note 18.
45. More on this, too, *infra* Chapter 6. *See also* FINANCING THE GREEN NEW DEAL, *supra* note 18; *Finance without Financiers*, *supra* note 15, at 41 (discussing how, in secondary markets, "endogenously generated credit-money can recursively drive prices to dangerous, crash-prone heights"); and Hockett, sources cited *supra*, note 1.
46. These terms stem from the work cited supra, note 1, and are reprised infra, Chapter 3.
47. More on Fedwire and its significance infra, Chapters 6 and 7.
48. As more fully discussed *infra* Chapters 6 and 7; *see also, supra* nn. 3, 4, and 17 (discussing developments in technology and fintech, and both U.S. and global financial architecture affecting economic development).
49. *See, e.g.*, *Finance Without Financiers*, *supra* note 15 (explaining how financial flows stem from public accommodation and monetization of privately originated loans). Also Hockett, *Capital Commons*, supra note 1; and Hockett, *Wealth of Our Commonwealth*, *supra* note 1
50. *Finance Without Financiers*, *supra* note 15, at 12–13 (explaining how financial flows stem from public accommodation and monetization of privately originated loans). Also Hockett, *Capital Commons*, supra note 1; and Hockett, *Wealth of Our Commonwealth*, *supra* note 1.
51. *See Finance Without Financiers*, *supra* note 15, at 1149 (outlining how the hybrid public-private franchise debunks a standard paradigm and the new interpretation redefines the dynamics of the financial system). Also Hockett, *Capital Commons*, *supra* note 1; and Hockett, *Wealth of Our Commonwealth*, *supra* note 1.

52. *See* FINANCING THE GREEN NEW DEAL (elaborating the NIC proposal), *supra* note 18. See also Robert Hockett, *An FSOC for Continuous National Development: The National Reconstruction and Development Council*, 10 MICH. BUS. & ENTERPRENURIAL L. REV. 1 (2020); and Robert Hockett, *The National Reconstruction and Continuous Development Act of 2021* (Cornell Rsrch Paper No.), https://papers.ssrn.com/sol3/papers.cfm?abstract_id=3775616.
53. *Money's Past*, *supra* note 3 (detailing the financial evolution towards a digital dollar).
54. *Id.* at 11 ("Direct central banking, in short, is thus apt to be far more effective, saving friendly and consumer-friendly even than indirect central banking has been.").

2

Money, Capital, and Investment: Fixing Some Critical Terms and Relations

Careful and suitably detailed exposition of the present nature and future potential of our commercial republics' digitizable money and capital stocks requires, among other things, that we understand some of the process of capital investment and capital accumulation themselves. Explicating and understanding that process in turn requires that we organize thought through the use of certain well-defined concepts or categories of thought that have application to the reality of monetary and financial practice.

In some cases, the concepts that we require are already well captured and conveyed by clear, unambiguous terms of art familiar to lawyers and financiers generally, and to economists occasionally. In other cases, the concepts that we require are presently named by ambiguous, equivocal, open-ended, or clearly-but-inconsistently employed terms of art. And in still other cases they have yet to be named by any useful terms at all.

Probably few fields of study are more plagued by this species of terminological Babel than the field of finance—unless it be economics. "Capital," "money," indeed the word "finance" itself … what does one mean when one uses such words? What shall they mean in the subsequent chapters of this book? I shall aim to define all terms clearly upon each occasion of introduction over the course of this chapter's discussion.

Let's start with "capital"—surely the single most mysteriously used term in the whole of finance, if not economics more broadly.[1]

R. C. Hockett, *The Citizens' Ledger*,
https://doi.org/10.1007/978-3-030-99566-9_2

2.1 Capital: A Crucial Yet Oft-Muddled Term

"Investment capital" lies at the core of this book's claims, analyses, proposals, and supporting arguments, so I'll commence by defining that term. In so doing, it proves helpful first to define "capital" generically as anything used in the "production" of something else, then to differentiate separate species of this genus through further distinctions and associated lexical refinements. "Investment capital," thanks to an idiosyncrasy of the terminological hand we are already dealt, then emerges as one of these species.[2]

2.1.1 Production: What Capital Is (Ultimately) *For*

Begin with the "production" in relation to which capital usually is understood. Most activity that we treat as bearing "monetary" or "economic" significance has some connection to "production" or "productive activity," and all forms of "capital" seem to be understood by reference to the same. We can define such "production" as the application of energy by some individual or collective agent—e.g., a business firm—either to transform given materials into other, more desired material "goods," or to generate desired material "services." Pictorially (Fig. 2.1).

Production on this rendering can be effected by individual agents or collective agents (commonly called "organizations," "associations," or "firms"), and can be pursued under any number of property, contract, or counterpart governance arrangements of the kind that we find in all societies, commercial or otherwise.[3] In this sense the term is meant very broadly indeed.

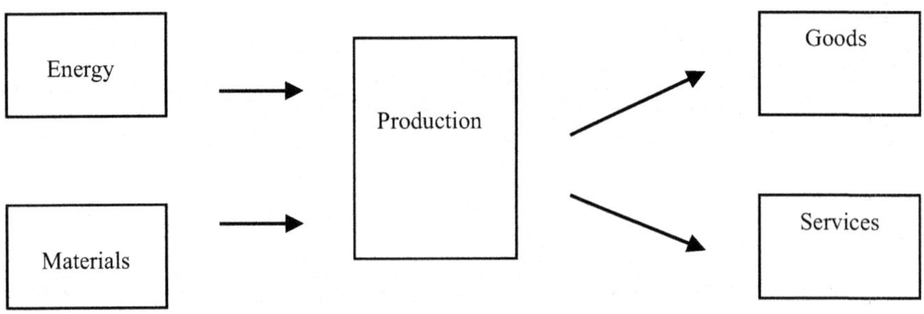

Fig. 2.1 Stylized production function

2.1.2 Generic Capital

In a society in which goods and services provision, transfer, or distribution is effected through direct rationing or apportioning by a central administration rather than through market exchange, "the capital stock" will simply be the aggregate of those material objects that the society as a singular collective agent deploys either in the production of other material objects or in the delivery of services. In Aristotelian terms, we might label these objects "means-goods" as distinguished from "ends-goods"—goods consumed only in the production of other goods or in the provision of services, rather than solely for survival, nutrition, or enjoyment.[4]

In a society where at least some goods and services provision, transfer, or distribution is effected through *exchange* rather than direct rationing or apportioning, and in which exchange is in turn effected through *barter*, the capital stock will simply be the previous aggregate, on the one hand, as differentiated on the other hand into (a) the still centrally rationed or apportioned stock, and (b) the portion of stock that the society does *not* apportion or ration directly as a singular collective agent, but instead assigns or consigns to the initiative of individual members of the society—thereby fostering "market exchange" (in this case, in bartering form) as a species of what is sometimes called, as in Chapter 1 above, "private ordering."

Finally and most saliently for our purposes, in a society where transfer or distribution is done at least partly through exchange and exchange is effected, in turn, not through barter but through a generic *medium* of exchange—a "money"—the capital stock will appear under *three* aspects. The first two will be those just formulated—capital as the sum of objects that either are or can be directly deployed by the society or its members in the production of goods or delivery of services—while the third will effectively amount to the quantum of *exchange media*, or "purchasing power," or "money" that private sector agents deploy to secure *command* over objects of the aforementioned kind. This third guise of capital is of course crucial, though surprisingly unremarked, in contemporary commercial republics.

2.1.3 Generic Capital in Production—Investment Capital

It is not uncommon to employ the term "investment capital" only to designate capital in the third guise just formulated, even while overlooking or making nothing of the fact that it is exchange *media*, or "money" of some form, that one is then typically talking about. The latter omission is perhaps

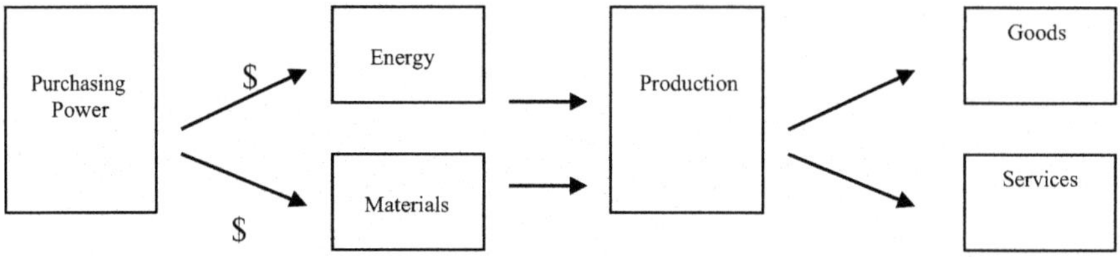

Fig. 2.2 Stylized production function in a monetary exchange economy

forgivable, however, in view of the multiple functions that money discharges *beyond* merely serving as medium of exchange.[5]

Hence we shall define the term here—again, "investment capital"—simply as purchasing power deployed to produce or provide goods, services, or, through sale of the same, yet greater purchasing power.[6] In such case, investment capital will be fully represented by the box to the far left of Fig. 2.2, while what we might then distinguish as physical capital will be represented by the two boxes stacked immediately to its right.

Generically speaking, "investment capital" on this understanding can also be thought of as "financial wealth" used to generate greater financial or material wealth.[7] Hence the many rough synonyms for "investment capital" in common usage, which include not only "money capital" and "finance capital," but also "liquid wealth" and the like. "Wealth" is an especially ambiguous term, however,[8] while "money" and "finance" discharge more functions than that which I wish here to single out with "investment capital," so I will be sparing in my use of those other terms. I will speak mainly of "investment capital."

On my rendering, then, the user of investment capital employs purchasing power to gain control over the disposition of objects or services (including energy supplies) purchased or rented, in order therewith to expend energy to generate what amounts, in commercial societies, ultimately to *more* potential purchasing power. This the user does through the production or generation of more goods or services that can be rented out or sold—that is, "liquidated" or "monetized"—even if some of the latter are *not* ultimately (even meant to be) rented out, sold, liquidated, or monetized.[9]

This is how we both generate and accumulate wealth—how we grow in "prosperity" or, in an earlier idiom, "opulence"—in any monetary exchange economy undergirding a commercial society.[10]

2.2 Investment: Antonym and Antidote to Speculation

In societies that consign a significant portion of investment decision-making to individual initiative prompted by individual incentive to profit, capital lends itself—pun now remorselessly intended—to "finance" and, through finance, what I'll call financial "stratification."[11] The latter emerges from individually rational efforts by individual agents to re-socialize risks that attend their privatized investment activities even when they are investing effectively public investment capital. These are efforts that we shall find often aggregate into collectively irrational, because of counter-productive and wealth-destructive, outcomes.

We'll come to that. The point to emphasize *here* is that multiple "levels" of capital contribution can interpose themselves—in finance parlance, "intermediate"—between initial disposers of capital on the one hand, and the processes of production that investment capital "capitalizes" on the other hand. This gives rise to more salient analytic distinctions and associated terms of art that prove useful at the expository stage to which we are headed in the subsequent chapters of this book.

2.2.1 Investment and Finance

While it is common in some contexts to employ terms like "finance" and "investment" more or less interchangeably, it will be best for present purposes to restrict use of the word "investment" to circumstances in which investment capital, as defined just above, is at work in financing production. Hence we'll use both "investment" and its cognates only in productive contexts, meaning in turn that it will serve as an antonym of sorts to "gambling," "gaming," "betting," "wagering," "speculating," or "mere speculation."

I am of course aware of the difficulties in some circumstances of sorting between "investment" and "speculation" given their overlaps rooted in risk, and hence am deliberately denigrating this form of skepticism in defining our terms as I do here. I do so because this alleged difficulty is much overblown (as we shall find further below), and then serves to provide cynical cover for what is no more than complacency or surrender in the task of reclaiming control for productive purposes of our public investment capital.

There will be more to say on this matter in due course. Suffice it for now to observe that, unlike Sorites, most of us are able to use words like "baldness" and "heap" sensibly notwithstanding there being no evident integer *n* such that fewer than *n* hairs definitively qualify Socrates as "bald," or such that fewer than *n* grains disqualify a quantum of sand from the status of "heap." "That's life," as one says—and so is it likewise finance.

"Finance" I shall use somewhat more generally, and indeed vaguely, than "investment." I will treat it as genus to investment's species, embracing all contexts in which purchasing power is deployed to produce goods or generate further purchasing power, irrespective of whether this be done through production or via other means—means that include gambling or speculating.

2.2.2 Stratification and N-ary (a.k.a. "Meta-") Markets

In what I and some others call the "primary" case of capital investment and production, the investment and production process as described above involves both material and juridical elements or "inputs"—physical objects or processes on the one hand, and legally enforceable claims to the right of their use or disposal on the other hand. In what I'll call the "secondary," "tertiary," or indeed any *n-ary* case, in turn, the process involves only juridical elements—claims on the claims generated in the $(n - 1)$-ary case.[12] In light of their essential reference to other, "lower level" markets in determining the money value of claims, we can call all such claims markets "meta-markets."

In a typical primary market case, for example, I will deploy purchasing power to take rights in "raw materials," which I will transform into "finished" goods or services through a production Process that might also involve my purchasing "labor services"—that is, renting labor.[13] The material elements here are—surprise—the mentioned materials: the goods or services. The juridical elements are my rights in the same, as well as to any surplus net of inputs—any "profits"—that I glean through a sale, should I sell.

In a typical *secondary* case, in turn, you confer *your* purchasing power upon *me*, whereupon I now proceed through the process that I've called the primary case. The contractual consideration that you have likely required of me as a condition for use of your purchasing power is now your legal entitlement—your right, your justiciable claim to agreed compensation—be that a debt claim, an equity claim, or some hybrid of these.

This is entirely "legal" or juridical, in the sense that you now need not "dirty your hands" with material objects or processes of any sort to take part in production. Secondary participation of this kind accordingly enables remote participation in material production—as do tertiary and other *n-ary* forms with $n > 3$.[14] And this form of meta-market remoteness from primary markets, we'll see, can lead to attenuation that need not but nonetheless often grows, not productive, but production-indifferent or counterproductive in speculation.

2.2.3 Intermediation, Derivation, "Financialization"

There is a tendency on the part of many who speak of finance, particularly those keen to convey an impression of being in possession of recondite knowledge, to speak of "financial intermediation" instead of "finance." There is nothing necessarily intermediating, nor should there be anything intimidating, about "finance," however—any more than there is about that species of finance which is productive investment. Intermediation is an artifact entirely of stratification as just defined, hence of remote and entirely juridical participation in production as just described.

In a typical *n-ary* case as just described, for example, someone confers upon you the purchasing power that you confer upon me in the scenario earlier specified (hence $n = 3$), or confers it upon someone else who confers it on you so that you can confer it on me ($n = 4$), etc. In all such cases intermediation emerges simply because n exceeds 1. The larger is n, in turn, the greater the margin by which meta-markets come to exceed primary markets in the notional value of money turnover, or what is more tellingly called "market churn." And that's all there is to it—apart from the dysfunction that such churn can foster...

When n grows very large, or when the number of remote participants in production at any stratum $n > 1$ grows very large, intermediation can grow more salient than production itself—it can grab our attention, generate problems, or otherwise get "in our face." Meta-markets, that is to say, can come to exceed primary markets in significance, whether we read significance in terms of the notional value of money turnover or in terms of the hours of human attention "paid" the markets in question.

This can in turn lead one to think that finance is all or primarily about meta-markets and intermediation. Conflation of finance with financial intermediation in this way signals thought of finance as abstracted, inadvertently or otherwise, from finance's foundational purpose, which is production through productive investment. That is unhealthy if our wish is to produce our own future, in which we must productively invest. We can usefully label the process through which this shift of attention and activity from productive investment to financial intermediation occurs—the process through which meta-markets come to exceed primary markets in significance—the process of "financialization."

Investment stratification is not the sole source of attenuated participation in production, hence of financialization. In a typical "derivative" case, for example, I purchase from you a contractually contingent claim referencing events that might befall my (or perhaps someone else's[15]) *n-ary* claim on

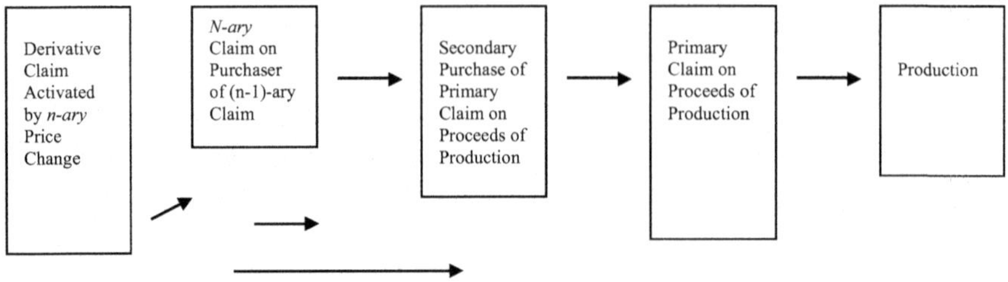

Fig. 2.3 Stylized representation of stratified and derivative markets

production. The contingency in question is then called a "triggering event," a "referenced event," an "insured event" or, in financial derivatives parlance, "an underlying." The "underlying" just is the claim one is effectively "hedging"—that is, insuring or betting upon—through purchase of further, now contingent and offsetting, claims.

Here too, as in the *n-ary* cases associated with investment stratification, only juridical elements—legally vindicable contractual claims—are involved, be they contingent or otherwise. Hence the less elliptical synonym for "derivative" that is "derivative contract." And hence the suggestion above both *n-ary* cases where n > 1 and derivative cases enable remote participation in material production (Fig. 2.3).

The more remote this participation, it should be noted, the more "intermediated" and, therefore, potentially "financialized" the relation between investment capital and real production becomes. For again, I shall define here the oft-used but seldom defined term "financialization" simply in terms of degrees of remoteness from production along either or both of two axes implicitly referenced already above—(a) the numerical value of *n*, and (b) the notional value, or "churn," of transactions occurring at any $n > 1$.

The participation in some of these cases out in "the real world" can become *very* remote. For in *n-ary* cases, remoteness grows directly in tandem with *n*. And in derivative cases, for their part, the claim-conferrers are typically interested in primary production not in the capacity of direct or indirect investors in production for production's (or sale's) sake, but instead in the capacity of agents who have wagered on the values or price paths of underlying *claims on the proceeds* of the production, or of claims on such claims, or on claims on such claims on such claims, … etc.

The short-term market values of these claims can vary, often enormously, from the longer-term market values of what is produced through production processes—a source of "slippage" we shall find to lie at the core both of the investment/speculation distinction and of the incapacity of our present system of outsourced management of public investment capital to allocate or modulate public capital productively and stably.[16] In effect, this dysfunction is simply the by-product of consigning public investment—that is, investment of public investment capital, as elaborated more fully in connection with "Money" directly below—to private sector agents, while permitting the same agents to re-socialize production-associated risk with abandon.[17]

We can say more: In view of the contractual nature of both derivative claims and *n-ary* claims in stratified financial markets, we can expect to see lawyers and financiers proliferate in number relative to engineers and applied natural scientists as an economy and society move from preoccupation with production to preoccupation with generic investment, thence from investment to finance, thence from finance to "financial intermediation," and thence from financial intermediation to full on financialization. These things are all of a piece, and proceed from that severing of finance from production which the consigning of public capital to private management through franchise and other forms of hybrid finance not only brings, but structurally *must* bring.

You read that rightly. The tendencies to which I refer are inherent in any system of investment that consigns the deployment of public investment capital to private initiative. And this suggests, as noted in Chapter 1, that privately ordering production, as "capitalist" economies do, might not be sustainable without publicly ordering finance. Demonstrating the inherence of the mentioned tendencies and thus the likely truth of the latter supposition, which requires explication of certain collective action predicaments latent in all forms of decentralized market exchange, takes us straight to the ultimately public source of literally all investment capital, as well as to the virtual impossibility of good private management of public capital.

2.3 Money: From Measure to Medium—and Back

Now is the time, counterintuitive as it might initially ring, to turn from "investment capital" to the "purchasing power" in terms of which I defined it above. For this affords us a crucial additional angle on investment capital itself, including not only its properties and behavior in its commercial and financial habitats, but also its source—*the public* that stands at the core of *every* republic, *including* every commercial republic.

2.3.1 Paying—Including Investing

"Purchasing" as used in the term "purchasing power" above presupposes exchange and hence payment. "Power" for its part suggests legal or normative efficacy[18] and variable quantifiability[19]—the prospect of holding or transferring "more" or "less" purchasing power. This in turn opens the door to some scale, measure, or metric's becoming useful or even necessary for purposes of *efficient* exchange in some societies.

Modern "financialized" societies in which investment capital "flows," like the populous commercial societies and complex exchange economies on which they are constructed, are such societies. We typically call the scales—the scalar measures of value—that they adopt "monies," in the "unit of account" sense of the word that is salient in accounting.[20].

Accounting ... This too is needed in all modern "financialized" societies in which investment capital tends to "flow," as in the complex commercial societies and exchange economies on which they are constructed. For it is simply the tracking of juridical claims—the contractual rights referenced repeatedly above, which will figure prominently in our "public accounting" below.

In commercial republics and the exchange economies in tandem with which such republics grow, transfers of most things, including contractual and hence juridical claims, are reciprocal. This is all that the doctrine of contractual "consideration," alluded to above, amounts to. And this practice is what underlies the practice of so-called "double-entry bookkeeping," or modern accounting, which is simply the application of algebra, first discovered in the Arab world, to matters commercial ever since Italian merchants began trading across the Mediterranean in the late Middle Ages.

2.3.2 Accounting

Accounting in exchange economies like those of modern commercial republics is the practice of tracking contractually exchanged reciprocal obligations—an obligation's being simply the flipside of a claim. (My obligation to you is your claim upon me. You "own" what I "owe.").

"Mental accounting" suffices to track claim- and obligation-flow in narrowly circumscribed, low transaction volume—that is, "low velocity"—contexts.[21] Such contexts typically also allow for exchange to be barter—hence for obligations and claims to be discharged as quickly as they are incurred. As transacting grows in complexity, volume, and turnover rate, however, mental accounting gives way to ledger accounting or "book-keeping," while the latter comes to employ a generic "unit" of account for purposes of simultaneous quantification and commensuration.[22]

What one is owed—that which one "owns"—per a ledger we call one's "credit," is accounted a "financial asset." That which one owes we call "debits," or "debt"—which is accounted a "financial liability." We call the discharge of credits and debits "payment." And when the debit arises from a sale, we call the payment a "purchase," in the sense used above in the phrase "purchasing power."

2.3.3 Crediting/Debiting

The fact that barter involves simultaneous discharge of mutual obligation is why instantaneous barter does not involve credit, debt, or, therefore, money. The latter arise only in cases of non-simultaneity, meaning in turn that they make use of time. Credit, debit, and time hang together. So then do *money* and time—"time is money"—since money comes into the picture only when credit and debit, and the accounting that tracks credits and debits, come into view. Hence the role played by *time* in the celebrated Swedish and Austrian accounts of capital outside of the Anglosphere, not to mention Fisher's, Keynes's, and Minsky's later Wicksellian and neo-Austrian accounts of money, in the late nineteenth and twentieth centuries, respectively.[23]

Because money is simply the measure of quantifiably variable credit and debit, it is "only natural" that money as unit of account should morph into money as "medium of exchange." For again, credit and debit arise from exchange, and one must exchange something for something else, which if not bartered can only be money.[24] This is why money is sometimes called "spendable credit." And it is why money can also be called what I called above "purchasing power." Money, purchasing power, the measure of both or of credit and debit ... these all come down to one thing. And all are embedded in "common practice"—practices of exchanging, paying, and deferring paying hence crediting, debiting, and accounting.

This tells us yet more about purchasing power and therefore investment capital. money as just described is just "that which pays" in a payment practice or "payments system," and "that which counts" in a system of debit and credit accounting.[25] And since, thanks both to payment practices and to the "legal tender" laws that typically sharpen them, money is purchasing power,[26] money is likewise investment capital as defined above.

We are now fully equipped to lay out and examine, then critique hybrid public–private finance in detail, this en route to developing its full digital cure. On, then, to financial hybridity.

Notes

1. *See, e.g.*, Robert Hockett, *From "Law In" to "Law And": Some Legal Foundations of Economic Analysis*, in LAW, ECONOMICS, AND CONFLICT (Kaushik Basu & Robert Hockett, eds. 2021). What about "finance" itself? Read on, McDuff.
2. The idiosyncrasy is that, strictly speaking, all forms of capital are by definition "invested," such that the prefix "investment" shouldn't do any work. As it happens, however, the prefix does do work because common usage has come implicitly to define "investment capital" simply as *non-material* capital, understood in contradistinction to "hard capital," "physical capital," "machine capital," and the like.
3. See generally Hockett, *Capital Commons*, *supra* note 1.
4. One could, of course, treat pleasure or welfare as "products," as orthodox welfare economists in effect do, but the object of the present exercise is precisely to separate out for its own treatment the raw and produced *material inputs* to these individual "utility functions."
5. *See* Robert Hockett, "Money in Context, Part 1," and Robert Hockett, "Money in Context, Part 2," *supra* note 111.
6. There is of course an isomorphism here with Marx's celebrated "M-C-M" rendering of capitalist production in KAPITAL, Vol. I.
7. This is effectively the mode of analysis employed in Staffa's monumental work. See PIERO SRAFFA, THE PRODUCTION OF COMMODITIES BY MEANS OF COMMODITIES (1960).
8. The word derives, of course, from the adjectival and adverbial forms of the word "good"—"well"—and accordingly associates terms like "commonweal" and "commonwealth" with "the common good."
9. See again the earlier remark on Marx's "M-C-M" formula, *supra* note 62.
10. Opulence of course figures as the proper object of economic policy in Adam Smith's WEALTH OF NATIONS, as well as the work of most other practitioners of "political economy" before the "marginalist" turn of the 1870s. That shift can accordingly be marked as the beginning of a move from preoccupation with material production to a strange new preoccupation with "subjective utility" a la Bentham. The corresponding terminological shift from "political economy"—that is, the "home economics" of the polis, or polity—to mere "economics" signals that change rather starkly.
11. See generally Robert Hockett, *Metamarkets* (working paper, 2010) (working paper, on file with the author).

12. *Id.*
13. The distinction nowadays drawn between "labor" and "material" inputs to production appears to be rooted in the repudiation of human ownership. Where there is chattel slavery, humans can be owned and hence figure among the objects consumed in production—*all* inputs are "capital" inputs. Where chattel slavery and similar forms of servitude are prohibited, humans are rented instead of owned and hence differentiated from physical objects—inputs divide into "labor" and "capital."
14. Care must be taken not to confound "primary" and "secondary" here with those terms as used in contemporary financial markets—a potentially difficult task inasmuch as the same sort of stratification is involved, with the difference residing simply in different "starting points"—different "primary cases" and hence different numbers assigned the successive layers in the hierarchy. In financial market parlance, the term "primary" refers to what I'm calling "secondary," while the term "secondary" refers to markets in which claims generated below are "negotiable"—that is, "alienable," "saleable," "tradable," "exchangeable," etc.
15. The parenthetical "someone else's" highlights a critical difference between primary insurance markets, in which the *Insurable Interest Doctrine* holds legal sway, and the secondary insurance—that is, derivatives—markets, in which it does not. In the first case, I can bet on—that is, insure against—my own property's being damaged, but not against yours being damaged. In the second case, I can bet on anything. This form of untethering is present not only in secondary insurance—that is, derivatives—markets, but also in repo markets that permit unrestricted rehypothecation of collateral. See general Hockett, sources cited *supra* note.
16. The recent brouhaha over GameStop's share price is only the most recent high- profile case. *See* Robert Hockett, "Wall Street's "OK Boomer" Moment," *Forbes*, January 31, 2021, available at https://www.forbes.com/sites/rhockett/2021/01/31/wall-streets-ok-boomer-moment–what-theyre-not-saying-about-gamestop/?sh=1490b97f49a6.
17. Re-socializing by hedging and thus pooling the relevant risk—in this case, with one's "insurers," a.k.a. derivative counterparties.
18. *See* Hockett, *Rousseauvian Money*, *supra* note 3.
19. *See* Robert Hockett, *Putting Distribution First*, 18 THEORETICAL INQURIES IN LAW 1 (2017), available at https://papers.ssrn.com/sol3/papers.cfm?abstract_id=2903624#:~:text=To%20attend%20systematically%20to%20this,policy%20are%20implicitly%20as%20equalizing.
20. *See* Hockett, *Money in Context*, Parts 1 and 2, infra note 111.
21. *See* again Hockett, *Rousseauvian Money*, *supra* note 3.
22. *See* again Hockett, *Putting Distribution First*, *supra* note 75.
23. *See* Robert Hockett, "Modern, Pre-modern, or Post-modern Money? A Guide for the Perplexed," *Forbes*, October 26, 2020, available

at https://www.forbes.com/sites/rhockett/2020/10/26/modern-pre-modern-or-post-modern-money-a-brief-guide-for-the-perplexed/.

24. Money-payment and barter jointly and complementarily determine the entirety of payment space. What is not one is the other.
25. *See* Robert Hockett, *Democratic Digital Dollar*, *supra* note 5; and Hockett, Financing the Green New Deal, *supra* note 18. Also Robert Hockett, *Money's Past is Fintech's Future: Wildcat Crypto, the Digital Dollar, and Citizen Central Banking*, 2 Stanford Journal Of Blockchain Law And Policy 1 (2019), available at https://stanford-jblp.pubpub.org/pub/wildcat-crypto-fintech-future/release/1; and Hockett, *Finance Without Financiers*, *supra* note.
26. *See* again Hockett, *Rousseauvian Money*, *supra* note 3.

3

Franchise Finance: A Brief Exposition and Exposé

Armed with the categories elaborated in Chapter 2, we are now equipped to understand the full nature of hybrid public–private finance as briefly described in Chapter 1, along with its ills and the cure promised by new digital savings and payments technologies that this book will proffer in Chapters 5–8. We'll start by describing the particular form of hybridity found in commercial republics' contemporary financial systems—a form that I long ago dubbed public–private "*franchise* finance."

Contemporary financial systems are essentially public–private franchise arrangements.[1] It is surprisingly easy, as a matter of technological history, to understand how these came about, as Chapter 4 will show. It is a bit harder to understand why we retain them, as Chapter 5 will explain. The work of both Chapters 4 and 5, however, as well as the more constructive work of Chapters 6–8, will be simpler if we first take a look at the primary details of this mode of finance, as well as its ills.

3.1 Hybridity in the Large: Exposition

Franchise arrangements are in effect quality-assurance arrangements. The good that franchise *finance* distributes is not hotel rooms, foodstuffs, or auto-parts that conform to reliably uniform standards across an integrated national economy. It is instead a national payment, credit, and value-storage medium—the monetized full faith and credit of the sovereign.[2] Our systems

R. C. Hockett, *The Citizens' Ledger*,
https://doi.org/10.1007/978-3-030-99566-9_3

distribute, in other words, uniform national currencies and their credit equivalents—in the U.S., for example, dollar-denominated debt—most in the form of what is alternatively called "credit-money," "bank money," "deposit money," or "broad money."[3]

Our sovereign republics issue this good, and like any franchisor promulgate and enforce certain "quality control" measures to ensure that specific exemplars of the good conform to a uniform standard.[4] Licensed private sector banking and other financial institutions in turn act as franchisees, distributing the good—again, monetized public full faith and credit—for the public sector franchisor and earning what I call "privatized seignorage" for their trouble by being permitted to charge interest for lending, and fees for managing, republic-issued credit-money.[5]

It is easiest to trace the truth of this claim in connection with commercial banks, which extend currency-denominated credit in the form of newly opened or credited deposits for borrowers.[6] These bank-issued deposits are immediately spendable ("drawable upon") as money—that is, as full payment equivalents of central bank notes, better known in the U.S. as dollar bills—in virtue both of the role that our systems confer upon banks in their national payments infrastructure, and of the role central bank accommodation plays in conferring money status on payments made out of licensed bank deposit accounts via those payments infrastructures.[7]

But effectively the same thing now happens in other subsectors of the financial sector—notably capital markets, money and commercial paper markets, repo markets, derivatives markets, and other shadow banking markets—as well as, thanks to the multilateral credit and payments linkages we now permit among all of these markets, private sector banks, and our republics' central banks.[8] The upshot is a cluster of financial systems that are far less about "intermediating" scarce private capital, as banking and financial orthodoxy still surprisingly proclaim, than they are about *generating* and *multiplying* often over-abundant, because misallocated, *public* capital, a.k.a. credit-money.

As just suggested, an unfortunate misconception, both assumed by nonexperts and reinforced by some lawyers, financiers, economists, and public servants who ought to know better, is that banks simply lend what others have antecedently deposited, and that other financial subsectors likewise just intermediate between such private sector accumulators of putatively scarce capital and end-users of capital.[9] In the case of the banking sector, the assumed picture is nicely captured by phrases like "loanable funds," on at least one unfortunate understanding of that phrase, and slogans like "deposits make loans."[10] In fact, however, it is far more accurate to speak of "loan-*generated* funds" and say "*loans make deposits,*" since most of what we see in the way of deposits is simply the bank balance sheet's liability-side equivalent of bank-disseminated, publicly enabled, currency-denominated asset-side *credit*.[11]

The real key to loans' spendability as deposit account "bank money" (again, that is a term of art) is not those loans' fictitious derivation from antecedently deposited private-sector-supplied funds, as the dominant misconception—what I call "the intermediated scarce private capital myth"—has it.[12] It is, rather, what I have elsewhere dubbed central bank "accommodation" and "monetization."[13] That is to say, CB-recognized clearing and settlement, through the public payments architecture that the CBs typically oversee and administer, of payments drawn upon deposit accounts maintained with publicly licensed and enabled banking and other financial institutions.[14]

The license in question, in turn—the best-known and most coveted "flavor" of which is known among specialists as the "bank charter"—is essentially a franchise contract.[15] Required reserves and capital buffers, like portfolio regulation, consumer financial protection, and other modalities of financial regulation, are in turn simply terms of that contract.[16] They amount to quality control terms meant to maintain the stability of the franchisee banks and other financial institutions, along with the payments infrastructure that they largely constitute, upon which the public relies, all while preventing both (a) exploitation of that same "general public" and (b) over-issuance (inflation) of the public money in relation to the quantum of available goods and services that this money can command.[17]

Thanks in part to their deliberately cultivated borrowing, other transactional, and affiliative relations with banking institutions, and in part to public backstopping of themselves along with the banks during times of financial distress, nonbank financial institutions have steadily become, as suggested above, de facto franchisee institutions as well.[18] They now issue and multiply public credit-money much as do banks, and do so far in excess of anything they borrow from depositors, investors, and other nonbank counterparties.[19]

Nonbank financial institutions assist, in a word, not only in credit-intermediation but in credit-multiplication and -generation too, again as our commercial banks do.[20] And this is made possible by public accommodation and facilitation of these institutions' transactions in manners that resemble or replicate public accommodation of banks' and their depositors' transactions. In short, then, money being simply "that which pays" in the making of payments, and "what pays" in turn mainly comprising as it does payments made out of loan-credited transaction accounts, our money systems boil down to our CB-overseen and -enabled payment and financial systems.[21]

The upshot of this set of arrangements is that even the capital and money markets, and even the repo and derivatives markets, and even the rest of the so-called "shadow banking" sector, are now franchisees in our public–private finance franchise too, albeit less carefully monitored than traditional depository institutions (that being part of their point).[22] All of these institutions are now privately owned and operated distributors of that endogenously generated public good which is the monetized full faith and credit of the sovereign, also known as the money supply.[23] And this is so even though these institutions continue also to intermediate.[24]

What I call credit-multiplication and -generation, in other words, now *accompany* and vastly *exceed or supplant* credit-intermediation *throughout* our financial system, with its share of transaction volume and the associated money supply growing ever larger through time to the point that it dwarfs what has been antecedently accumulated.[25] And thanks to our systems' ties to our central banks, the *credit*-share's growth is the *public*-share's growth.[26] The overwhelmingly greater part of that monetized full faith and credit which is our money is, in other words, quite literally *ours—our republic's.*

3.2 Hybridity in Detail: Exposé

Were banking and finance merely "intermediation," as Chapter 2 indicated that bankers want us to think, most if not all investment capital in commercial republics would be in a certain sense private, and unproblematic. For there would be inherent limits. All that was lent would have to have been preaccumulated—deposits *would* "make" loans, and meta-markets of the kind modeled in Chapter 2 wouldn't be able to grow and proliferate out of hand. But this is not how banks or most of finance work—it is how mutual funds work. Where banks are concerned, it is as noted above truer to say "loans make deposits."

3.2.1 Credit-Money's Endogeneity: Private Lending of Public Capital

The key point you must bear in mind is that we, the public, supply most of any contemporary republic's investment capital by monetizing our public "full faith and credit." This takes a wee bit of detailed tracing to substantiate, both because it is counterintuitive at first—we've been trained through such words as "intermediation" to think differently—and because the process of monetization occurs in "black boxes" that we call "banks."

You've heard the phrase, "the alchemy of banking." You're about now to learn that alchemy. This is how we turn trust—public trust—into gold. Just watch …

You go to a bank for a loan to finance a remunerative project—a project you're sure will be profitable. You need purchasing power to purchase your project's inputs, but all that you have is your own private promissory note. Your note is not legal tender—it's not recognized money—hence can't serve directly as monetized investment capital. So you go to the bank to exchange it—as noted above, to swap it—temporarily for *public* promissory notes. These *do* count as legal tender, as money, and hence purchasing power usable to finance production.

Look at a U.S. dollar, for example, read across the top. A dollar is a Federal Reserve Note—a "note" as your promissory note is a note. But it is more widely usable. That's why it's money—public money. The bank is going to evaluate your proposed project before approving your proposed swap. I will talk about how it does that in a moment, for much hinges on that. But first let us see how the swap works and how it turns privately approved loans into publicly issued capital.

If the bank approves your swap application, it is going to trade for your promissory note not quite literal public promissory notes, but what used to be called their fiduciary equivalent. It is going to open an account in your name, credit an account already there in your name, or provide you a check—another variant on our old friend the promissory note—that instructs someone else to credit you.

Now for the kicker: you can immediately *spend* this credit—it is monetary from the get-go, requiring no antecedent accumulation of gold in a sack, bills in a vault, or whatever. You simply insert a chip, swipe a strip, or key a blip and you've paid for the inputs to your bank-financed project, be they machine tools or a ticket to Vegas (we'll come back to that).

What makes this possible—what makes it a private note / public note swap—is that the bank is a publicly licensed institution networked into the commercial republic's national payments system. At the center of that system sits … wait for it … the republic's *central* bank. In the U.S., again, that is the Fed, a public instrumentality that oversees banks chartered by yet other public instrumentalities—again, the suggestively named "Comptroller of the Currency" for national banks, and state banking commissioners for state banks.

A functioning money, again, is just "that which pays" in a payments system—"that which counts" in a system of debit and credit and value accounting. And in a republic it is we, the public, who legislate what shall pay, what shall count, and who shall disseminate it when we generate it, *ex nihilo*, through public–private note swapping. And in the U.S., again, the public have legislated that the public sector Fed shall generate and hence modulate it, while private sector banks shall allocate it.

I am not a licensed bank, so I can only *purport* to lend to you by "opening an account" in your name and handing you a chip card or strip card to "swipe the swap." But when you swipe it to purchase your inputs—machine tools or plane tickets or otherwise—precisely nothing will happen. It "doesn't count." It will not pay. It is not money, it's not a public capital instrument swapped for your private capital instrument. Nor is it that instrument's instantly generable and indefinitely extensible fiduciary equivalent—a "bank account." For again, I'm not a bank.

3.2.2 Endogeneity's Blessing—And Curse: Production and Wealth, Speculation and Recursive Collective Action Problems

The role of publicly licensed banks in commercial republics' payments systems lends to bank loan money a peculiar attribute, depicted in Fig. 3.1: While some of it is privately intermediated in the form of exogenously deposited funds, most of it is endogenously generated in the form of bank-conferred loan proceeds in newly opened or credited spendable deposit form. In this sense, most money in contemporary commercial republics is effectively public capital. Diagrammatically, this point is captured by the fact that

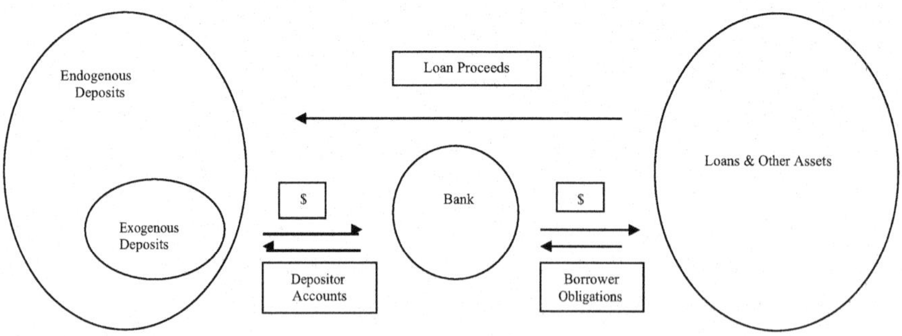

Fig. 3.1 Exogenous deposit and endogenous bank money

none of the flows represented by arrows in Fig. 3.1 need be temporally prior to any others.

This form of monetized public investment capital changes everything where money is concerned, and has done for centuries. For it not only enables productive investment, but also allows effectively infinite, hence infinitely wasteful and counterproductive, speculation in meta-markets.

For this reason, its analysis lay at the core of the work of the greatest economist you've perhaps never heard of, Sweden's Knut Wicksell (1851–1928), who called this stuff "bank money," which I generalize by calling it "credit-money" and "endogenous money."[27] You've heard of Keynes, and "the Austrians," though. Fragments—and alas, *only* fragments—of Wicksell's insights found their way into contemporary thinking through Keynes in the Anglosphere and "the Austrians" beyond. But Wicksell's followers drew only modulatory, not allocative, lessons from his work on endogenous money. And that is our tragedy, as we're nearly now ready to see—a tragedy that new payment technologies now will allow us to rectify.

We can see what's at stake here by highlighting the blessings and curses that credit-money's and hence public capital's endogeneity brings. The blessing is easiest to see—which might be why we retain this form of money even while not having yet succeeded in mitigating its curses. Quite simply, money's endogeneity enables tremendous productivity economy-wide. The reason is simple: To produce requires command over resources—the inputs to all forms of production. But in a monetary exchange economy such as those of the world's commercial republics, command over resources is secured by purchase or rental of the same. This in turn means that only those with money are able to produce—"it *takes* money to *make* money."

Commercial republics could, of course, respond to this fact conservatively by settling for productive arrangements under which only those who have already accumulated material wealth and its monetary correlate are thus able to produce additional wealth. But this would needlessly curtail and limit productive activity and associated wealth-generation. By enabling people to monetize now the production they've yet to accomplish, we fuel much greater production and growth. And that is just what productively lent credit-money does. It disseminates means by which even the non-wealthy majorities of our populations can monetarily secure command over resources that can then be deployed in production.

This is precisely why economies with well-developed banking system develop and grow so much more rapidly than do economies without such systems. These systems enable the public at large, through its banking system, to "bet on" its own citizenry's productive potential—a form of betting that, with careful project evaluation and associated sound allocation, pays off both individually and collectively.

That caveat, however—"careful project evaluation" and "sound allocation"—also signals the curse that endogenous money can bring. If the public allows its franchisee institutions to allocate public investment capital—again, that's what endogenous money in our licensed bank systems amounts to—not with a view only to profitably productive projects, but also with a view to profitably speculative gambles, there is practically no limit to how much new money can be generated and misallocated to destructive bubble- and bust-causing purposes. To see why, I shall have to note one more feature of decentralized market exchange—its susceptibility to what I long ago dubbed "recursive collective action predicaments."

A collective action predicament—call it a "CAP"—is a choice situation in which individually rational decisions aggregate into collectively irrational outcomes.[28] Think of the rush to the theater door after "fire!" is shouted, or of everyone's standing at once to "get a better view." A CAP is in this sense a "tragic situation," tragic in the classical Greek—"damned if you do, damned if you don't"—rather than in the trivial, "bad news" sense. (I harp on this because the *structure* of the situation is what is critical, and only "predicament" and the Greek sense of "tragedy," not the imprecise "problem" or "disaster," convey that.)

CAPs are familiar enough generically—again, "fire!"—but their pervasive affliction of decentralized market exchange seems to be strangely underappreciated, even in the commercial republics where they're ubiquitous. And what I have dubbed their far worse *recursive* renditions—let's call them "ReCAPS"—seem to attract no notice at all. This, I believe, is why we don't solve them. It's why we keep getting finance and, accordingly, production all wrong.

A few examples will sharpen understanding …

The most salient *non*-recursive CAPs where production is concerned stem from what I call "controllability" and "capturability" problems, respectively, in economies in which production is delegated to decentralized private ordering. *Controllability* problems induce collectively irrational underinvestment in productive *industry*—why individually invest in a firm, for example, if underemployment, deflation, or inflation in the macro environment make future sales uncertain? *Capturability* problems induce collectively irrational underinvestment in *infrastructures* necessary to production—why individually invest if the "positives" yielded by the investment are mainly "external"?

Recursive CAPs—again, ReCAPs—are collective action problems with "feedback effects." They are self-worsening in consequence of their structure, which drives an iterative process pursuant to which individual reactions at time $t + 1$ to events that occur at time t do not mute, nullify, or counteract those events, but repeat them in more acute and collectively devastating form. Examples abound in decentralized markets, especially but not solely in banking and capital markets. A few more familiar examples will make the point …

Inflation: You and I see prices rising, hence rationally buy more now rather than waiting till later; but this just makes prices rise faster. *Deflation*: You and I see prices falling, hence rationally defer buying or hiring till later; but this just makes prices fall further and unemployment rise faster. *Bank Run*: You and I hear that our bank is faced with liquidity trouble, hence rationally "run" there to withdraw our funds; but this simply hastens the eventuality we fear. *Asset Price Bubble*: Simply a hyper-inflation in capital markets. *Market Crash* or *Asset "Fire Sale"*: Simply a debt-deflation or "bank run" on assets. And so on…

The story of financialization, productive atrophy, and crash-to-crash lurching on the part of many of our *macro*economies over the past 50 years just is the story of unnoticed collective action predicaments endemic to the *micro*structures of those economies. And that microstructure is a structure of scattered nodes of individual agency actuated by individual "interests." That needn't be a problem for production. But it *will* be a problem for production if we let it act as a problem for production *finance*.

As noted in Chapter 1, it is one thing to decentralize production, it is another to decentralize the *financing* of production—at least when we do so with public as well as private capital. The first simply isn't compatible with the second. That's apt to strike you as counterintuitive at first—again, we've been taught otherwise, and have been taught not to think of production and production finance separately. But disaggregate and then think of them separately, and you will see this is right…

Simply remind yourself that if finance is for profit, and profit is possible without production, then production will tend to be under-financed, while unproductive and even counterproductive profiting will be over-financed—indeed *vastly* over-financed once indefinitely extensible public capital ("bank money") gets into the act. Hence my earlier mention of Vegas, where people go not to produce, but to win from others what they already have. But what can we do about it?

Keynes and the Austrians "got" the endogenous money and consequent bipolar financial "swinging" to which Wicksell attended with ceaseless attention to detail. That's all that Keynes's "credit-money" spin on Wicksell's "bank money," and Austrians' "business cycle" spin on his "cumulative process" effectively were. That is why "neo-," "post-," "classical-," and others whom

I call "*x*, *y*, *z*-Keynesians" of all stripes fixate on the "*macro*economics" that they credit Keynes with inventing. And it's why Austrians fixate on "taming" endogenous money by shackling it to finite-supplied shiny metals or "rules."

None of these bromides helps much, however, as surely the past eighty years should have demonstrated. And this is because you cannot get the macro right without getting the micro right. We cannot well modulate until we well allocate.[29]

What then to do? The key is to reattach macro to micro—that is, modulation to allocation. For while those are analytically distinct, as I have argued for years now, they are practically inseparable. And to see how to do this—how to reunite modulation and allocation—we'll do our best to return to your swap for a moment…

In evaluating your swap application, the bank asks itself whether you're apt to succeed with your project. That is a micro-, not macro question. And the bank will unpack and address this question by reference not to production, but to profit. That is the rational thing for the bank to do in a system where not only production, but also production finance, is left to market exchange as it is in commercial republics. The bank survives and keeps its shareholders happy in our fragmented system only as it profits.

Our systems of bank regulation—in the terms used above, our bank-licensing regimes—publicly endorse this. They police primarily bank "safety and soundness"—again, that's a regulatory term of art—and aims above all else to … another term of art … "prevent bank failure."

None of this would be problematic were profits and producing identical or even proximately linked, such that production would "take care of itself" just so long as we ensured profitability. But alas, the monetization of investment capital as noted above *enables* a divergence, while the outsourcing of public capital management to profit-driven private sector financiers *guarantees* that divergence. In fact, it guarantees not only that this divergence can and will happen, but also that it will steadily widen through time, "feed on itself" without limit till terminal collapse.

That sounds apocalyptic—it should, for it is—and this might have led you to think I'll now posit some "radical," exotic, or "heterodox" idea in explaining myself. Something about "dialectic," "deconstruction," "Minsky Moment" or some such thing …

But I'm not.

The crowning irony of our present-day financial mess is that the dysfunction endemic to decentralized private management of centrally supplied public capital is entirely accessible to orthodox intuition. It is, in other words, attributable to variants on orthodox "market failure" more familiar in both "freshwater" and "saltwater" precincts even than in hotbeds of heresy like late nineteenth-century Paris or London, or late twentieth-century Annandale-on-Hudson or Tennessee.

I am referring to ReCaps as modeled above, which loom around any setting in which people decide things individually that can affect all collectively. The garden-variety renditions of these challenges are familiar, while what I have long called their iterative, recursive renditions for some reason are not. As a consequence, the form of their solutions all take escape notice as well.

To solve a collective action problem, you have to exercise collective agency.[30] We used to have a word for this—we called such agency "governance," and called its agents—our republics' agents—our "governments."[31] The chief secret of capital, I think, is that ungoverned production is in the long-run incompatible with ungoverned finance. And by "governing" I don't mean reactive regulation. I mean proactive *allocation*—allocation on which production and, in the end, modulation itself depends.

And this takes on to our solution in Chapters 6–8. But first a bit more on why we still linger where we do.

The brief functional trajectory that I will now narrate addresses these questions. More importantly, it shows that what I propose in this book "fulfills," in a sense, our commercial republics' monetary, commercial, and financial histories—histories from what I call "ledger money" to "token money" and back that manifests a distinct teleological pattern in its steady "dialectical" unfolding.[32]

Notes

1. *See* Hockett, *Finance Without Financiers, supra* note 15. Also Hockett, *Capital Commons, supra* note 1; and Hockett, *Wealth of Our Commonwealth, supra* note 1.
2. *See Finance Without Financiers, supra* note 15, at 6 (defining the franchise arrangement). Also Hockett, *Capital Commons, supra* note 1; and Hockett, *Wealth of Our Commonwealth, supra* note 1.
3. *See Finance Without Financiers, supra* note 15, at 11. Also Hockett, *Capital Commons, supra* note 1; and Hockett, *Wealth of Our Commonwealth, supra* note 1.
4. *See Finance Without Financiers, supra* note 15, at 26 ("[Repo transactions] have not yet become subject to the 'quality control' standards that the franchisor imposes upon those forthright franchisees."). Also Hockett, *Capital Commons,* supra note 1; and Hockett, *Wealth of Our Commonwealth, supra* note 1.

5. *See id.*, at 11 (describing how private franchisees earn profits—"privatized seignorage"—by dispensing a good provided by the sovereign franchisor). Also Hockett, *Capital Commons*, supra note 1; and Hockett, *Wealth of Our Commonwealth*, *supra* note 1.
6. *Id.*, at 8 (using commercial banks as a counterexample to the intermediation interpretation). Also Hockett, *Capital Commons*, *supra* note 1; and Hockett, *Wealth of Our Commonwealth*, *supra* note 1.
7. *See Finance Without Financiers*, *supra* note 15, at 12 ("Accommodation and monetization are the processes through which the sovereign enables credit to be indefinitely generated in immediately spendable form, by committing ex ante to convert certain private liabilities into public liabilities that serve as money."). Also Hockett, *Capital Commons*, *supra* note 1; and Hockett, *Wealth of Our Commonwealth*, *supra* note 1.
8. *Finance Without Financiers*, *supra* note 15, at 40 ("In sum, then, all of the shadow banking channels enable the capital and money markets to amplify and replicate, in all salient respects, the functions of traditional banks."). Also Hockett, *Capital Commons*, *supra* note 1; and Hockett, *Wealth of Our Commonwealth*, *supra* note 1.
9. *Finance Without Financiers*, *supra* note 15, at 4, 6. Also Hockett, *Capital Commons*, *supra* note 1; and Hockett, *Wealth of Our Commonwealth*, *supra* note 1.
10. *Finance Without Financiers supra* note 15, at 14. Also Hockett, *Capital Commons*, *supra* note 1; and Hockett, *Wealth of Our Commonwealth*, *supra* note 1.
11. *Finance Without Financiers*, *supra* note 15, at 15 (explaining bank lending transactions—the bank will record the loan as an asset and the deposit as a liability). Also Hockett, *Capital Commons*, *supra* note 1; and Hockett, *Wealth of Our Commonwealth*, supra note 1.
12. *See Finance Without Financiers*, *supra* note 15, at 5–9 (showing that the "intermediated scarce private capital orthodoxy" view is false). Also Hockett, *Capital Commons*, *supra* note 1; and Hockett, *Wealth of Our Commonwealth*, *supra* note 1.
13. *Finance without Financiers*, *supra* note 15, at 11 (explaining public "accommodation" and "monetization" of initially privately extended credit.).
14. *Finance Without Financiers*, *supra* notes 15, at 17. Also Hockett, *Capital Commons*, supra note 1; and Hockett, *Wealth of Our Commonwealth*, *supra* note 1.
15. *Finance Without Financiers*, *supra* note 15, at 6 ("[C]ontemporary financial systems as we now find them are best interpreted as public–private franchise arrangements."). Also Hockett, *Capital Commons*, *supra* note 1; and Hockett, *Wealth of Our Commonwealth*, supra note 1.
16. *See id*. Also Hockett, *Capital Commons*, *supra* note 1; and Hockett, *Wealth of Our Commonwealth*, *supra* note 1.

17. *See id.* at 16. Also Hockett, *Capital Commons, supra* note 1; and Hockett, *Wealth of Our Commonwealth, supra* note 1.
18. *See id.* at 23 (explaining "capital, and now also money, markets amplify and replicate the role of banking and Treasury securities markets as channels for dispensing the full faith and credit of the sovereign" just as banks do under their franchise arrangements). *See also id.* (discussing the financial crisis of 07–09 that shed light on so called, "shadow bank[s,]" that replicate the banking industry and similarly promote public accommodation and monetization). Also Hockett, *Capital Commons, supra* note 1; and Hockett, *Wealth of Our Commonwealth, supra* note 1.
19. *Id.* ("[Nonbank financial institutions are] now a critically important complement to the traditional banking sector where credit-money proliferation is concerned.") Also Hockett, *Capital Commons,* supra note 1; and Hockett, *Wealth of Our Commonwealth, supra* note 1.
20. *Id.* (explaining how "credit-money proliferation" complements our traditional banks). Also Hockett, *Capital Commons, supra* note 1; and Hockett, *Wealth of Our Commonwealth, supra* note 1.
21. *See Democratic Digital Dollar, supra,* note 5, at 1; also *Finance without Financiers, supra* note 15, at 30 (explaining how a non-bank derivative transaction replicates bank lending and "necessarily augments public accommodation and monetization as described" above).
22. *Finance Without Financiers, supra* note 15, at 6 ("[C]ontemporary financial systems as we now find them are best interpreted as public–private franchise arrangements.") Also Hockett, *Capital Commons, supra* note 1; and Hockett, *Wealth of Our Commonwealth, supra* note 1.
23. *Id.* ("Under the terms of the franchise, the sovereign public effectively licenses private financial institutions to dispense a vital and indefinitely extensible public resource – the sovereign public's monetized full faith and credit.") Also Hockett, *Capital Commons, supra* note 1; and Hockett, *Wealth of Our Commonwealth, supra* note 1.
24. *Id.* at 5 (explaining that many financial institutions intermediate). Also Hockett, *Capital Commons, supra* note 1; and Hockett, *Wealth of Our Commonwealth, supra* note 1.
25. *Id.* at 9 ("Finance capital in the form of credit might instead be more accurately said to be 'generated' by lending institutions than 'intermediated' or 'multiplied' by them."). Also Hockett, *Capital Commons, supra* note 1; and Hockett, *Wealth of Our Commonwealth,* supra note 1.
26. *Id.* at 34 ("The Fed's converting both private borrower liabilities and private insurer liabilities into public liabilities amounts to its monetizing that much more public full faith and credit, and injecting it into the financial system."). Also Hockett, *Capital Commons,* supra note 1; and Hockett, *Wealth of Our Commonwealth, supra* note 1.
27. *See* Knut Wicksell, Geldzins Und Güterpreise (1898).

28. See Robert Hockett, *Recursive Collective Action Problems: The Structure of Procyclicality in Money Markets, Macroeconomies, and Formally Similar Contexts*, 3 Journal Of Financial Perspectives 1 (2013), available at https://papers.ssrn.com/sol3/papers.cfm?abstract_id=2239849.
29. The distinction between and relations among what the present author calls "credit- modulatory" policy on the one hand and "credit-allocative" policy on the other are fundamental to the author's work of the past 12 years, and failure to attend carefully to their relations accounts for a surprisingly large portion of the most salient financial and macroeconomic disasters of the past century. For essential background, see Hockett, *Fixer-Upper, supra* note 13 (introducing the distinction and proposing 'regulation as modulation' as preferred model of financial supervision); and Hockett, *The Macroprudential Turn, supra* note 13. For discussion of the practical inseparability of the conceptually distinct allocation and modulation functions, and of the consequences of this inseparability for the sustainability of our present practice of assigning allocation to Treasury and modulation to the Fed, see Robert Hockett, *Scissors Require Two Blades: Central Bank Independence with (Principled) Central Bank Allocation*, 65 Challenge (2022) (forthcoming), at https://papers.ssrn.com/sol3/papers.cfm?abstract_id=3918988. Also Robert Hockett, "Money in Context, Part 1," *Law & Political Economy*, April 8, 2020, available at https://lpeproject.org/blog/money-in-context-part-1/; and Robert Hockett, "Money in Context, Part 2," *Law & Political Economy*, April 9, 2020, available at https://lpeproject.org/blog/money-in-context-part-2/.
30. *See* Hockett, *Finance Without Financiers, supra* note 15.
31. The "Austrians"—Böhm-Bawerk, von Mises, Hayek, Schumpeter ...—kind of "got" this. But unlike the Swedes—principally Wicksell and Myrdal—who tipped them off, all of them save Schumpeter seem to have had Freudian 'issues' with authority. Hence they overlooked this solution, which is the only solution. In fine Habsburg fashion, they re-fetishized metal finery instead. Fisher, more on whom presently, 'got' it as well, but he seems to have thought we could get on *without* public capital. We can, provided we're cool with subsistence-level production.
32. I allude to the familiar "Hegelian" pattern pursuant to which, as societies develop, solutions that they have earlier developed to particular challenges grow obsolete as the forms that those challenges take themselves develop, then are updated to address the new forms that the challenges take. *See* G.W.F. Hegel, Phänomenologie des Geistes (1807). In the present context, I will be showing in Chapters 1–4 how monetary relations within any community begin as informal accounting—credit, debit, and hence "payment"—relations tractable on mental or paper "account books," or ledgers; then move to circulating currencies that function as payment ledger substitutes when societies grow too large and productively complex for their credit and debit—their "payment"—relations to be tracked mentally or on paper

account books; and then return, in a sort of "higher synthesis," to ledger accounting once communications and payment technologies grow sufficiently sophisticated to track even complex and far-flung sets of credit and debit relations.

4

Franchise Finance: Why and How We Got Here

Why we first instituted de facto public–private finance franchise arrangements, and why we have allowed them to radiate steadily outward from their banking and payments system cores to the farthest reaches of our shadow banking and broader financial systems, can be gleaned by addressing three questions. All three are implicated by the opening remarks in Chapter 3, where I said that our system distributes a uniform national currency and its credit equivalent, and the answers to all three implicate technological limitation that once constrained us but no longer constrain us.

The pertinent questions to which I allude are: first, why "currency and its credit equivalent"; second, why uniformity; and third, why uniformity through franchising rather than through direct distribution? My replies to these questions indicate not only why we now publicly franchise, but also why we both can and now ought to move on to a more thoroughly republican form of digitized ledger finance such as Chapters 6–8 describe and prescribe.

4.1 Why Credit and Currency

I begin with a brief reminder of what a financial system is for, and the roles credit, money, and payments play in any such system. This reminder, in turn, makes use of the concepts and categories defined above in Chapter 2.

R. C. Hockett, *The Citizens' Ledger*,
https://doi.org/10.1007/978-3-030-99566-9_4

4.1.1 Credit: Production and Payment in Time

As I suggested in prior chapters, finance is the means by which people or entities presently lacking in resources necessary to engage in productive activity secure temporary or ongoing access to those resources from others who have them. It is, in other words, the means by which productive units productively borrow.[1] One way to do this would be for the would-be user of resources simply to borrow them directly from their possessors, then return them as-is or in-kind.[2] A credit transaction then would occur, with the lender conveying the needed resource and the borrower conveying a promise to return the resource as-is or in-kind at some later date, perhaps with a premium couched as a "rental" payment.[3]

This would amount to a borrowing rendition of barter, as inconvenient and transaction-slowing, and therefore production-slowing, as barter is in any exchange economy with a complex division of labor and resources deployed in productive activity.[4] Non-stone-age economies accordingly employ, as noted earlier, some form of fungible *money or ledger accounting* in exchanges of resources and repayment promises just as they employ money or ledger accounting in exchanges of goods and services.[5] It is how they efficiently transfer and track mutual credits and debits among transacting parties.

The same medium that is used to *purchase* goods or services for production or consumption is accordingly *lent*—or "advanced"—for the purchase of goods and services; indeed the latter appears historically to precede the former.[6] We call that medium "money," which amounts among other things to a universally usable mode of payment for—or claim upon—resources.[7] Money is how, or that with which, we pay—it is that which "counts" for purposes of our "accounting" to one another where mutual exchange and attendant obligations—credits and debits—are concerned.[8]

4.1.2 Currency: From Ledgers to Tokens—And Back

Money of course need not take any particular physical form. Where societies are small enough, or claim-tracking technologies sophisticated enough, a formally or informally kept "account book" or "mental ledger" suffices to "keep score"—that is, to keep track of everyone's claims and counterclaims, credits and debits, assets and liabilities.[9] Coin and currency get into the act only when societies grow large and complex enough to render informal "mental" accounting and even paper "book-keeping" incapable of tracking all transactions, while still being technologically underdeveloped enough to render a single formally kept *digital* social account book or ledger not yet practicable.[10]

Currency and coin are in this sense intermediate-stage payment technologies in monetary evolution.[11] They are means of "*keeping* accounts" with each other in a common "*unit* of account"—a "common currency" or "coin of the realm"—even when we do not all know one another or have means of recording and tracking our many exchanges with one another on one common ledger or spreadsheet.[12] They are in other words primitive *ledger-substitutes*, we might say.[13]

This observation affords us a clue as to why coin and currency issuance typically become sovereign functions—in a commercial republic, republican functions—as economies and the polities in which they are always embedded grow ever-more populous, socially complex, and technologically advanced.[14] Just as people in very small societies or proto-polities could in theory keep accounts with one another through debit and credit entries in a common mental or paper book-like ledger, so could they decentralize that account-keeping as they grew larger and no longer able to use the same physical book.[15] They could do so by conveying individually issued promissory notes to one another, with holders understood to have claims upon issuers.[16]

This is essentially how wooden "tally sticks" and breakable clay, then metal, tablets, and bars—the first circulating currencies—functioned in ancient societies.[17] The break pattern clearly identified who owed whom by reference to who held each half of the broken token.[18]

The problem this left was that the same growth in population and economic complexity that prompted the move from mental accounting to what we might call "metal accounting"—that is, to commercial- and financial-instrument-issuing—ultimately rendered *private* instrument-issuing, like mental accounting, unsatisfactorily transaction-limiting and hence production-limiting too.[19] Broad transferability and hence usability of claim tokens was limited to those able to "credit"—that is, to believe in the *credibility* of—the token-issuer.[20]

It was natural in this circumstance to begin centralizing token-issuance, which for present purposes is best seen as a step toward reinstituting centralized bookkeeping to societies that have grown beyond *both* informal account-keeping *and* private token-issuing.[21] This form of centralization has historically taken two forms.[22] And the second of these forms can be viewed in principle as the near-completion of the first, even though in some cases it has in practice chronologically preceded the first, owing to late discovery of the need for currencies to become "elastic," as I will explain.[23]

The first mode of centralization was the establishment of institutions with which large numbers of people could maintain monetary—that is, again, credit and debit—relations, which then could act as account-keepers for all of them, transferring credits and debits among them on single account books.[24] Call this "the physical ledger strategy," a more broadly usable digital rendition of which I will be schematizing and advocating below in Chapters 6–8.[25]

The second mode of centralization was for sovereign or quasi-sovereign authorities themselves to issue tokens that could function as claims and payment media far more widely—at the limit, throughout their jurisdictions or realms—than could privately issued tokens.[26] Subjects or citizens then could lay hold of such tokens either by making tax payments in kind—for example, in the form of crop shares paid the local liege lord, or grain bushels requisitioned by a priestly authority—or by temporarily swapping private promissory tokens for public promissory tokens.[27] Here centralization of issuance substitutes for centralization of account-keeping. Call this "the sovereign issuance" strategy, which I shall show now to be digitally mergeable with the ledger strategy when I get to Chapters 6–8.

In most societies still in existence, the second mode of re-centralization seems to have preceded the first, with the first added on only later as societies groped toward recognition that money supplies must be elastic and what I call "modulatable"—that is, adjustable to accommodate fluctuating transaction and productive credit demand.[28] Authorities dispensed tokens as evidences of payment-obligations'—in effect, tax obligations'—fulfillment.[29] Because the mentioned obligations were universal and ongoing, the tokens, as de facto tax receipts representing the authority's obligation to recognize payments' having been made, were universally desired.[30]

These tokens of "vertical" credit/debit relation between sovereign and subject or republic and citizen accordingly came to function as means of discharging even "horizontal" credit/debit relations among subjects or citizens *inter se*.[31] Originally fashioned of clay into which sovereign seals could be stamped before baking for purposes of authentication, in time they came to be fashioned of more durable yet malleable metals resistant to corrosion, for which purposes gold and silver were most suitable.[32] Here lies the origin of sovereign-stamped metal coinage—not to mention of coin-metals' perceived preciousness.[33]

Banks got into the money business—indeed, came even so much as to exist—in these societies much later than tribute-requisitioning and receipt-issuing sovereigns and quasi-sovereigns.[34] They began as metalsmiths whose business required the keeping of safes.[35] Safe-ownership led naturally to a sidelight, that of metal storage for a fee—bailment.[36] Holding metal in trust for many people in time came to recommend issuance of "claim checks" used to keep track of whose metal stores metalsmiths held.[37] Some smiths—the most trusted ones—might well have simply kept books.[38] Others, with clients less trusting, issued verifiable claim tokens.[39]

In time it came to be recognized that claim tokens could substitute, as payment media, for the heavier metal coins or other objects that they represented claims upon, and then that they also could be issued in excess of those metal stores themselves.[40] The life of fully functional "elastic currencies"—moneys whose supply could in theory be modulated more readily than metals could be mined and then minted—effectively commenced at this juncture.[41] Metalsmiths who had banked soon became bankers, full stop.[42] These bankers could spend their own claim checks as money or lend them to others at interest so long as they did not issue too far in excess of metal stores.[43] Fractional-reserve banking was born.[44]

Public authorities appear to have permitted this eventually burgeoning private practice owing to the advantages an elastic currency afforded.[45] Money supplies could grow to accommodate growing transaction volume as economies grew, even when metal-mining couldn't keep pace.[46] All that was needed was to ensure that they did not grow *too* fast—at rates that brought excess inflationary pressure, excess liquidity risk, or both.[47] (Excess metal-mining, which did sometimes happen even if but rarely, could exert similar inflationary pressure. This seems to have happened, most notably, after Spain and Portugal struck silver in conquered South American territories.) So sovereigns allowed, but also regulated, private bank currency issuance based upon sovereign coin issuance.[48] And they let bankers lend in those currencies at interest so as to facilitate trade, investment, productive activity, and growth.[49] In effect, they shared their seigniorage, which their coin issuance long had afforded, with bankers in the form that new note issuance afforded.[50]

This privatized "note seigniorage" was meant to serve as an incentive to bankers to lend prudently and productively—that is, in ways that were well calculated to prove wealth-generating.[51] In effect, sovereigns were outsourcing the role of productively issuing and lending sovereign claims upon resources, money—in elastic, readily multipliable, hence modulatable paper form—to their citizens.[52] And they were controlling the quality of the multiplied money by requiring licensure of its private disseminators and regulating their activities.[53] In effect, what I call the finance franchise was born.[54]

But with the currency elasticity and prudent lending incentives this system brought came to a vulnerability as well, the seriousness of which varied inversely with the effectiveness of sovereign franchisor monitoring of franchisee institutions' activities.[55] That was the danger of losing, through the franchise arrangement itself, precisely that form of monetary uniformity and associated de facto account centralization that sovereign coin issuance had afforded in the first place.[56]

This takes us to a closer look at the need for monetary uniformity, as well as at the single most idiosyncratic historical attribute of the American rendition of the finance franchise: its having had, until late in the game, a multitude of ersatz-franchisee money-issuing institutions under the control of no single coherently acting franchisor money-modulating institution.[57] This is important in understanding both the nature of the present American financial system and the necessity of that modernization of this system which Chapters 6–8 propose below.[58]

4.2 Why Uniformity

Franchises, as noted above, are among other things uniformity—maintenance regimes.[59] The reason for *monetary* uniformity is not unlike that for hotel room or foodstuff uniformity of the sort that franchise arrangements in those industries ensure.[60] But it also is much more compelling. A well-functioning and fully integrated economy, in both its productive and its distributive functions, requires a common unit of account and a common payment medium whose value as measured in that unit is reasonably insensitive to variations among issuers, users, transaction locations, and time intervals.[61]

These are the twin needs that necessitate "account uniformity" of the kind that I noted above as economies grow in both size and complexity—the kind that amounts to the keeping of a single ledger or the using of its functional equivalent, a uniform coin or currency.[62] We can think of these as forms of what I will call spatial and temporal uniformity. The story of the *American* republic's gradual securing of those forms of uniformity for its money and, through that, its commercial and financial systems, is illustrative of this evolution across jurisdictions—many of which modernized their systems well before the U.S. managed to do so. It is also a story of long struggle.[63] And this is because the story of America's gradual attainment of coherent national *sovereignty itself*, like most other countries', is a story of long—and at times tragically violent—struggle.[64]

4.2.1 Spatial Uniformity: Payments and "Universal Equivalents"

Before U.S. federal passage of a sequence of mutually complementary legal tender, currency, and banking acts in the early 1860s, there was neither a single national payment ledger nor any national "dollar bill" worth the name in the U.S.[65] The circulating medium—the token-form substitute for a centralized ledger—took the form primarily of privately issued banknotes.[66] These were effectively paper "claim checks" or currencies representing claims upon private sector banking institutions.[67] The claims they betokened were in theory redeemable in precious metal specie minted by many different sovereigns or, as time went on, various forms of primarily but not solely publicly issued debt.[68] Banks for their part were kept local by the only public authorities then legislatively authorized to license and regulate them: sub-sovereign U.S. state governments.[69]

This arrangement, because it fell short both of a national ledger and of any uniform national currency that could serve as that ledger's circulating functional equivalent, posed two challenges to efficient transcontinental market integration across the still young U.S.[70] First, payment in one state out of accounts held in another state was fraught with uncertainty.[71] Differing states regulated banks with differing degrees of strictness and effectiveness.[72] New York and New England, for example, appear to have been doing quite well by the mid-nineteenth century, while Nebraska and Michigan did notoriously poorly at that time.[73] This meant in turn that the practical redeemability, and hence ultimate reliability, of notes issued by, or of drafts drawn upon accounts maintained with, banks in one state could appear "iffy" to counterparties domiciled in other states.[74]

In effect, every state had its own licensed private purveyors of private money variously backed, with purveyor reliability varying according to backer liability and of course charter address.[75] This in turn meant that the dollar, though in theory a national unit of account, could not in practice serve either as such a unit—there *was* no centralized national account amalgamating all citizen accounts—or as a bona fide national currency *substituting* for credits and debits on a national account.[76] A nominal dollar note issued by, say, Wyatt Earp Bank in Kansas might circulate at par or near-par, while another nominal dollar note issued by Jesse James Bank in Texas might circulate at but 20% of par; that is not good for Kansas-to- Texas cross-border transacting.[77]

The second challenge posed by spatial non-uniformity in the U.S. was the intrastate counterpart of the interstate challenge just noted. It was that, in states where bank chartering and regulation were lax, currencies could vary in value relative to one another even *within* states.[78] Wildcat Bank's dollar might trade at twelve cents up in Omaha, while Eagle Bank's dollar might trade at par in the same general vicinity. This patchwork form of reliability found reflection in merchants' having to maintain periodically updated discount schedules for locally used currencies, advising for how many cents on the dollar to count various private bank currencies when these were offered in payment for goods or services.[79] That too, of course, operated as an impediment to (intrastate) transaction activity—an impediment more pervasive than that to what was then still only nascent interstate commerce.[80]

In many ways, this "wildcat" era in banking—called "free banking" by its advocates during the rare intervals that it was not in crisis—confronted market participants with a bewildering array of wildly fluctuating payment media reminiscent of that which confronts those who use newly issued privately issued cryptocurrencies today.[81] I will have more to say on that later when I propose, in Chapters 6–8, a publicly administered Democratic Digital Currency associated with my proposed system of digital Citizen and Resident Wallets. For present purposes, what matters is what ultimately emerged as the nineteenth-century U.S.'s imperfect paper currency substitute for my proposal, which latter simply brings systems like that of the former into the twenty-first century.

I allude to the institution, through the Legal Tender Act of 1862,[82] the National Currency Act of 1863,[83] and the National Banking Act of 1864,[84] of a nationwide network of federally chartered National Banks, located all over the U.S., all subject to the same regulatory standards and all issuing notes convertible into the very same Treasury-issued currency—tellingly called then "the Greenback."[85] This was effectively the birth of the U.S. dollar as we now know it—a centrally issued and universally employed money that is not only a unit of account, but also a bona fide payment medium circulating throughout the entire republic.[86] It was a centralized ledger-substitute,[87] a uniform currency whose nationwide uniformity in effect substituted for the "centrality" of a centralized national ledger that at the time was not technologically feasible but now is in the way that Chapters 6–8 will elaborate.[88]

The new 1860s regime marked the commencement of the American republic's rendition of the full finance franchise described above.[89] It delegated quality control duties to a newly established federal instrumentality whose name becomes comprehensible against the backdrop just narrated; I refer to the OCC.[90] It is instructive that this agency, contemporarily described simply as a bank regulator, was originally a *currency* regulator.[91] The Comptroller, whose name derives suggestively from an archaic English word for controller, was essentially the agent through whom our finance franchisor, the sovereign public, "controlled"—that is, maintained the quality of—that which it franchised, the dollar.[92]

Of course, this involved maintaining what we have ever since called the "safety and soundness" (believe it or not, that is a term of art) of the franchisee institutions—the banks—in the U.S.[93] But the primary reason for federally maintaining that safety and soundness was precisely the fact that, as distributors of that public good which is the public's currency, these institutions were in effect privately owned public utilities.[94] They were accordingly locked into partnership with the designated agent of the American public itself—its Currency Controller.[95]

The American banking and currency reforms of the 1860s comprehensively transformed the U.S.' interlinked banking, financial, and monetary systems.[96] In very short order there were federally chartered banks in most states and territories of the American Union, all of them subject to uniform regulatory standards—including that every $100 in notes be backed by $111 in U.S. sovereign securities—and all of them issuing, accordingly, a de facto uniform national currency with a uniform value.[97] These banks also sold U.S. Treasury securities, effectively making them a system of outlets for the issuance of *both* of our federal government's principal circulating liabilities at the time—Greenbacks and T-Bills.[98] In very little time, "wildcat" banknotes lost value and drained out of circulation.[99]

4.2.2 Temporal Uniformity: "Sound Money" and "Elastic Currency"

The foregoing paragraphs implicate two of money's oft-noted functions—its serving both as a "unit of account" and as a "medium of exchange."[100] The other role typically observed to be played by money—its function as a "store of value"—is what lay behind the U.S. polity's later replacement of the Comptroller as money-modulator by a new central bank, the Fed.[101]

Key to maintaining a currency's stable value over time—that is, to preventing inordinate inflation and deflation—is the capacity to fine-tune and regularly readjust the supply of that currency as transaction volume in the "real" economy grows, shrinks, or fluctuates.[102] The currency must, in the words I used earlier, be elastic and modulatable.[103] Its supply must be adjustable (a) to accommodate, while not *over*-accommodating, transaction and credit demand, and (b) to counteract sudden and destabilizing credit expansions or contractions.[104]

> The idea is to maintain just enough credit-money supply to accommodate desired transaction volumes and enable productive investment, so as not needlessly to squelch either, while at the same time preventing over-issuance of the sort that can spark inflation—the classic problem of "too much money" chasing "too few goods." A money whose supply can be "modulated" in this way … is essential if we're to avoid needlessly disrupting either transaction activity, investment activity, or currency value. And that is to say it's essential [if people would maintain smooth, steady growth of their national wealth and productive capacity.[105]

This is why, as noted above, polities in the early modern era tolerated metalsmiths' and then bankers' issuances of what came to be widely spendable "claim checks" in excess of their sovereign-issued metal coin stores.[106] It is also why they regulated them carefully; regulation was as much about monetary control—what I call "money modulation"—as it was about consumer protection.[107] But the American republic, founded partly by landed aristocrats who were suspicious of centralized political governance and centralized banking alike, had to rediscover for itself the dependence of money's temporal uniformity upon public money modulation.[108]

> The OCC in particular and Treasury more generally were not well equipped, operationally or transaction- technologically speaking, to engage in the daily money- modulatory task that maintaining a value-retentive elastic currency requires—particularly not so long as state-chartered banks now offering checkable deposits in lieu of private banknotes continued to operate alongside the new national banking system.[109]

The Second Bank of the U.S. from 1816 to 1836 on the one hand, and the central banks familiar to the rest of the world since the late seventeenth century, on the other hand (notably the Swedish Riksbank, the Dutch Rijksbank, the Bank of England, and the Banque de France), had shown the means of performing that function.[110] In serving as "banks to other banks," they had developed methods by which publicly to modulate private bank currency-issuance in ever more finely tuned and sophisticated ways, including a "public market-actor" role.[111] In a similar but unavoidably less complete manner, clearing house arrangements among U.S. private sector banks had developed means of at least partly buffering note-issuing private sector banks against periodic liquidity shocks.[112]

The U.S. thus patterned its own version of a central bank partly on its own earlier Banks of the U.S., partly on European—especially German—models, and partly on these clearinghouse arrangements. This it did with the

Federal Reserve Act of 1913, which like the banking acts of the 1860s was proximately occasioned by a crisis—this time the market panic of 1907.[113]

The Federal Reserve Act, especially as supplemented by further legislation during the New Deal, established the Fed of today, and transferred de facto and de jure administration of the U.S.'s national money supply from the Comptroller to the new instrumentality.[114]

Yesterday's "Greenback" Treasury notes became today's green "Federal Reserve Notes" [(Fed Notes)].[115] That means that while Americans are still using "banknotes" of a sort as currency much as they did in the nineteenth century, the notes in question are now *public* banknotes—"central" banknotes—rather than *private* banknotes.[116] We might even call them *Citizen* Notes, or claim-check equivalents of dollar-denominated credits in incipient Citizen Wallets tracked on an implicit or incipient Fed-administered Citizens' Ledger of the kind I shall design and advocate below.[117] They are issued and spent in the name of the citizenry.[118] And so Americans now have a publicly franchised good—a sovereign currency—that is more or less uniform not only across space, but also across time, as the Fed engages in daily monetary operations aimed at preventing inflation and deflation alike.[119]

It bears repeating that what is true of Federal Reserve Notes in this connection is true of *credit* extended in Fed Note denominated increments too.[120] The loan that a private sector bank or other Fed-accommodated financial institution makes in the form of a newly opened or credited deposit is made in the form of dollar-denominated drawing or spending rights—credits, or "assets." By accounting convention (again, double-entry bookkeeping), these correspond to counterpart dollar-denominated bank debits, or "liabilities."[121] Since the Fed-administered payments system recognizes payments made out of these deposits as settling transactions, dollar increments of these bank liabilities are functional equivalents of dollar bills.[122]

Once we appreciate this, and once we remind ourselves both that those dollar bills are Fed Notes and that one gives the bank a signed *promissory* note for one's *loan*, we are able to see something else in addition: a loan is simply a *temporary swap* of a *citizen's* promissory note for *central bank* promissory notes—of one's privately issued money for more widely spendable publicly issued money.[123] This is the contemporary form taken by what I labeled above "vertical" tokens coming to function as "horizontal" tokens. Modern bank lending is in this sense just temporary private–public currency swapping.[124] That is how things have long been in Europe and, for less long, in the U.S. and the rest of the world as well.[125] The reasons are found in the tale just told.[126]

But why do Americans and their counterparts in other commercial republics worldwide *still* operate in this way? Why do we all still franchise finance and in effect outsource much of our payment infrastructures' provision to the private sector institutions whose managed accounts we use as its pillars? Must we continue to do so? Why not make publicly issued money elastic and modulatable, not by supplementing it with dollar-denominated *bank*-ledger credit-money, as we all now do, but with *central bank*—or *finance ministry*-ledger money—digitized *Public* or *Citizens'* Ledger money, as we will be able very soon to do?[127]

As it happens, there once were good functional reasons for incremental resort to public–private franchising where our republics' financial and commercial infrastructures were concerned—reasons rooted in the early modern polities' incomplete sovereignty during their first centuries, give or take.[128] But those reasons have by and large long since receded, as I will now indicate. This means our civilization's long detour in the realm of ledger-substitute coin and currency can end. It means that fully public-administered digital Citizens' Ledgers and associated Democratic Digital Currencies are now possible and indeed easily instituted, as I shall demonstrate.

Notes

1. There is, accordingly, a trans-temporal element baked in to the concept of finance, as the word's etymology—"fin," meaning "finish" or "end"—itself suggests. I refer here primarily to "productive" finance rather than finance for consumption because productive activity is in an important sense "prior" to consumption activity. Any economy that has moved beyond gathering to hunter-gathering or more is an economy in which that which is consumed has been grown, killed, constructed, or otherwise produced. Indeed, even much gathering is in a certain sense producing. *See Rousseauvian Money, supra* note 3 at 37–38 (describing financial institutions as making productive activity possible, whereby productive activity "allow[s] us … to spend now (part of) what we won't actually have until later.").
2. *See Rousseauvian Money*, *supra* note 3, at 38–41 (explaining that "when you borrow money … you just temporarily trade your own notes for Fed notes").
3. *Id.*
4. *Id.* at 13 ("And because we organize productive activity, in a decentralized exchange economy such as our own, largely by swapping obligations—that is, by contracting—the principal medium through which such organizing is done is our money.").

5. I intend this less as a historical claim than a functional one. Nor do I mean by "exchange economy" a "private ownership economy." With respect to the latter point, communal economies involve exchange just as private property economies do. And as to the first point, no historical evidence supports the common economist's argument that money "was invented to improve upon barter," or even that barter occurred much at all. Indeed all available evidence suggests that monetary arrangements grew out of highly "networked" state, social, and religious authority-maintained credit systems. *See, e.g.*, PETER EINZIG, PRIMITIVE MONEY 316 (2nd ed. 1966) (illustrating several definitions of money, including "means of purchasing goods and services and of defraying social costs" and "a commodity which is habitually and without hesitation taken by anybody in exchange for a commodity"); DAVID GRAEBER, DEBT: THE FIRST 5,000 YEARS 21–23 (2011) (describing the forms money has taken, including as a "medium of exchange, unit of account, and store of value"); A. HINGSTON QUIGGIN, A SURVEY OF PRIMITIVE MONEY 3–4 (Barnes & Noble, Inc. 1970) (1949) (categorizing money as a "recognized medium of exchange, a standard of value and a symbol of wealth"); MICHAEL HUDSON & MICHAEL VAN DE MIEROP, DEBT AND ECONOMIC RENEWAL IN THE ANCIENT NEAR EAST 165–69 (2002) (summarizing seventeenth- and eighteenth-century financing, including the credit system that supported the natural resources market); Alfred Mitchell-Innes, *What Is Money?*, 30 BANKING L.J. 377, 377–78 (1913) (describing that "by common consent one particular commodity is fixed on which is generally acceptable and which therefore, everyone will take in exchange for the things he produces or the services he renders and which each in turn can equally pass on to others in exchange for whatever he may want; That this commodity thus becomes a 'medium of exchange and measure of value.' That a sale is the exchange of a commodity for this intermediate commodity which is called 'money'").
6. *See Rousseauvian Money*, *supra* note 3, at 38 (explaining that "money's being a kind of circulating credit/debit is part of what enables it to function as an inter-temporal claim—a 'store of value'—in the first place").
7. *Id.* at 34–36 ("Insofar as money functions as a medium of exchange, it can be thought of as a claim upon what it's exchanged for. It's status as legal tender makes it a legal claim upon what it buys—a claim upon resources.").
8. *Id.* at 16–17 ("The next thing to note is how readily our obligations here—what is due, what is owed—will be 'cashed out' at discharge into something like money. In so doing, we'll see not only money's rootedness in normativity, obligation, accountability and associated accounting, but also its elaboration into the notions of credit, asset, and liability that populate the familiar legal and financial 'universe'").
9. *Id.* at 38 ("And just as your merely 'mentally tracked' promise did in our you, me, and Jean-Jacques story, where scale was sufficiently small, trust

sufficiently high, and matters sufficiently simple as to allow for the keeping of mere 'mental accounts.'").

10. *Id.* at 24–25 ("When populations grow larger and asset/liability relations grow more farflung and complex, however, things must be 'formalized' and 'regularized.' That is so if for no other reason than to enable us all to 'keep track' and 'verify.'"); *see also* QUIGGIN, *supra* note 71, at 4–5 (describing general difficulties in a bartering system and that such problems were later avoided by "elaborate customs of credit, deferred payments or payment by services.").
11. *Rousseauvian Money*, *supra* note 3, at 28 (describing the process by which currency can be introduced and formalized until it is officially made commonplace).
12. *Id.* ("What we do is develop means of converting small-group-recognizable 'horizontal,' or 'private,' IOUs into full-polity-recognizable 'vertical,' or 'public,' IOUs. Then we have truly common 'common currency.'").
13. *Id.* at 18–19 (illustrating informal ledgers via running chores hypothetical).
14. *Id.* at 24–26 ("When populations grow larger and asset/liability relations grow more farflung and complex, however, things must be 'formalized' and 'regularized.' That is so if for no other reason than to enable us all to 'keep track' and 'verify.'").
15. *Id.* at 9 ("Productive and distributive activity in decentralized exchange economies pervasively involves joint exchanges of promises, hence joint issuance of countless reciprocal obligations ... Citizens authorize one another to demand that such promises be honored and obligations be met.").
16. *Id.* at 26–27.
17. *Rousseauvian Money*, *supra* note 3, at 44 ("The important thing about claim checks was never their material form, but the fact that they reliably represented claims. 44 Receipts of this kind actually took many different material forms over time. In the early Near East, clay tokens stamped with the grain authority's seal were the most convenient form.").
18. Mitchell-Innes, *supra* note 71, at 395 (describing the process by which a coin was broken to serve as a tally for a debtor-creditor relationship); HENRY DUNNING MACLEOD, THE THEORY OF CREDIT 83–84 (2nd ed. 1889) (illustrating the different types of substances used to represent currency).
19. *Rousseauvian Money*, *supra* note 3, at 46–47 ("The credit-money—the 'finance capital'—supply must be able to grow at a rate that allows for this resource stock to grow through the productive activity of those who need claims upon current such resources—that is, again, money—in order to produce future resources"); Mitchell-Innes, *The Credit Theory of Money*, 31 BANKING LAW JOURNAL 151 (1914) (discussing how buying and selling are really only exchanging promises to pay); N.T. Skaggs, *Debt as the Basis of Currency*, 57 AMERICAN JOURNAL OF ECONOMICS AND SOCIOLOGY 453,

456–59 (1998) (discussing the disadvantages of a metallic currency, and the evolution of money).

20. *Rousseauvian Money*, *supra* note 3, at 47 ("It's all about optimizing productive capacity ... Too little money—too little finance capital—diminishes such capacity... Too much money—too much finance capital—diminishes the reliability of money as a claim-transfer device, hence again productive capacity.").
21. *Id.* at 14 ("... [J]ust as state and economy emerge, respectively, out of the (contract-like) authority and (contract-like) obligation birthed by the joint 'we,' so is money simply the authoritative means of signifying and discharging the multiple (contract-like) obligations ...").
22. *Id.* at 37 (discussing the purpose of financial institutions, especially in regard to enabling productive activity).
23. *Id.* at 39–40 (explaining the dual private promissory note and public promissory note system).
24. *See id.* at 19 (explaining the concept of a ledger as a set of accounts through which multiple parties owing obligations to each other another transfer debt and credit).
25. *Rousseauvian Money*, *supra* note 3, at 19 ("[W]e'll call it a *ledger*.").
26. *Id.* at 26 ("[M]odern societies deem certain 'privately'—that is 'horizontally'—incurred obligations 'publicly recognized' and hence 'vertically' enforceable in special adjudicative institutions we call 'courts.'").
27. *See id.* at 43 (observing receipts can function as assets to their recipients and as liabilities to their issuers). *See also* EINZIG, *supra* note 71, at 316 (illustrating several definitions of money, including "means of purchasing goods and services and of defraying social costs" and "a commodity which is habitually and without hesitation taken by anybody in exchange for a commodity").
28. *Rousseauvian Money*, *supra* note 3 at 42 (on how civilizations heavily dependent on agriculture stored grain during "fat years" in anticipation of "lean years" due to fluctuating crop yields).
29. *Id.* at 42 ("Growers were required to make 'grain deposits' into a community pool, which requirement operated as a kind of tax or mandatory social insurance premium, both of which boil down to essentially the same thing").
30. *Id.* at 43 ("These are public liabilities that circulate as private assets, so everyone uses and accepts them.").
31. *Id.* at 43 ("Once 'tax receipts' become 'vertical claim checks' ... they begin circulating as 'horizontal claims' too among those who need them ...").
32. *Id.* at 43 (explaining claim checks represented by many different material forms such as clay tokens in the early Near East and overtime by precious metals).
33. *Id.* at 44 (["T]hese metals *became* 'precious' largely because they came to be used widely as material representations of money claims."). An irony

here is that these 'precious' metals, rather than becoming money because they were precious, instead became precious because they were money. *See* Daniela Pylypczak-Wasylyszn, *The Historical Value of Silver: A 2000-Year Overview*, CommodityHQ.com (June 24, 2015), https://commodityhq.com/education/a-brief-2000-year-history-of-silver-prices/ [https://perma.cc/734G-UPLC] (documenting declines in money-price of silver when it has ceased to be used as a money medium).

34. *Rousseauvian Money*, *supra* note 3, at 45 ("The benches—or '*banca*,' as benches are still called in Italy where this practice first developed—on which metalsmiths did their smithing gave their name to what we now call 'banking'.").
35. *Id.* ("People began 'depositing' their metal with metalsmiths who happened to have safes, for 'safe-keeping.'").
36. *Id*. (explaining how once claim checks began circulating as paper currency metalsmiths could issue checks for lending at interest).
37. *Id.*
38. *Id.* (explaining the smiths' move from metal to banking).
39. *Id.* at 45.
40. *Id.* ("It also didn't take long for the metalsmiths to discover …[o]nce their claim checks began circulating as paper currency, they could issue such checks *to themselves* in order to buy things.").
41. *Id.* (explaining how coins were magnified by practice of issuing derivative paper claims as multiples of metallic claims, causing the money supply to increase many-fold).
42. *Id.* ("[P]eople began 'depositing' their metals with metalsmiths who happened to have safes …. The smiths issued paper claim checks upon the deposited metals.").
43. *Id.* ("Once their claim checks began circulating as paper currency, they could issue such checks to themselves in order to buy things. They could also issue such checks for lending at interest. As long as the checks were not issued too far in excess of the metal in store, there was no danger in doing this, and there was much gain to be had.").
44. *Id.* ("[T]he practice of issuing more notes than one had metal became known as 'fractional reserve banking.'").
45. *Id.* ("In time this line of work unsurprisingly became much more lucrative than metalsmithing.").
46. *Id.* ("[T]he elastic currency could be 'over-stretched,' issued too far in excess of the metal that 'backed' it.").
47. *Rousseauvian Money*, *supra* note 3, at 45–46 ("One could 'over-promise' by issuing too many promissory notes, which would undercut the value of promise and promissory note alike.").
48. A banker who over-issued and went insolvent in consequence was deemed "bankrupt"—a term that derives from the practice of public officials ceremonially—*rupta*, from which the English word "rupture" derives—the

benches—*banca*—on which metal-smith bankers plied their trade in late Medieval Italy, where modern European banking originated. (The Italians were first among Europeans because they were first to trade extensively with Asia and North Africa, where commercial and associated financial practice were then far in advance of their European counterparts.) *See id.* at 46 (observing much of bank regulation during olden days involved licensing requirements and reserve regulations to avert risk of elastic currency being issued too far in excess).

49. *Rousseauvian Money*, *supra* note 3, at 46 (explaining how various jurisdictions permitted banks to issue claim tokens for promoting growth).
50. *Id*. at 45 (stating that note issuance allowed for "a currency whose supply could be grown both to accommodate growing transaction activity and to finance growing productive activity").
51. *Id.* at 45–46 (observing that "this practice of issuing more notes than they had metal made banker's business … profitable").
52. *Id.* at 40, 45–46 (theorizing that publicly licensed private banks act as outsourced credit checkers for the central sovereign entity).
53. *Id.* at 40 (stating that federally regulated banks "assist our Fed … in temporarily transforming private money into public money").
54. *Id.* at 41 (stating that reliance on the "public full faith and credit" of the sovereign allows for "the franchise" of proliferated private banking by a multitude of financial entities).
55. *See Rousseauvian Money*, *supra* note 3, at 45–46 (observing that franchisee lending of sovereign tender was "risky—both for the banker and for society—because the elastic currency could be 'over-stretched,' issued too far in excess of the metal that 'backed' it"); *see also Finance without Financiers*, *supra* note 1 (stating that "the public franchisor … retains primary responsibility for preventing both under- and over-generation of credit").
56. *See Rousseuvian Money*, *supra* note 3, at 45–46 (stating that "bank-licensing requirements and reserve-regulation" appeared at attempts at maintaining through the financial franchise the uniformity once afforded by sovereign coin issuance).
57. *Money's Past*, *supra* note 17, at 4 (observing that, in the early days of the U.S., "the U.S. Mint minted coins [and] the Treasury issued some paper… [b]ut paper money—'notes'—were issued primarily by private banking institutions until late in the nineteenth century").
58. *Id.* at 4–6 (providing an overview of U.S. currency issuance from the late eighteenth century through twentieth century).
59. *Id.* at 3 (explaining that "banks are franchisees, while we the sovereign public are the franchisor and our national money—the dollar, the monetized full faith and credit of the United States—is the franchised good").
60. Fast food and hotel franchises emerged and spread through the American economy, for example, at the same time that the U.S. interstate highway

system developed across the country and newly affluent Americans began taking road trips and family vacations. However good or bad the accommodations or foodstuffs might be in the places one visited or re-provisioned at, one could at least rest assured they were no more undesirable than their counterparts back home. That is the sense in which franchises were "quality control" compacts. *Id.* ("You can think of the uniform value and appearance of our currency as being a bit like those identical sandwiches and golden arches you see all around the country (and world) if you like: They serve to let everyone know that the item's the same irrespective of just where you are in our nation—New York, California; Florida, Alaska ... They are always and everywhere the same: green notes, worth no more and no less that they purport to be worth.").

61. *Rousseuvian Money*, *supra* note 3, at 35, 37 (stating that money "can be thought of as a claim upon what it's exchanged for" and by virtue of its stability is "ultimately meant to make possible more productive activity across time").
62. *Id.* at 25, 27–28 (noting that as a financial system becomes widespread and complex, the sovereign must "'formalize' and 'regularize' ... which obligations shall 'count' for purposes of 'accounting' and public 'accountability,' ... [and] where to track and enforce such obligations and their discharge").
63. *See Money's Past*, *supra* note 17, at 4–8 (explaining the history of U.S. currency issuance from the late eighteenth century through twentieth century).
64. Jane Kamensky, *The American Revolution: A History of Violence*, NY TIMES (May 19, 2017), https://www.nytimes.com/2017/05/19/books/review/scars-of-independence-americas-violent-birth-holger-hoock.html (discussing America's violent beginning).
65. *See id.* at 6 ("The banking and currency acts of the 1860s transformed our interlinked banking, financial, and monetary systems. In very short order there were federally chartered banks in most states and territories of the Union, all of them subject to uniform regulatory standards.").
66. *Id.* (explaining that before the reforms of the 1860s, "America's paper money supply was primarily a plethora of privately issued 'bank notes'").
67. *Id.* (stating that banks' "notes were their own liabilities—hence liabilities of private issuers").
68. *See id.* (explaining that "differing state willingness or readiness to regulate" privately issued banknotes "could bring differing values to currencies issued in different locales"); *see also* CHARLES A. CONANT, A HISTORY OF MODERN BANKS OF ISSUE, WITH AN ACCOUNT OF THE ECONOMIC CRISES OF THE PRESENT CENTURY 310–85 (1896); *Rousseauvian Money*, *supra* note 3, at 44 (stating that "just as the paper memorialized promises, so did the metal—it's just that the paper memorialized private bank promises").

69. *Money's Past*, *supra* note 17, at 4 (stating that "banks then were chartered and regulated … by states rather than by our federal government"); *Rousseauvian Money*, supra note 67, at 46 (explaining that, until the establishment of the Fed and its uniform currency regulations, currency was backed by local institutions that varied in authority from jurisdiction to jurisdiction).
70. An integration, one might add, the need of which grew all the more poignant when the nation slipped into civil war over precisely the question of how much sovereignty the federal government was authorized to exercise and how much was "reserved to the states." *Money's Past*, *supra* note 17, at 4 (explaining that with no national ledger "[t]wo banks might both promise redeemability of their notes into the same quantum of something more solid—gold, for example, or U.S. Treasury certificates—but might well be differently able to live up to their promises.").
71. *Id.* (explaining that redeemability of banknotes issued by state-regulated banks were not reliably redeemable in other jurisdictions).
72. *See id.* (explaining how the reliability of different banks depended on the individual state's regulation).
73. *See id.* (describing how Nebraska and Michigan banks were unreliable because of the state regulation); *Rousseauvian Money*, *supra* note 3, at 46 (observing that in the early nineteenth century, "New York and New England banks, for example, were often reliable. Nebraska or Michigan banks, by contrast, not so much"); CONANT, supra note 134, at 311–312, 328–29 (commenting on the varying reliability of early banks' notes); RONALD E. SEAVOY, THE ORIGINS OF THE AMERICAN BUSINESS CORPORATION, 1784–1855 149–90 (1982) (providing an overview of early currency stability in the U.S.).
74. *See Money's Past, supra* note 17, at 3 ("Two banks might both promise redeemability of their notes into the same quantum of something solid—gold, for example, or U.S. Treasury certificates—but might well be differently able to live up to their promises. Some might be sound, other might be less so. Some might be sound this year but not so much next year.").
75. *Money's Past*, *supra* note 17, at 3 (noting that banks' reliability varied with states' charters); *Rousseauvian Money*, *supra* note 67, at 40 ("In doing so, banks decide whose private promissory notes will be temporarily tradeable for public promissory notes. They thereby assist our Fed, and hence 'us,' in temporarily transforming private money into public money—purely horizontal claims into vertical or verticallyenhanced horizontal claims.").
76. *Money's Past*, *supra* note 17, at 4 (discussing how banknotes fluctuated in value. "Needless to say, private banknote money did not make for an optimal payments system. It was good that the nation had a *unit of account*—the dollar—but unfortunately it still lacked a widely usable national *currency*."); *Rousseauvian Money*, *supra* note 3, at 23–24 (using

hypothetical to explain single, unified ledger necessary for creation of functioning unit).

77. *Money's Past*, *supra* note 17, at 3–4 ("The upshot of this 'Banking Babel' was that the nation's currency supply largely consisted of hundreds or thousands of distinct bank notes all trading at various discounts to stated par. A dollar note issued by Bill the Kid Bank or Sidewinder Bank might trade at 50% of par, for example, amount to no more than 'four bits,' not a dollar. A dollar note issued by Wyatt Erp Bank or Bald Eagle Bank might, by contrast, go for 90% of par, or even full par.").
78. *Money's Past*, *supra* note 17; *Rousseauvian Money*, supra note 67, at 24.
79. *Money's Past*, *supra* note 17, at 4 ("Shopkeepers and tradesmen in consequence had to maintain regularly updated discount schedules behind their counters, instructing clerks how much to discount different banks' notes in determining 'how much' (of what) to charge buyers for goods or for services.").
80. *Money's Past*, *supra* note 17, at 4.
81. *Money's Past*, *supra* note 17, at 7 ("We are amidst, that is to say, digital currency's 'wildcat' era. For one thing, there are *many* such currencies—indeed, a bewildering and seemingly all-the-time growing array of them.").
82. Legal Tender Act of 1862, ch. 142, 12 Stat. 532 (1862).
83. National Currency Act of 1863, ch. 85, 12 Stat. 665 (1863).
84. National Banking Act of 1864, ch. 106, 13 Stat. 99 (1864).
85. *Money's Past*, *supra* note 17, at 4 (explaining that notes were converted into Treasury-issued currencies called Greenbacks after legislation); *Rousseauvian Money*, *supra* note 3, at 44 (stating that Greenbacks were seen as uniformed currency); CONANT, *supra* note 134, at 345–46 (stating that after Federal regulations notes were replaced with bills of credit).
86. CONANT, *supra* note 134.
87. *Rousseavian Money*, *supra* note 3, at 24 (highlighting usefulness of a shared ledger).
88. *Rousseavian Money*, *supra* note 3, at 30; CONANT, *supra* note 134, at 344.
89. *Money's Past*, *supra* note 17.
90. *Money's Past*, *supra* note 17, at 5 (describing OCC's job).
91. *Money's Past*, *supra* note 17, at 5 (outlining history of OCC).
92. *See Money's Past*, *supra* note 17, at 5 ("The name is telling because 'comptroller' is merely archaic English for 'controller.' The OCC, housed in Treasury, was effectively the 'controller'—the administrator—of our national currency system."). *see also Rousseauvian Money*, *supra* note 3, at 45 ("One could, in other words, 'over-promise' by issuing too many promissory notes, which would undercut the value of promise and promissory note alike.").
93. "Safety and soundness" is a ubiquitous banking law term of art, used by legislators and all U.S. bank regulators to designate a sort of regulatory touchstone by reference to which banks are to be supervised. *See Making*

Sense of the Federal Reserve: "Safety and Soundness," FEDERAL RESERVE BANK OF ST. LOUIS (October 15, 2019, 5:45 PM), https://www.stlouisfed.org/in-plain-english/safety-and-soundness [https://perma.cc/DXN4-K2GF].

94. *Money's Past*, *supra* note 17, at 6 (describing current money system as "public–private franchise system."); *Rousseauvian Money*, *supra* note 3, at 39 (explaining that when one borrows money, one transforms "private money into public money" and effectively exchange "your ... promissory obligations" for "our promissory obligations."); *Finance Franchise*, *supra* note 1, at 1151 ("Private parties essentially borrow from or invest in *one another*, and one can only invest or borrow what is 'already there' in previously accumulated, privately-owned form.").
95. *Money's Past*, *supra* note 17, at 6 (describing our system as 'outsourcing' "credit-checking and public money-dispensary functions to private institutions."); *Rousseauvian Money*, *supra* note 67, at 40 ("One way of thinking of 'private' (yet always publicly licensed) banking and other financial institutions against this backdrop, as noted earlier, is as 'outsourced' credit-checking offices of the Fed and, in consequence, of Us (our joint political 'we,' our 'We, the People')—all Americans in their capacities as citizens of one shared republic (one *res publica*, or public thing), whose central bank the Fed is.").
96. Richard Sylla, *The U.S. Banking System: Origin, Development, and Regulation*, THE GILDER LEHRMAN INSTITUTE OF AMERICAN HISTORY (last visited November 1, 2019), https://ap.gilderlehrman.org/history-by-era/economics/essays/us-banking-system-origin-development-and-regulation (discussing the changes in American banking from 1781 to the present).
97. *See* BENNETT MCCALLUM, MONETARY ECONOMICS: THEORY AND POLICY 318 (1989) ("The mechanism was simple: national banks were required to hold $111.11 worth of government bonds for each $100 of bank notes issued"); BORIS P. PESEK & THOMAS R. SAVING, THE FOUNDATIONS OF MONEY AND BANKING 397 (1968) ("For each $100 of bank notes produced, the national bank had to deposit with the U.S. Treasurer 'eligible' U.S. bonds promising repayment of $111").
98. *See* MCCALLUM, *supra* note 163, at 318–319 (discussing the issuance of greenbacks and T-Bills).
99. PESEK & SAVING, *supra* note 163, at 391–95 (illustrating the change from "Greenbacks" to the "Gold Standard"); *Money's Past*, *supra* note 17, at 6 ("In very little time, 'wildcat' banknotes drained out of circulation"); *Rousseauvian Money*, *supra* note 67, at 19 (discussing liabilities and assets).
100. *Rousseauvian Money*, *supra* note 3, at 23 ("Our 'chore money' now will be transparently functioning not only as a 'medium of exchange' usable in 'settling [chore] accounts,' and not only as a 'unit of account' used in keeping such accounts, but also ....").
101. *Money's Past*, *supra* note 17, at 7 ("The Federal Reserve Act ('FRA') of 1913 established the Fed that we all know today, and transferred de facto and

de jure administration of the national money supply from the Comptroller to this new entity"); *Rousseauvian Money*, *supra* note 3, at 35 ("The 'value' component of money as 'store of value' stems from money's status as a claim …").

102. *Money's Past*, *supra* note 17, at 7 (summarizing what an elastic currency is intended to do); *Rousseauvian Money*, *supra* note 3, at 45–46 (discussing the danger of oversupplying currency into the market).
103. *Money's Past*, *supra* note 17, at 7 ("A money whose supply can be 'modulated' in this way, as I call it, is essential if we're to avoid needlessly disrupting either transaction activity, investment activity, or currency value"); *Rousseauvian Money*, *supra* note 3, at 45 (expounding on the importance of an 'elastic' currency).
104. *Money's Past*, *supra* note 17, at 7 ("An elastic currency is a currency whose supply can be adjusted (a) to accommodate, while not over-accommodating, transaction and credit demand, and (b) to counteract sudden credit expansions or contractions").
105. *Id.*
106. *Rousseauvian Money*, *supra* note 3, at 45 (explaining how bankers began issuing more notes than they had metal).
107. *See id*. (discussing metal and regulation).
108. *See Pre-Liberal Autonomy*, *supra* note 10, at 113 ("Second is an attendant suspicion of large aggregations of financial capital"). *See also Materializing Citizenship*, *supra* note 10, at 2075 (discussing suspicion of large aggregating entities).
109. *Money's Past*, *supra* note 17, at 7. *See also Rousseauvian Money*, *supra* note 3, at 45 (discussing elasticity of currency); Conant, *supra* note 134, at 20 (explaining the need for elasticity); Seavoy, *supra* note 139, at 150–67 (discussing the development of the free banking system).
110. *Money's Past*, *supra* note 17, at 7 ("The Second Bank of the U.S. from 1816 to 1836, and especially central banks of the kind found all over the 'developed' world circa 1913, by contrast, had shown themselves well suited to the task."); Richard Timberlake, Money, Banking, and Central Banking 163–71 (1965) (discussing the development of the Second Bank of the U.S., which was chartered in 1816).
111. *Money's Past*, *supra* note 17, at 7 ("By acting as 'banks to the banks,' these institutions were able to modulate private bank money-issuance in ever more 'fine-tuned' manners, using 'carrots' as effectively as 'sticks'").
112. Eugene N. White, The Regulation and Reform of the American Banking System, 1900–1929, 63–74 (1983) (discussing the development and impact of the Federal Reserve Act of 1913); *Money's Past*, *supra* note 17, at 4 (explaining how New York and New England banks were reliable); *Rousseauvian Money*, *supra* note 3, at 46 (highlighting how the U.S. Fed followed actions taken by the Bank of England).

113. *Money's Past*, *supra* note 17, at 7 ("Like the banking acts of the 1860s, this change too was proximately occasioned by a crisis—in this case, the panic of 1907").
114. *Id.* ("The Federal Reserve Act ["FRA"] of 1913 established the Fed that we all know today, and transferred de facto *and* de jure administration of the national money supply from the Comptroller to this new entity.").
115. *Id.* ("This is why the 'Greenbacks' you now find in your pocket call themselves, not 'Treasury Notes', but 'Federal Reserve Notes'.").
116. *Id.* ("It is just that they are *public* bank notes—'central' bank notes—rather than *private* bank notes now.").
117. *Id.* ("They are Citizen Notes, you might say.").
118. *Money's Past*, *supra* note 17, at 7 ("They are issued and spent in the name of us all.").
119. *Rousseauvian Money*, *supra* note 3, at 37 (observing that financial institutions enable "more exchange to take place across space by enabling exchange across time").
120. *Money's Past*, *supra* note 17, at 8 ("And what is true of Federal Reserve Notes here is true of bank credit extended in Fed Note—that is, dollar—increments too.").
121. *Id.* ("The loan the bank makes to you in the form of a newly opened or credited deposit it 'makes' in the form of dollar-denominated withdrawal or spending rights.").
122. *Money's Past*, *supra* note 17, at 8 ("The deposits, in other words, are functional equivalents of dollar bills."). What makes this possible, again, is that a bank-issued card that you swipe in a machine at a retail outlet hooked up to the Fed-administered payments system "counts" as a payment and accordingly both debits your account and credits the retail outlets. Were I, who am not licensed as a bank, to issue you an identical card, nothing would happen other than that I would be arrested for fraud or counterfeiting.
123. *Id.* ("Once you realize this, and once you remind yourself both that those dollars are Fed 'Notes' and that you give the bank a signed *promissory* note for your *loan*, you are able to see something else too: This is that a loan is simply a *temporary swap* of your promissory note for Fed promissory notes—of your privately issued money for more widely spendable publicly issued money."). This point is emphasized, and its significance more fully elaborated, in *Rousseauvian Money*, *supra* note 3, at 39–40 ("When you borrow money, then—which you often do in this country by handing a bank your own promissory note in exchange for Fed promissory notes (or their depository or cashier's check equivalents)—you just temporarily trade your own notes for Fed notes. It's just a temporary swap.").
124. *Money's Past*, *supra* note 17, at 8 ("Bank lending is just temporary private–public currency swapping.").

125. *See e.g.*, CHRISTINE DESAN, MAKING MONEY: COIN, CURRENCY, AND THE COMING OF CAPITALISM 295–329 (2014) (discussing the history of currency in England and its origins in the seventeenth century).
126. *See generally id.* (tracing the history of currency and the reasons for its development).
127. *Money's Past*, *supra* note 17, at 10 (discussing the potential adoption of a Fed-issued digital currency and the subsequent feasibility of a Fed-administered central banking ledger).
128. CONANT, *supra* note 134, at 311 ("A new country, poor in specie and in loanable capital, is almost forced by the necessities of her situation to adopt monetary devices which would not be tolerated under better conditions.").

5

Franchise Finance: Why We Retain It—And Why We Need Not

I have now elaborated both why a geographically and temporally uniform, elastic currency was necessary when consolidated nationwide ledger-accounting was not yet feasible and why it was all but inevitable that our sovereign republics would ultimately issue it.[1] In this sense my account embeds a teleology. It tells a tale of steady development and improvement through a course of alternating improvisation and consolidation—a tale that, I argue below, will almost certainly be replicated in the space of digital payments technology and associated digital currency. There should be, and will be, central bank- or finance ministry-administered Democratic Digital Currencies affording the same spatial and temporal uniformity that the U.S.'s previously Treasury-administered and now Fed-administered "green paper" dollars, and their counterparts in other commercial republican jurisdictions, afford at present.[2]

Matters are different when we turn from monetary *uniformity* and *elasticity* to monetary and financial *hybridity*. While the first two seem to be ultimately necessary in all times and places, and in this sense essential to commercial and financial optimization themselves, the third is historically contingent, a product of political and technological under-development and associated ideological inertia.[3] And *here* the best explanation of *what has been* recommends *change* in *what soon shall be*.

The story is still teleological, to be sure, but now the story of *money's* returning to being fully public figures as simply the penultimate chapter in

R. C. Hockett, *The Citizens' Ledger*,
https://doi.org/10.1007/978-3-030-99566-9_5

the story of *finance's* returning to being fully public—in the form of a consolidated digital public ledger. We can see why when we ask ourselves what accounts for hybridity in the first place, then ask whether that which accounts for it continues to necessitate it.

5.1 Why We Retain It: New Facts, Old Ideas

Why did we first take to publicly franchising money and finance? Why do we *still* do so now? Why do our sovereign republics still *out*source the allocation of their *re*source—their monetized full faith and credit —and privatize the *seigniorage* rents earned on its rental?

In light of the foregoing discussion, it will not be surprising to suggest that the best explanation stems from popular assumptions that once were well founded in political and technological "facts on the ground," but which have long since receded.[4] Since the receding of those facts, popular beliefs have not yet been updated, and it is part of the purpose of this book to instigate just that updating.

The two most foundational popular assumptions to which I allude are that what Chapter 2 labeled investment capital—a.k.a. "finance capital"—is both inherently scarce and unavoidably privately supplied.[5] These two assumptions underwrite a third assumption which stems also from other assumptions—namely that capital *allocation* decisions are most justly and efficiently made in the private sector, with the public sector playing at most a supportive and modulatory role in respect of credit aggregates so as to smoothen "the business cycle." These assumptions all jointly underwrite the picture that I call the "intermediated scarce private capital myth."[6]

Investment capital, probably not accidentally, seems to figure almost like precious metal money in the intermediated scarce private capital picture. It is as if the publicly issued coins discussed above were both (a) not multiplied by paper currency, bank credits, or other tokens, and (b) not issued by republics or other sovereigns at all. There seems to be assumed, in other words, a finite and determinate quantity of metal money capital at any one time in the intermediated scarce private capital picture, and most if not all of it is viewed as rightfully owned and hence lent by domestic or foreign persons in the private sector.[7] When you think about money in this way, it is easy then also to think that "intermediaries" can only "lend out" what they antecedently "take in," and that those who supply what is lent are thus both entitled and best suited to directing it.

The "sanctity of property" and "common sense about incentives" alike, the intermediated scarce private capital story accordingly continues, recommend leaving investment decisions to those who *own and provide* the putatively scarce money capital.[8] These *rentiers* have every right to charge rents and every reason to do their homework and lend their money out cautiously only to those who will put it to productive use, using the temporary claims to productive resources that lent money affords them to add to the stock of society's wealth over time, pay back their lenders, and pocket rich profits while at it.[9]

Et voila, the miracle of "finance and development"—a tale told often in textbooks, journal articles, white papers, and speeches all valorizing the role of "financial liberalization" in fueling economic growth miracles.[10] The public sector typically is admitted into this picture at best as an afterthought, or as a necessary evil.[11] The story begins with the need to standardize the monetary units into which precious metal capital, already used as a private money-form thanks to its putatively "intrinsic" value, is to be parceled.[12] (Money as a unit of account, as noted above.) Standardization is an orthodox public good, the solution to a coordination problem. So is enforcement of standards. So the public can be permitted these roles, hence the role of a franchisor in the *standard*-maintenance, *quality*-control sense of the word.[13]

The story might then reach, if narrated by people cognizant of the need for a currency that is not only spatially uniform but also temporally uniform (again, "elastic"), the need also to standardize *paper representations* of precious metal coins once it is recognized that wealth expansion is outstripping metal money supply expansion.[14] Such imbalances are addressed, the story will continue, with adoption of an elastic currency that can be issued in excess of the metals that "back" it, so long as the currency volume isn't allowed to become too great a multiple of the metal reserve.[15] (Money as an elastically expansible means of exchange and a reliable store of value, again as noted above.)

In both cases the publics in our commercial republics are grudgingly seen as providers of an orthodox public good that they are suited to providing—standard-setting and enforcement—while private sector agents are viewed as still acting as ultimate providers of the "monetary base," hence the "real capital," and thus as the proper deciders as to that capital's disposition or allocation.[16] Here is the kernel of the franchise arrangement to which I have referred, as it would be described by our still-ubiquitous purveyors of the intermediated scarce private capital myth.

What escapes notice in this picture, however, is that (a) what is monetary about the metal coin base is the stamp *of* the coin, not the metal *in* the coin[17]; and (b) that once the money supply comes significantly to outstrip the coin supply, the putative "base money" does no real work any longer.[18] It grows ever more vestigial as real wealth and its monetary representation—the full money supply—grow ever larger in relation to it.

The real monetary work is thus done by the multiplier from putative "base" to full money supply, and that means that this work is done by the *decider of the multiplier*—that is, the *public*, which sets and enforces required reserve ratios in the first place in every commercial republic.[19]

In effect, then, the moment we move from putatively private moneys used among some people to public–private *franchise* money used among all people is the moment we move to the prospect of cutting out private moneys, and with them private payment platforms and private finance, altogether.[20] For it is the moment we recognize money's ineluctably public, and hence ineluctably "fiat," character.[21] Now that we know it is *possible*, all that remains is to decide whether it is *desirable*. In other words, now that we know assumptions (a) and (b) above to be false and (c) therefore to be weakened, should we bring money and finance back "in house" and stop franchising it out to privately run institutions?

5.2 Why We Need Not: New Facts, New Prospects

It seems clear that the answer to that question is now largely, if not wholly, "yes." My reasons stem partly from changes in those facts on the ground that I alluded to before in accounting for assumptions (a) through (c) of the intermediated scarce private capital myth. I'll explain this first before turning to additional reasons that I maintain militate in favor of bringing money, payment, and finance back in-house for the public that is each of our commercial republics.

Let's take the early U.S. again as an illustrative mid-modern case study—a study whose counterparts elsewhere began centuries earlier.

During the first century of the American republic, metal coin money was still, by tradition, the preferred form.[22] And specie was indeed scarce, especially in North America.[23] In this sense there was indeed capital scarcity.[24] This meant, ironically, both that non-metal expedients grew urgently necessary quite early on in American history once economic growth had got underway, and that hastily adopted non-metal money expedients came often to grief in those early days, ironically reinforcing beliefs that metal moneys were somehow inherently more "sound" (another term of art).[25]

Just as its supply of reliable money had difficulty keeping up with its economic growth, moreover, so did the new American republic's governance structures at first have difficulty keeping up with its geographic and populational growth.[26] It proved as difficult to integrate the nation politically and administratively as it was to integrate the nation monetarily.[27] Indeed, the latter difficulty, in large measure, both stemmed from and reinforced the former difficulty in ways noted above. Incomplete sovereignty and incompletely sovereign money were mutually complementary and mutually exacerbating.[28]

Partly this was a matter of antecedent political ideation and attitude—southern plantation owners' suspicions of centralized federal government and centralized finance continued to hold sway in the years that culminated in the Civil War.[29] Partly it was also a matter of consequent incapacity's—"imbecility's," as the U.S. Constitution's co-drafter and the nation's first Treasury Secretary Alexander Hamilton called it—seeming to validate those suspicions in self-fulfillingly prophetic fashion. And partly it was a matter of communications infrastructure, fiscal infrastructure, and other technical determinants of governmental capacity's still being underdeveloped in the first seven decades of the American republic.[30] A federal government without deep reach or a widely used currency of its own could take but a minimal role in the allocation of investment capital throughout its own territorial jurisdiction.[31]

The upshot was a system of commerce and finance in which inherently imperfect private ordering was bound to play a key role until such time as the nation's sovereignty and capacity both fiscally and physically to *act* as a sovereign, in respect of both money and beyond, had fully coalesced.[32] The divided sovereignty of the pre-Civil War era, pursuant to which the states ironically were constitutionally barred from issuing currencies even as they retained (a) sufficient powers to prevent the federal government from doing so and (b) the sole power to charter banking institutions, was effectively incomplete—indeed impossible—sovereignty.[33] And incomplete sovereignty meant incomplete money and incomplete commerce and finance.[34]

Once both national and monetary sovereignty finally were settled by the non-accidentally concurrent Civil War and banking-cum-currency reforms of the 1860s, however, the American commercial republic's monetary and financial system moved into its present version of the hybrid state described above. The public sector grew steadily better able, through practice and time, to handle the money-modulatory task.[35] Establishment of the Fed—the U.S.'s present-day public sector money-issuer and money-modulator—in 1913 marked the American republic's monetary coming of age, centuries after its European antecedents, and it took very little time from then on for the new institution to begin in effect calling the shots even in the putatively private sector money and financial markets. As early as the 1920s, foreign central bankers were noting how U.S. Fed open market operations had become the primary determinants not only of the American, but indeed also of the global money supply.[36]

The American commercial republic also developed, initially at least, considerable facility with the money *allocative* task *complementing* the modulatory task. For the U.S. Fed, as noted earlier, actually began as a network of national development banks patterned after German models of the late nineteenth century (themselves inspired by the model of Alexander Hamilton via the great German-American national development economist Friedrich List).

Some sophisticates probably understand, at least obliquely, that the Fed is a kind of public capital manager—that is more or less what credit modulation and monetary policy are all about once public capital has been monetized—but they won't get the development bit. That is because we have severed capital from its original productive purpose, as noted above in Chapter 2, while relatedly severing modulation from allocation and macro from micro, as discussed in more detail below, In Chapter 7. These three divorces are all of a piece. They are faces of one schizophrenia, a state of mind in which finance and commercial republics' continuous productive development are unrelated or even at war.

Now if you want to find words like "finance" and "development" joined in one title or phrase, you have to read journals like "Finance and Development"—the joint publication of the IMF and the World Bank, legally known as the "International Bank for *Reconstruction and Development*" (emphasis added). You won't find these things tied together in any self-styled "*developed*" society. We didn't *used* to think development something only for "underdeveloped countries." Nor, accordingly, did we think of "development finance" as a special kind of finance only for underdeveloped client states. *All* finance used to be "development finance," just as all capital was productive capital, in the manner described above in Chapter 2.

That was back when we understood public investment capital had to be not only publicly modulated, at the macro level, but also publicly allocated, at the micro level. You can tell that in the American case, for example, by looking at its Fed's "federation"—its federated structure—which dates back to its establishment. People often seem confused by the Fed. They speak of "the Federal Reserve Bank" (not "a thing"), then "the Federal Reserve Board" ("a thing," but only as part of a bigger thing). When you then tell them that the U.S. has a "Federal Reserve System" (*that's* the thing), they wonder how a "System" can regulate or conduct monetary policy as if it had agency. Was Alan Greenspan "a system"? Was Janet Yellen?

The U.S.'s central bank is a "system" because it comprises multiple distinct nodes of agency at two distinct "levels"—one corresponding to what I've been calling macro and modulatory, the other corresponding to what I've been calling micro and allocative. The Fed Board is the first of those, while the Regional Federal Reserve District Banks constitute the second. The Regional Feds were meant originally to help finance development in the U.S.'s many still "underdeveloped" regions circa 1913, which they did by monetizing—"discounting," in the parlance of German-American Paul Warburg, one of the Fed's founders—productive commercial paper.[37] That is a credit -allocative function—it's about productively directing the flow of public investment capital as I defined it above in Chapter 2.

The Board was in turn meant to coordinate all of this regional development financing, to ensure that its partial decentralization across separate regions didn't fall prey to CAPs and ReCAPS as defined above in Chapter 3, and in consequence generate nationwide modulatory dysfunction—inflation, deflation, hyper-inflation or debt-deflation. This is a credit-*modulatory* function—it's about centrally orchestrating, via control of the national credit pipeline, the coherent functioning of regional public capital disseminators to avoid misallocation and, with it, mis-modulation.

This was a brilliant arrangement—maybe more brilliant even than its founders fully realized. In a single organizational stroke, it offered institutional means of solving the ages-old allocation/modulation conundrum, while relatedly defusing America's ages-old national ambivalence over the dangers of capital concentration on the one hand, capital over- or under-generation on the other hand. That conundrum and associated ambivalence had been the twin drivers of a strange national oscillation in the U.S. between central banking and de facto monetary anarchy from the era of Hamilton on down through the gilded age, and at last they were institutionally solved—in potential, at least.

The institutional solution, moreover, took a form that bridged not only macro and micro, not only modulation and allocation, but also *public and private*. For productive initiative was left to private sector producers and entrepreneurs, while decisions whether publicly to monetize project-associated private paper in the form of publicly issued endogenous credit-money were assigned to institutions that were themselves hybrid entities—the Regional Fed Banks being, as they were, overseen by Boards of Directors with membership two-thirds determined by private sector entities subject to Fed Board approval.

And so there it was, a network of public–private regional development banks overseen by a nationwide public investment capital overseer. And hence an optimal half-centralization of public development finance in the cause of decentralized private productive activity.

So what happened? It grows a bit complicated here, as I've written at greater length elsewhere.[38] The allocative Fed as originally founded reflected the influence of a once globally popular, half-right idea known as the "Real Bills Doctrine" ("RBD"). Prominent among the Fed's founders were the RBD adherents Paul Warburg (who'd learned the doctrine in Germany) and Carter Glass (the latter of course better known now in the States for the Glass-Steagall Act). The RBD in its crude form suggested that productively lent credit-money could not fuel inflation or deflation. For the productivity requirement would ensure that lent funds stayed in primary market investment, not meta-market speculation.

But in fact there are other possible sources of monetary disturbance than mere fad investment and meta-market speculation, the effects of which demand-responsive endogenous lending can then procyclically amplify pursuant to the recursive dynamic outlined above, as readily as if they were the latter. A sudden petroleum price hike by OPEC nations as in the 1970s, for example, or an influx of New World silver into Spain 400 years earlier, can quickly alter the money-goods balance, commencing a self-amplifying inflationary or deflationary episode. In short, exogenous factors can spark endogenous self-amplification.

In effect, this is the "cumulative process" that the Swede Wicksell identified in the late nineteenth century, but of which Anglo-Americans, notwithstanding Adam Smith's having also spotted it, tragically didn't take systematic heed until decades later when Wicksell was translated from Swedish and German into English. Something much like it happened in the early 1930s after (a) an influx of European gold sent in payment of war debt and (b) the twinned real estate and stock market crashes of the late 1920s. Exogenous money supply changes were amplified by endogenous lending and contracting before and after 1929.

A savvy Fed after 1929 would thus have supplied a countercyclical exogenous money infusion, a boost to the by-then only transaction-driven money supply, to counteract the contraction in the money supply wrought by the Crash and ensuing Fisher-style debt-deflation. But the Fed of the time, mistaking productive lending's necessity to monetary stability for sufficiency to the same end, assumed that the money supply must by definition be right. It accordingly took no countercyclical corrective action. (The gold standard didn't help either.)

So how did this lead to the U.S.'s separating modulation and allocation, monetary and fiscal policy, and hence its Fed and Treasury? It overreacted. It effectively decided that, since productive allocation was not *sufficient* to afford optimal modulation, it was not *necessary* either. This was only half-right, just as the crude form of the RBD had been half right. The upshot was the U.S.'s Banking Act of 1935.

Under the influence of Irving Fisher's rendition of the quantity theory of money, the Banking Act focused almost exclusively on monetary modulation, eschewing credit allocation. The act accordingly established an independent Federal Open Market Committee ("FOMC") in Washington to formulate and execute monetary policy (good), while sidelining the Federal Reserve District Banks and their discounting role (bad). It switched out, in other words, one blade of the modulation/allocation scissors for the other.

This change opened the door for the Fed massively to enter the credit markets at the behest of speculative financial institutions that misallocate endogenous credit-money. Glass-Steagall prevented, for a time, this misallocation by restricting speculative bank lending, and other parts of U.S.C. Title 12 (the U.S.'s Banking Code) limited interstate banking and branching. Fed Chairs who understood their modulatory roles, and a very actively allocating fiscal state operating through many institutions, especially the War Finance Corporation ("WFC"), the Reconstruction Finance Corporation ("RFC"), and their progeny—the Federal Housing Authority ("FHA"), Fannie Mae, and the Small Business Administration ("SBA") prominent among them—up to the 1990s, kept markets relatively stable during the so-called Great Moderation.[39]

But when those fell away over the 1990s, the U.S. like many other jurisdictions fell into continual private misallocation of endogenous public credit-money. Multiple life-, wealth-, and polity-destructive crises have been the upshot. Continual misallocation of public capital by privately profit-, not production- driven financial institutions; consequent capital mis-modulation by timid or ill-informed stewards of our capital commons; and thus perpetual under-production, over-speculation, and secular stagnation have ben America's, and much of the world's, lot ever since.[40]

A resurgence of nineteenth-century folk belief about finance as intermediated scarce private capital in the 1950s, perhaps partly brought on by Cold War fears in the commercial republican West of Soviet "socialism," didn't help in this process. They brought about a winding-down of the U.S.'s RFC and counterpart institutions elsewhere.[41] Popular conceptions of money and finance formed during the pre-sovereign period had apparently continued to linger as a sort of "lagging indicator," and thus preserved supposedly indispensable roles for both *rentiers* and what came to be called a "financial services" industry, in the minds of those ignorant about money, banking, and finance in some precincts of the academy, the professions, and the lay public alike.[42]

And so here we still linger both as polities and as economies over which our commercial republican polities preside, as described above in introducing this book. We seem to oscillate continually between misallocation and consequent under-modulation and associated asset price inflation on the one hand, and bust and ensuing debt-deflation on the other hand. And it is all because the job that we all started in the nineteenth century, though haltingly improved and fine-tuned through the 1910s, 1930s, 1940s, early 1970s, and 2010s, has still to be finished, with even the good done quite often being *un*done.

The job that remains to be done is that of finally more fully republicanizing and democratizing finance as we have republicanized and democratized money and governance in the two centuries past the 19th, leaving private players to play with their own private money holdings but not ours—the publics'. To that task of completion I now turn, beginning with the general form of the solution, followed by a more detailed exposition.

5.3 Ending Hybridity—Citizen Ledger Finance in Broad Outline

We can digitally restore "two-bladed scissor" central banks and finance ministries of the kind that the U.S. and other commercial republics have had in the past as described just above, both modulating *and* productively allocating the public investment capital that all publicly enabled endogenous money amounts to, while leaving only preaccumulated private capital to private sector allocators. In so doing, we will be ending franchise finance; we will be ending dysfunctional hybridity.

This will be a generalized rendition of what I have elsewhere proposed for the U.S. as a once again Treasury-complementing "Spread Fed" that *modulates* from the nation's capital against *exogenous* shocks, while *allocating* in *endogenously productive*, *counter-speculative* manners from distinct *regional district* branches. I'll limit myself here to a schematic description and explanation, in order to set the stage for the full digitized elaboration that is the task of Chapters 6–8.

Let us start with some simple accounting along the lines described above in Chapter 2, doing so here specifically in connection with the republic's endogenously generated money—that is, again, its public investment capital stock—and its proper purposes. To do this is effectively to imagine, through double-entry bookkeeping, a consolidated public balance sheet that includes all central bank and finance ministry assets and liabilities. The latter in turn can be disaggregated at will for particular purposes into a sheaf of distinct interlocking, sub-public *partial* balance sheets, but that prospect can wait until later for now.

Now suppose, for example, that the public capital stock is managed by a public bank or ministry—at the national level of any commercial republic, what will amount to the "central" bank or the central bank and finance ministry both as one consolidated office of public finance ("OPF")—say, in virtue of its operation as the sole "financial intermediary" between, or "at the center of," parties who transact in public investment capital.[43] The central bank or OPF in such case will have assets and offsetting liabilities as does any bank—or, for that matter, any person or entity that experiences capital inflows and outflows.

In the case of ordinary commercial banking institutions, the greater part of liabilities are of course deposit liabilities—the obligations, under which banks operate, to enable withdrawals or payments from out of depositor accounts. There are other liabilities too, of course—obligations on bonds sold in bond markets, for example—but again, deposit liabilities will make up the lion's share. This, you'll remember, is how banks play the role that they do in constituting the national payments and hence credit dissemination system described above. (Recall what your loan is, and how it's extended to you.)

On the asset side of any bank's balance sheet, in turn, are the bank's many "investments," which might or might not be *productive* (as distinguished from merely speculative) investments. Among these, of course, is your promissory note as described above. Likewise all other investments that the bank has made—additional loan promissory notes, more negotiable debt instruments like corporate bonds and sovereign debt instruments, ... all manner of bank betting, investing, or both.

But now note: the recursive collective action predicaments noted above in Chapter 3 and after tend to lead, we observed, to underinvestment in long-term industrial and infrastructural improvements, hence in production and productivity. In many cases those who run banks will hope instead to place bets on price-swings in secondary securities and tertiary derivatives markets. These meta-markets are after all, as noted in Chapter 2, where the "quick buck" is found, and that's what the commercial bank's individual shareholders, both individually rationally and collectively irrationally, are after.

For again, as explained in Chapter 3, they cannot control the macroenvironment that enables investments to be profitable, and cannot individually capture most of the value that's generated by primary investment. So the collective action problems that plague decentralized capital markets will find expression on "short-termist," hyper- "financialized" (in the terms of Chapter 2) private sector bank balance sheets.

Now return to the balance sheet of a central bank or finance ministry managing the public investment capital stock, and imagine what *this* might look like. Unlike the case of the private sector commercial bank, in the case of the public sector central bank or finance ministry there is no pressure exerted by shareholders for whom it is individually rational to insist on a quick buck. Rather, those who manage the public capital stock do so with a view to the stably and steadily growing long-term real wealth and well-being of the republic's constituents—those in whose name the central bank or finance ministry acts.

Moreover, because it is unitary and is the society's most inclusive collective agent in the investment realm, the central bank or finance ministry faces no collective action challenges what ever, and likewise is able both to control the macro environment in the relevant respects and to capture and monetize gains. None of the dysfunctions that we found above to plague private sector capital allocators, in other words, are present here. The central bank or finance ministry, in effect by definition, just *is* the *solution* to those problems. It is the republic's duly authorized collective agent in the realm of money, finance, and bona fide investment.

Does that mean there's no place for private sector capital allocation, or that a central bank or like instrumentality should altogether replace or in essence displace private sector banks and other financial institutions? No. But it does mean the relation between central and non-central banks, and the relation between that bank and households and firms, should be different than it is now, as we'll now see.

Let us start with the asset side of the public balance sheet. If public investment capital is to flow solely into productive, not speculative investments, we shall require democratically accountable institutions that specialize in identifying veritably productive investment needs and opportunities. Some such needs and opportunities will be "macro" in character—the infrastructures and heavy industries of tomorrow, say—while others will be "micro" in character and thus possibly best identified by publicly assisted private and non-profit sector entrepreneurs. Central banks are ideal for handling the latter public role—via their "discounting" activities as described above—while finance ministries in collaboration with more broadly based executive agencies are ideal for the former public role.

Taking them in reverse order for expository purposes, then, first configure all members of the national executive's cabinet who have jurisdiction over the commercial republic's primary infrastructures and heavy industries into a National Investment (or "Development") Council (again, "NIC," or "Council"). The Council will be chaired *ex officio* by the nation's chief executive and vice chief executive (if there is one), and officially by the heads of the central bank and finance ministry—a bit like the U.S.'s Financial Stability Oversight Council ("FSOC"). Its task will be to formulate and regularly update a "National Investment [or "Continuous Development"] Strategy" ("NIS")) analogous to the National Defense Strategy updated each year by the U.S.'s defense and security agencies. The NIS identifies ongoing national development imperatives and accordingly determines what counts as "productive" in a democratically accountable manner (owing to its primarily executive cabinet-determined composition). It is a latter-day counterpart to the U.S. WIB's old Production Index described above.

The NIS will identify the sustainable infrastructures and heavy industries of the future that are in need of jump-starting or up-scaling in the present, and will likewise identify the most economically "left-behind" regions of the commercial republic in question and segments of its citizenry in need of new productive opportunities. It will earmark specific project fields and public investment projects—e.g., medical technologies; transportation and communications networks and platforms; wind, solar, geothermal, and electric power generation and storage; etc.—in which to invest, since incumbent firms often won't, to make ongoing technical and productive development in all of our commercial republics both sustainable and never-ending.

A cardinal intellectual and policy blunder in the "developed" world over the past 50 years has been both to segregate "national development" from justice and sustainability, and to treat it as a one-off achievement instead of a perpetual process of technical and productive renewal. We can probably thank the U.S. Defense Department's Cold War era economist Walt Rostow for that. Going forward, developed countries will do well to remember the words of the far greater 1960s era development economist Bob Dylan—"he not busy being born is busy dying"—and remind themselves that these words are as true of commercial republics and other societies as they are of individuals. The Council will be the embodiment of that recollection. And comprising a subset of the executive cabinet as it does, it will be both democratically accountable and able to plan ongoing development coherently instead of in "siloed" fashion.

Second, establish or use a preexisting public investment institution—in the EU, that could be the EIB; in the U.S., the U.S. Treasury's already-existing Federal Financing Bank ("FFB") as the Council's investment arm. Currently many such institutions—including the U.S.'s FFB—use legislatively appropriated funds to finance administrative agencies through lending and credit support. Two simple tweaks, one at the intake and one at the output end, can ensure such institutions' status as permanent national development banks alongside the Councils.

At the output end, authorize the investment bank to invest in sub-national units of government, and public–private development partnerships, as well as in executive agencies as currently. Let it also take equity stakes in addition to credit instruments, where appropriate, as financing instruments. For in some cases boardroom "voice" will be helpful in overseeing projects, and earned revenue will be welcome as well.

At the input end, authorize these banks also to issue their own credit instruments, and to form Special Purpose Trusts ("SPTs") to fund fully diversified portfolios of specific project types. Let private sector investors purchase stakes in these funds too, so as both to add private to public capital in financing perpetual national development, and to give pension funds and other "patient capital" investors something more productive than Wall Street, Lombard Street, or like places in which to invest.

The U.S.'s aforementioned World War I era WIB and WFC, as well as the World War II era WPB and RFC, paired up much as I am envisaging here. In the case of those earlier pairings, the U.S. had to finance and ramp-up war production quite quickly. These institutions accordingly planned and financed both conversion of existing factories and the establishment of new factories to produce steel, rubber, jeeps, tanks, ships, and planes, taking both debt and equity stakes in the relevant firms. They financed these operations, in turn, with public investment capital, private investment capital, and retained earnings.

Today the world's commercial republics are faced, thankfully, not with literal war, but with what the American philosopher William James called "the *moral equivalent* of war." Working together, then, NICs and their associated public investment banks can, from the output end, plan and finance decarbonizing projects from municipal installation of electric vehicle charging ports at all parking meters, through the building of multiple battery and wind turbine factories in scores of impoverished communities, on down to the retrofitting of all sizable buildings in each country in question. And at the intake end they can form investment pools for all project types—e.g., "solar funds," "battery funds," "wind power funds," etc.—in which any citizen or investment institution—including the central bank—can invest.

Third, on behalf of smaller firms, start-ups, and veritably productive entrepreneurs rather than infrastructural and heavy industries, conduct a nationally appropriate rendition of "Spreading the Fed" along the German-inspired lines described above. Do so especially with all central banks in large, diffuse economies like those of the U.S. and E.U. That will assure adequate liquidity and short-term funding to our commercial republics' primary drivers of new technological development and productivity growth—their small, nimble, and start-up firms. Today's central banks by and large do not operate this way any longer, yet their enabling acts—certainly the U.S. Fed's—in many cases still authorize this form of development support the importance of which commercial republican citizens worldwide seemed to understand prior to the late twentieth century.

All that the U.S. Fed, for example, would have to do is once again to open its "discount window" to businesses of the kind that it used to support, while in this case "prioritizing" firms that the Council finds to be developing new technologies and socially just labor practices—including worker ownership or codetermination. Socially just and environmentally friendly small firms all over our commercial republics would then benefit. A start-up firm developing new air- or water-treatment methods, for example, or perhaps better solar power or battery technologies, would be the new paradigms of "productive" for central bank lending purposes.

If newly "spread" central banks limit their facilities to financing only such NIC-endorsed productive green project types in their "Main Street" economies rather than speculative gambles in their "Wall Street" or "Lombard Street" economies, they will both (a) more productively deploy their nations' public investment capital and (b) take the wind out of overblown Wall Street or Lombard Street sails. And since the central bank chairs will be co-chairs of the aforementioned NICs, they will have no trouble discerning what has been democratically determined to "count" as justly and sustainably *productive*.

Turning now to the *liability* side of the public balance sheet, provide smartphone-accessible digital banking, in Democratic Digital Currency units (again, "2DC") to all citizens, businesses, and legitimate guests of our republics, and conduct all of the aforementioned asset-side activities over this new national digital platform—this Citizens' Ledger. An NIC-recommended investment in a new green-tech firm, for example, could be made instantly over the new digital platform. Ditto central bank discount lending and open market operations, which now will be "leak-proof" in the manner described in the Prologue above.

In effect, then, this platform will be the full liability-side counterpart to the asset-side augmentation entailed by the first three plan-planks just elaborated.

Private sector payments over the platform will occur on the liability side of the public balance sheet, just as accounts and payments now respectively subsist and occur on the liability sides of combined private sector bank balance sheets which themselves are in effect on the central bank balance sheet at one remove, via the banks' own reserve accounts with their central banks. In effect, this will give perfect account-book reflection to the fact that, in trading with one another "severally" in our *private* capacities, we commercial republican citizens are all trading liabilities that we all "jointly" issue—central bank promissory notes—in our shared *public* capacities.

The full plan is really that simple. And this should not be surprising. For, think about it: presently private sector banks hold privately extended loans on the asset sides of their balance sheets, and corresponding privately owned demand deposits on the liability sides of their balance sheets. All we are doing is removing those portions of both of these that involve *public* capital to the *public* balance sheet, leaving all that involves only private capital as is.

All private sector payments, then, will occur on the liability side of the central bank or OPF balance sheet, just as accounts and payments now subsist and occur on the liability sides of combined private sector bank balance sheets which themselves are in effect on the central bank balance sheet at one remove via the banks' own reserve accounts tracked on the central bank balance sheet. In other words, they will occur within the small box in the right hand side of the stylized balance sheet that is Fig. 5.1. The small box on the left-hand side, meanwhile, indicates what will be added to what's already held, more on which in Chapter 6.

This is what needs doing in broad outline to end financial hybridity—to reclaim all publicly franchised functions "in house"—and reassume public

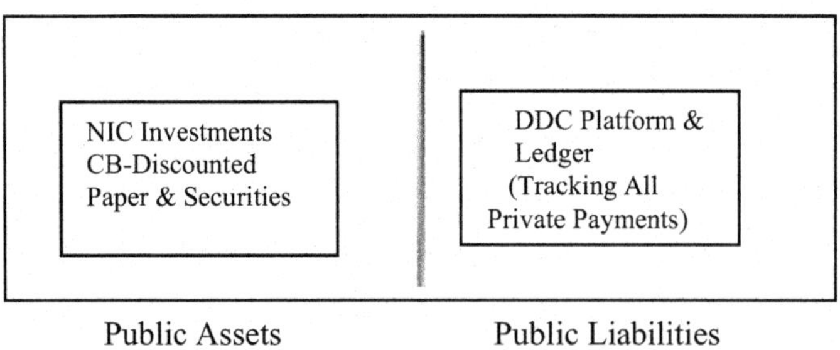

Fig. 5.1 Consolidated public balance sheet

control over the public investment capital that all publicly licensed bank-issued credit-money amounts to.

But how will this look in detail, and how, precisely, do our new digital finance technologies enable it? To that—to digitized Citizen Ledger Finance—we now turn.

Notes

1. *Rousseauvian Money, supra* note 3, at 26–27 (discussing the modern societal trend of centralizing and formalizing currency arrangement).
2. *Money's Past, supra* note 17, at 10–11 (concluding that a Fed-issued digital currency would be "more effective, saving-friendly and consumer-friendly" than the current system).
3. *Id.* at 4 (discussing the historical necessity of U.S bank franchising).
4. *Id.* at 5 ("It is at best a holdover from earlier times: times when currencies were pegged to exogenously given stocks of precious metals, finance was indeed by and large privately supplied, and capital—at least liquid capital—was indeed scarce.").
5. *Finance without Financiers, supra* note 15, at 4–5 ("The dominant intermediated scarce private capital view of finance is, then, a *myth.*").
6. *See Finance without Financiers, supra* note 15, at 4–5 (arguing that financial institutions do indeed intermediate, capital is not actually "scarce *see also Rousseauvian Money,*" *supra* note 3, at 33–34 (explaining misconceptions of the government's role in managing markets).
7. *See Rousseauvian Money, supra* note 3 (noting that financial intermediation theories "conflate[-] an indefinitely extensible resource—finance capital—with a (momentarily) scarce resource—physical capital").
8. *See Finance without Financiers, supra* note 15, at 4–5 (debunking the intermediated scarce private capital myth).
9. *See id.* at 5 ("[Intermediated scarce private capital view] is a myth whose widespread acceptance is no doubt convenient for certain rentier interests in contemporary 'financialized' societies, but is a myth nonetheless.").
10. *See id.* at 4 (explaining the intermediated scarce private capital "view is routinely stated in treatises, textbooks, learned journals, and the popular media.").
11. *See Rousseauvian Money, supra* note 3, at 41–42 (explaining early development of standardized monetary systems and the need for currency uniformity in commerce).
12. *See Rousseauvian Money, supra* note 3, at 44–45 (discussing the origins and history of metal capital as backing for paper currency).
13. *See Money's Past, supra* note 17, at 3 (discussing the consistent standards across franchisors).

14. *Rousseauvian Money*, *supra* note 3, at 47–48 (describing how inflation results from printing more money without having additional backing for it).
15. *Id.* at 45 (explaining the risk that "elastic currency could be 'over-stretched,' issued too far in excess of the metal that 'backed' it").
16. *Id*. at 45–46 (tracing the historical risks of unregulated private banks over-stretching their currency leading to the development of national standards and bank regulations).
17. *Id.* at 44 and 51 (explaining that the stamp on the precious metal coin gave it recognition and value as currency; "currency and coin are not money, they represent money").
18. *Id.* at 46 (discussing the move from the metallic constraints of issuing notes to "credit-money").
19. *Id*. at 45–47 (describing the loss of the metallic constraints).
20. *See Rousseauvian Money*, *supra* note 3, at 40 ("For in effect private banking institutions are simply distributing that public resource which is the monetized full faith and credit of the U.S., earning privatized seignorage for doing the credit checks while being publicly licensed to play this role only so long as they maintain the 'quality standards' we demand through our franchisor Fed and its co-regulators.").
21. *Id*. at 46–48 (discussing the history of gold currency and sovereign backing of the same).
22. *A History of American Currency*, AMERICAN NUMISMATIC SOCIETY (last visited November 1, 2019) (discussing the evolution of currency in the U.S.).
23. *See* CONANT, *supra* note 134, at 311 ("A new country, poor in specie and in loanable capital, is almost forced by the necessities of her situation to adopt monetary devices which would not be tolerated under better conditions."); SEAVOY, *supra* note 139, at 154 (describing banking policy in the early 1830's as responsive in part to the scarcity of specie at several distinct financial crises).
24. *Id.* (describing banking regulations regulating the denominations of paper bills to be circulated in response to the shortages of coins). Treasury Secretary Alexander Hamilton's fiscal and banking plans were all about simultaneously addressing this scarcity and the incomplete centralization and sovereignty that perpetuated it. *See, e.g.*, *Pre-Liberal Autonomy*, *supra* note 10; *Materializing Citizenship*, *supra* note 10, at 2077–79 (describing the decentralized early American financial landscape preferred by the government at the time, to which Hamilton's banking plans responded); *Jeffersonian Republic*, *supra* note 29 (describing the "Hamiltonian spirit" of developments in American financial policy encouraging access to capital and diversified sources of wealth amidst a backdrop of a decentralized, agrarian early economy); *see also* Robert C. Hockett, *When All Enterprise Was "Social,"* in CAMBRIDGE HANDBOOK OF SOCIAL ENTERPRISE (2018) (referencing the "free banking" period of American financial history that lasted from 1836–1863).

25. *See* Conant, *supra* note 134, at 286, 291, 346, 356 (discussing the early money-printing policies of the banks of several early states and the abrupt and adverse regulatory reactions to the influx of new capital therein and the American public's general trust in a metallic currency standard); Seavoy, *supra* note 139, at 154 (describing a collective national "panic" due to the shortage of metal currency and its replacement with paper currency).
26. *See Rousseauvian Money*, *supra* note 3, at 25 ("When populations grow larger and asset/liability relations grow more far-flung and complex, however, things must be 'formalized' and 'regularized.'").
27. *See* Sylla, *supra* note 162 (discussing the history of American banking).
28. *See generally* Conant, *supra* note 134 (arguing the decentralized political structure of the early U.S. served as an impediment to effective centralized banking and financial policy).
29. *Id.* at 345 (comparing the state banks of northern, midwestern, and southern states).
30. *Id.* at 108–114 (detailing how the early policies of Alexander Hamilton addressed structural perceived weaknesses in the American economy to create the idea of centralized finance as we know it in America); *see generally* Conant, *supra* note 134 (arguing that the agrarian, decentralized nature of early American society created myriad challenges to creating an effective, centralized financial system).
31. *See* Conant, *supra* note 134, at 311 (positing that the U.S. government was severely restricted in its early years because of its lack of centralized currency and capital).
32. *Id.* at 310–35 (describing the proliferation of small banks in early decades of the American Republic, which had four systems of note, and the diversity of their charters and loaning practices).
33. *A History of American Currency*, *supra* note 220 ("With the adoption of the Constitution, monetary production was redefined and restricted as a national prerogative.... Although the actual states were constitutionally forbidden to issue their own money, hundreds of private firms circumvented the law by producing what became generally known as "broken-bank notes.").
34. *See Rousseauvian Money*, *supra* note 3, at 14–15 (arguing that money, in any form of 'commercial exchange' is necessary for any political or social entity to exist).
35. *See* Feliks Mlynarski, Gold and Central Banks 33–34 (1928) (demonstrating the steady increase of gold reserves and deposits during the 1920s in America).
36. *Id. at* 52–70 (discussing effects of open market operations).
37. Another tragically forgotten bit of Fed—and hence our Republic's financial—history. And an ironic one at that, given the near-obsession with discounting commercial paper as the right way to central-bank on the part of Paul Warburg, the most influential Fed founder. See the brilliant Paul M. Warburg, The Discount System in Europe (1910), and try not to

weep. See generally Robert Hockett, *The Once and Future Fed—and Treasury*, 65 Challenge 1 (2021), available at https://papers.ssrn.com/sol3/papers.cfm?abstract_id=3808792. Also Robert Hockett, *Spread the Fed: Distributed Central Banking in Pandemic and Beyond*, 19 VA. J. BUS. L. 1 (2021), at https://papers.ssrn.com/sol3/papers.cfm?abstract_id=3597724; and Hockett, *Scissors Require Two Blades, supra* note 111.

38. *Id.*
39. The RFC in effect made partial amends for earlier switch-sleeping by the Fed during the bubble-inflating "Roaring '20s." During its twenty years of operation, the RFC was by far the world's largest financial institution, with a portfolio dwarfing those of all private financial institutions combined. That portfolio included assets as small as micro-loans to Watts (Los Angeles) barbershops and as large as multimillion dollar debt and equity holdings in banks, thrifts, railroads, power and light companies, and such still-operating entities as the U.S.'s Federal Housing Administration (FHA), the Federal National Mortgage Association (FNMA; Fannie Mae), the Small Business Administration (SBA), and the Export-Import Bank (Ex-Im Bank). And in all of these investments, the RFC made substantial profits, all of which were either plowed into further investments or remitted to the Treasury. See Hockett, sources cited *supra*, notes 1, 111. The WFC and, especially, the RFC showed decisively that the public finance franchisor even in the U.S., and hence surely elsewhere, ultimately needs private finance franchisee institutions little more for the allocative task than it does for the modulatory task, not to mention that getting modulation right requires getting allocation right. They showed that public–private finance-franchising, however useful it might have been during the early years of the new national money regime in the final decades of the nineteenth century, was no longer necessary for the bulk of financing by the second decade of the twentieth century, and that it was downright dysfunctional in any economy beset by coordination needs and recursive collective action problems of the kind that afflict all decentralized markets—especially those in which credit is endogenously generated. See Hockett, sources cited *supra*, notes 1, 111. Indeed, perhaps partly in recognition of this very fact, influential British economist John Maynard Keynes began advocating a "National Board of Investments" for the United Kingdom in the same period, predicting that it would naturally come to account for some two-thirds of Great Britain's total investments. *See* John Maynard Keynes, The Collected Writings of John Maynard Keynes 384–395 (Donald Moggridge ed., Cambridge Univ. Press 1978) (developing Keynes' economic theories); *see also* John Maynard Keynes, The General Theory of Employment, Interest, and Money 336 (Palgrave Macmillan 2018) (1936) (discussing the same).
40. See, e.g., Robert Hockett & Richard Vague, *Debt, Deflation, and Debacle: Of Private Debt Write-Down and Public Recovery*, White Paper, Global Interdependence Center, Federal Reserve Bank of Philadelphia (2013), available

at https://www.interdependence.org/wp-content/uploads/2013/04/Debt-Deflation-and-Debacle-RV-and-RH1.pdf.

41. *See Finance without Financiers*, *supra* note 15, at 1–7 (explaining the intermediated scarce private capital myth and the finance franchise).
42. *See generally* John G. Gurley & Edward S. Shaw, *Financial Aspects of Economic Development*, 45 AM. ECON. REV. 515 (1955); John G. Gurley & Edward S. Shaw, *Financial Intermediaries and the Savings-Investment Process*, 11 J. FIN. 257 (1956); James Tobin, *Commercial Banks as Creators of "Money"*, COWLES FOUNDATION PAPER 205 (1963) (representing examples of 1950s and 1960s economic theory).
43. Note that in a certain sense that will be recognizable thanks to the foregoing, we all do that every day in spending dollars, which are tradable liabilities issued by the Fed as surely as bluechip Apple bonds are tradable liabilities issued by Apple.

6

Digitized Citizen Ledger Finance: What We Now Can and Must Do

The foregoing discussion culminates in three suggestive conclusions. The first is that the sovereign—in a commercial republic or indeed any republic that is the public—must issue and modulate the supply of the polity's sovereign credit-money, its public investment capital.

The second is that the sovereign public both can and should actively *allocate* much of that vital resource, in particular toward productive primary and away from speculative secondary and tertiary meta-markets—partly in furtherance of the modulatory task itself, and partly for reasons quite independent of that task, including reasons of justice, macroeconomic stability, and the solving of ubiquitous recursive collective action problems that impede productive investment.[1]

And the third is that sovereign coin and currency represent what I have here been calling an "intermediate stage" monetary technology, necessary for purposes of monetary uniformity and elasticity only (a) after populations outgrow mental or paper account book ledger-money practicability and (b) before those populations develop *digital* account book ledger-money capacity.

I have more fully elaborated and argued for the truth of these propositions, as a theoretical matter, both in the previous two Chapters and in prior work.[2] And above I have also now provided a brief explanatory historical narrative showing both how and why we as contemporary commercial republics arrived at our present sets of no longer necessary or even desirable hybrid finance

R. C. Hockett, *The Citizens' Ledger*,
https://doi.org/10.1007/978-3-030-99566-9_6

franchise arrangements. What remains to do now is to show how to integrate the modulatory and allocative functions practically in the design of fully republicanized and democratized systems of digital finance—what I shall call, since we are republics, digitized "Citizen Ledger Finance." That is the task of this chapter.

What I shall sketch here is a system of digital "Citizen" and "Resident" Wallets maintained on single digitized national account books—consolidated public ledgers—to which will correspond public assets that will be generated by public investment and publicly backstopped productive private investment along the lines indicated above. These will fall into three classes.

One will be public "discount window"-style loans to both public and private sector lending institutions, which will take the place of much in the way of deposit liabilities currently owed by contemporary private sector commercial banks to the borrowers whose accounts they credit.

Second will come issuances of National Investment Councils (again, "NICs)" of the kind mentioned above, along with other public investment institutions such as the U.S.'s Small Business Administration ("SBA"), all as more fully described below.

And third will come other assets that central banks and finance ministries will hold and deal in in the interest of socially just credit allocation and stability-maintaining credit modulation, as I shall also describe below.

The implications of these changes for private sector banking, capital markets, and "shadow banks," not to mention traditional distinctions between central bank and finance ministry monetary and fiscal policy instruments and operations, will be extensive, as I shall show.[3] But what they will all have in common is one simple feature.

Private sector finance in all subsectors of our financial sectors now will indeed be *private*, and hence veritably preaccumulated and "intermediated" as orthodoxy now falsely describes, not endogenously generated. *Public* credit-money, for its part, which is publicly *generated* rather than privately "intermediated,"[4] will flow only toward publicly approved bona fide productive, not speculative, projects, meaning that public allocation will be forthrightly embraced and central bank/finance ministry operations accordingly by and large consolidated as described in Chapter 7.

Off then to the proverbial races in full detail.

6.1 Liability-Side Reform: Reserve Accounts, Citizen Wallets, and Resident Wallets

Let us begin on the liability side of present-day public sector balance sheets. Taking specific examples as case studies will aid intuition, so I shall again for the moment use the U.S. Fed and Treasury, whose operations I'm able to describe best. On the liability side of a digitized U.S. national account ledger, which can constitute either the Fed's balance sheet, the Treasury's balance sheet, or a consolidated balance sheet comprising both,[5] my proposal is quite simple. Indeed it is surprisingly so because, once one sees just how simple it is, the wonder is that the U.S. has not done something like it since 1913 or, at latest, 1918 or 1935. Indeed, for some institutions, the U.S. *has* been doing it since then, as I will indicate in the course of my exposition.

6.1.1 What the U.S. and Others Do Now: Reserve Accounts

Begin with what the U.S. does now. All nationally and most state-chartered banks, including U.S. affiliates of foreign banks, hold Reserve Accounts with the Fed.[6] It is through these accounts that the Fed manages its day-to-day bank reserve requirement and liquidity management regime, to which all banks chartered or operating in the U.S. are subject.[7]

Bank reserve accounts with the Fed are essentially deposits, hence assets of the banks and liabilities of the Fed.[8] The private sector banks stand to the public sector Fed, in other words, as ordinary citizens with demand deposits stand to their private sector banks.[9] The Fed in this sense truly is a "bank to the banks"—a *central* bank like other central banks worldwide—and has been since its inception.[10]

Since the crash of 2008, the Fed has paid interest on bank reserve accounts held with it—so-called interest on reserves, or IOR.[11] This is another respect in which Fed reserve accounts are like bank deposit accounts, save that the Fed pays much more than private sector banks do.[12] It also confers upon Fed reserves a characteristic once limited to Treasury securities—IOR is effectively the coupon on a bond.

Interest on reserves affords the Fed a liability-side monetary policy tool supplementing its ample kit of asset-side tools and renders Fed reserves rather like coupon-bearing Treasury securities to their holders—one reason I will keep saying "central bank or finance ministry" in what I elaborate immediately below, and suggest Fed/Treasury consolidation, as well as other central bank/finance ministry consolidations across all commercial republics, a bit further below.[13] Other such tools in the U.S. include the federal funds rate the Fed sets in the interbank lending market, open market operations in Treasury securities and some other instruments, repo and reverse repo transactions on various forms of collateral, and of course discount rates that the Fed applies when purchasing eligible instruments through its asset-monetizing discount window.[14]

All of these tools, some of long standing and others more recently developed in the face of financial exigency,[15] are means by which the Fed engages both in liquidity-maintenance and in what I have been calling its money-modulatory task in the name of the American republic.[16] Some of these tools also have been used in more recent times in pursuit of what I have been calling the credit-allocative task.[17] A conspicuous case of the latter in recent years has been the third round of quantitative easing—QE3—initiated in the autumn of 2012.[18] Through QE3, the Fed committed to purchasing $85 billion in mortgage-related assets in order to establish and then raise a floor under housing prices, until such time as residential real estate markets would stabilize.[19] I will have more to say about the importance of this as a precedent below.

Now as noted a moment ago, some of the Fed's monetary policy instruments operate on the asset side of the balance sheet, while correspondingly affecting the liability side of that sheet.[20] Other instruments work in the other direction.[21]

Fed open market operations in Treasury securities, or in mortgage instruments pursuant to QE3, commence with a purchase of instruments into or sale of instruments out of the Fed's asset portfolio, to which correspond creditings or debitings of "primary dealer bank" reserve accounts on the liability side of the Fed's balance sheet.[22] Interest paid on reserve accounts held with the Fed, conversely, are immediate creditings of banks' deposits on the liability side of the Fed's balance sheet, which will be balanced by additions the Fed makes to its asset portfolio.[23]

As a general matter, the liability side of the Fed's balance sheet consists of (a) its note issuance, (b) the sum of reserve account moneys, and (c) repo and swap line liabilities to dealer banks and other central banks.[24] The asset side, for its part, consists primarily of financial instruments the Fed holds in the form of Treasury securities, mortgage instruments, reverse repo claims, Special Drawing Rights ("SDRs") with the International Monetary Fund ("IMF"), and accounts with the Bank for International Settlements ("BIS").[25]

Needless to say, as with other central banks worldwide, the Fed is a very large balance sheet—especially since the crash of 2008 and its aftermath, which required significant Fed intervention to prop up both failing franchisee institutions and plummeting financial assets.[26] To track this balance sheet's changes over time is essentially to track the Fed's operations as the American republic's primary money-modulator and, ever more both of late and of necessity, credit-allocator.[27] It is to track, in other words, an incipient form of a full citizens' account book or ledger.[28]

Diagrammatically, things presently look in the U.S. as depicted in Fig. 6.1.

One feature of the liability side of the Fed's balance sheet is of particular interest for present purposes. This is that apart from the note issuance, the liabilities in connection with which run to all holders of U.S. currency, the Fed's liabilities run solely to public instrumentalities and a privileged few private sector financial institutions—what I have been calling finance franchisee institutions.[29]

This fact, arresting once one thinks about it (why *Note* and *Treasury security* availability for all but not *Wallet* availability for all?), underwrites three lines of criticism easily directed at the "developed" world's present way of doing things, lines that converge with those I laid out in introducing this book. None of these criticisms would be warranted where the national or central bank ledger to be digitally opened to all citizens, qualified residents, and business firms in the way I shall momentarily be advocating, rather than merely a privileged few banking and other financial institutions of large size.

First, the present arrangement needlessly privileges large, systemically important financial institutions, affording them a form of "public banking option" not offered to other firms, local governments, citizens, or legal residents.[30] It also affords those institutions a gratuitous rent in the form of

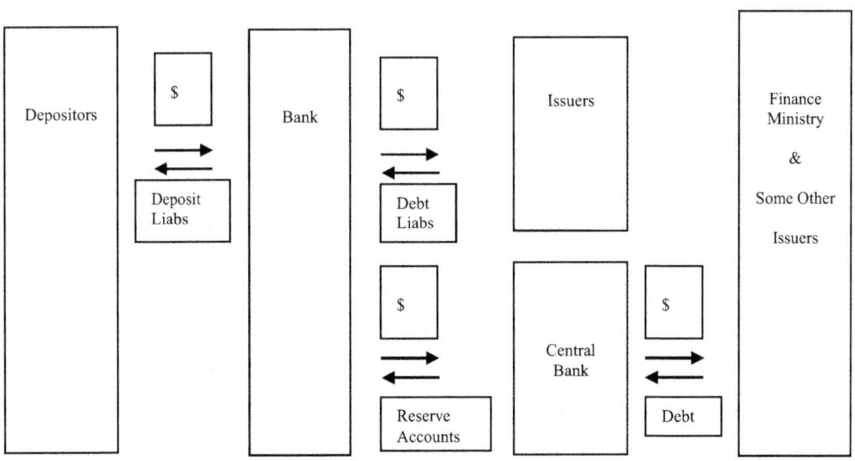

Fig. 6.1 Regular central bank/bank arrangements and financial flows

IOR, which they do not pass on to depositors in the form of equivalent IOD—interest on deposits.[31] This is strikingly inequitable, particularly under circumstances in which "the government" often looks to be in bed with "Wall Street," "Lombard Street," or "high finance," all while significant sectors of the population are unbanked or underbanked, hence commercially and financially disenfranchised.[32] Call these the financial–commercial inequity and exclusion problems.

Second, the present arrangement enables large franchisee institutions to spend or dispense public credit with abandon, particularly when central bank leadership, as it did, for example, in the U.S. during the Greenspan era, loses understanding of our central banks' modulatory and associated allocative and quality control responsibilities as our primary finance franchise administrators. That fuels financial market volatility, asset price bubbles, and catastrophic busts, not to mention an associated egregious misallocation—a *counterproductive* allocation—of our commercial republics' credit supplies. I call this the "rogue franchisee problem." It is especially galling in juxtaposition with the financial–commercial inequity and exclusion problems just noted.[33]

Finally, third, conducting monetary policy—that is, money modulation and credit allocation—through intermediaries, as using the medium of dealer banks amounts to, is an inefficient and leak-prone mode of operation, as noted above in this book's Prologue. Part of the idea behind both quantitative easing and other extraordinary measures taken by the U.S. Fed and Treasury alike in the public's name from 2008 to 2012, for example, was to pump liquidity into the financial system by enabling banks to keep lending even in the face and aftermath of the 2008 credit crunch.[34] There were three glitches, however, that impeded the efficacy of money modulation and allocation via private intermediary during times of crisis.

The first glitch was that many banks preferred simply to hoard their additional liquidity while fearfully riding out the continuing storm.[35] The second was that other banks found it more promisingly lucrative to speculate with their additional liquidity on secondary and tertiary financial, commodities, and derivative markets than to lend to would-be producers and consumers in primary markets, especially in the absence of any commitment to aggregate demand support or debt-cancelation by federal authorities.[36] And the third was that many citizens, left owing more than they owned in the debt-deflationary aftermath of the national housing and financial market crashes, were not keen to borrow more during the protracted slump anyway.[37]

These problems all added up to what came to be known as the "pushing on a string" problem, the insight essentially being that supply-side solutions are not well adapted to addressing demand-side disasters.[38] In response, many critics argued that monetary policy alone does not suffice to address crises, particularly in a liquidity trap. Fiscal measures also were needed. I agree with that criticism but note also that the weaknesses of monetary policy observed during 2009–12 are more rooted in *franchised* monetary policy than in monetary policy as such. This book's insourcing and digital national ledger proposal shows why—in effect, to take out the middleman institutions is to narrow the space between fiscal and monetary policy, potentially even to the point of consolidating them. But more of that in due course, specifically in Sect. 3.

6.1.2 What We Must Add: Digital Citizen Wallets, Resident Wallets, and Their Common Digital Ledger

I find all three of the foregoing criticisms of present-day Reserve Account arrangements compelling and see no downside to cutting the ground out from under them with one single stroke. That is simply to offer *all* citizens, along with the U.S.'s state and local governments, small businesses, and other nonbanking firms too, digital wallet accounts with the central bank or finance ministry much like the Reserve Accounts privileged U.S. banks have enjoyed with the Fed now for well over a century.[39]

In effect, parties depicted on the far left side of Fig. 1 in Chapter 2 would "bank," instead of with the private sector institutions depicted immediately to their right, with the central bank or finance ministry one step to the right of those institutions in the same diagram. Wallets would also enjoy peer-to-peer ("P2P") interoperability just as do paper currency and bank-issued strip cards and chip-cards, meaning that wallet-holders would transact with one another simply through simultaneous debiting of payor and crediting of payee wallets.

In other words, ignoring for the moment Fed and Treasury assets and looking only to the liability sides of their balance sheets, the primary national money and payments system, instead of being built upon transaction accounts held at multiple banking institutions, payment cards associated with the same, and the plethora of now proliferating "Venmo", "PayPal," "Apple-Pay" and the like, would be instantly streamlined into looking as depicted in Fig. 6.2.

In short, the "Master Account" depicted here would simply be one of the liability portfolios on the liability side of the central bank's or finance ministry's balance sheet—the portfolio to which the Depositors at the left of Fig. 1 in Chapter 2 would now directly connect rather than only indirectly

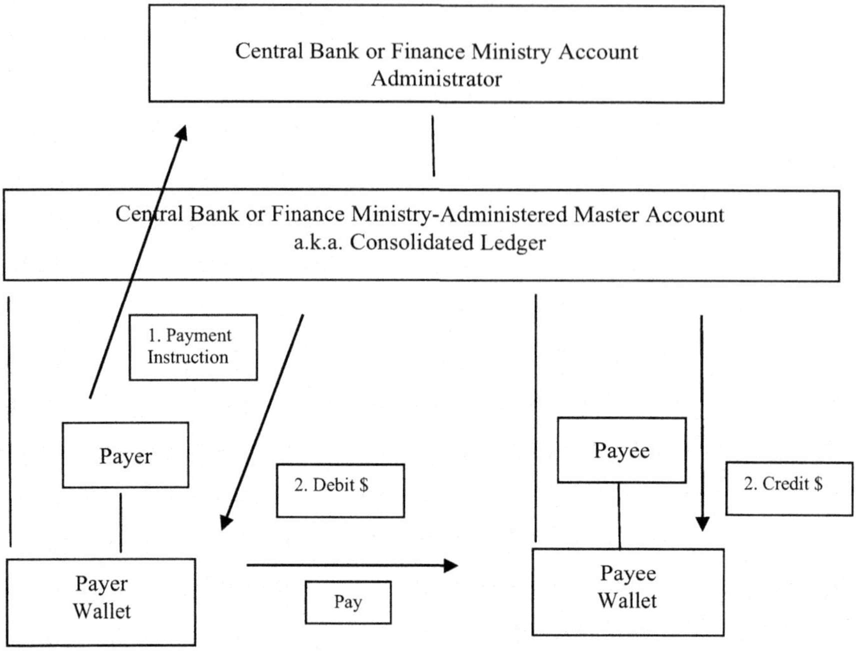

Fig. 6.2 Central-bank- or finance-ministry-administered democratic digital currency payments system

connecting via the medium of private sector banking institutions as depicted immediately to their right in that same diagram. Payments *inter se* would simply be simultaneous creditings and debitings within that portfolio, effectively replicating, in more direct and consolidated form, what is now done indirectly via the medium of private sector bank accounts (bank liabilities) balanced against reserve accounts (bank assets) held with the central bank. (I pay you by instructing my bank to debit my account held with it and simultaneously credit you via your account at your bank, with these changes to banks' accounts then registering in their accounts on the liability side of the central bank balance sheet.)

It bears noting in this connection that Americans can hold accounts with their Treasury Department already, which could be upgraded to P2P wallets of the kind I'm describing. I refer to the TreasuryDirect system, which presently permits "banked" citizens to purchase and redeem Treasury securities online, provided that they hold bank accounts from which dollars can be spent and into which dollars can be paid. U.S. Digital Service reports to this author TreasuryDirect Accounts ("TDAs") could be converted into P2P digital wallets that hold both Treasury securities and Fed Notes (dollars) in as few as three months. That is the basis of this author's "Digital Greenbacks" plan now before the U.S. Congress.[40]

In effect, then, this portfolio on the liability side of the central bank or finance ministry's balance sheet will constitute a single, uniform national payment ledger and associate system of digital wallets. In this sense, it will amount to a return to ledger money of the kind that Chapter 4 above indicated societies and smaller groups historically have maintained before growing too large and complex to maintain comprehensive account books on paper yet too technologically underdeveloped to digitize and thus avoid circulating uniformly valuable public IOUs as public ledger-entry substitutes. It will also amount to a form of digital sovereign-issued cash, as all digital wallet dollars will be direct issuances of the central bank or finance ministry. There will be no more "bank money" here other than literal "central bank money" or "finance ministry money."

This in turn will offer not only the benefit of banking and commercial inclusion and a simplified, far more efficient payments architecture than our present ones have become, but will also bring multiple advantages where transaction volume and thus economic growth, monetary policy, productive national investment, and financial stability are concerned. We will get to all of that, in addition to anticipated objections about privacy, "Big Brother," and so on. But first, we must fill out a bit more in the way of mechanical and logistical detail.

Now I referred to "offering" digital wallets before. This can take either or both of the two forms. One form would be to make wallets available to all and only those who might ask. The other form would be to open such wallets automatically, with beneficiaries free at any time to activate or not as they prefer. Probably the most sensible option will be to open the wallets automatically upon birth or naturalization for individuals born in or recently become citizens of the republic and to offer such wallets upon request to subnational units of government, businesses, and other institutions, and resident aliens who do not pose security threats.

I call wallet accounts of the first kind Citizen Wallets, which can be credited automatically with public benefits that citizens regularly receive such as social insurance payments, tax refunds, and the like.[41] This will simplify the task of sovereign payments to—that is, crediting of—citizens. Citizen Wallets also can receive "baby bond" or sovereign wealth fund proceeds,[42] if and when sundry republics adopt such things, not to mention earnings on public investments, more on which presently. And, of course, Citizen Wallets can and should earn interest, just as bank reserve accounts held with the U.S. Fed and as U.S. Treasury securities do.[43] These rates, along with direct "QE for the People" or "helicopter drop" measures in extremis, can then serve as central bank or finance ministry monetary policy instruments far more direct and effective in their operation than can our current sets of intermediary-dependent "string-pushing" tools.[44] I'll return to this too when I turn to a systematic tracing of the systemic ramifications that will flow out of full implementation my full proposal.

I call accounts of the second kind Resident Wallets, which beneficiaries can use as ordinary deposit accounts and which the central bank or finance ministry also can use, like Citizen Wallets, for monetary policy purposes. For most if not all intents and purposes, Resident Wallets will function identically to Citizen Wallets. The principal differences will be (a) that they are opened on request rather than automatically upon birth or attainment to citizenship and (b) that they close out more frequently, at least in the case of some short-lived business enterprises and other institutions.

One additional difference might be (c) that "QE for the People" or "Citizen Helicopter Drop" measures, should they at any point be taken, probably ought to be either restricted to Citizen Wallets, or restricted to Citizen Wallets and the Resident Wallets only of (a) subnational units of government and (b) such private sector entities as can verifiably commit to spending the proceeds of drops on real goods and services rather than speculative securities or derivative instruments.[45]

Affording digital central bank or finance ministry Citizen and Resident Wallets to all in the way here proposed will visit several immediate effects on the liability sides of the central bank's and other banks' balance sheets.[46] It will of course also bear corresponding implications for the asset sides of these balance sheets, and for the regulatory *apparati* through which banks and other financial institutions and markets are regulated. And, of course, it will raise various systemic, logistical, technological, and related questions that will have to be addressed before or during the course of implementation. None of these, however, are especially thorny or difficult, as I shall now show.

To begin with the liability side, the central bank or finance ministry's balance sheet will quickly begin to expand, as some—probably many—citizens and other residents switch from holding barely remunerated funds with privately owned banking institutions, money market funds, and other bank deposit substitutes to holding interest-bearing wallets with the central bank or finance ministry.[47] This they will do in virtue both of the rates earned on Wallet savings and of the immediate free access to the economy-wide, universal payments platform that the system of Wallets will constitute.

Banks, in turn, as their deposit bases shrink, will replace customer deposits with "discount window"-style loans from the central bank or counterpart loans from the finance ministry, which will be the new and sole "choke point(s)" through which the public sector allows for any private sector role in "gate-keeping," "credit-checking," or "project-evaluating" assistance in the productive channeling of public credit, more on which immediately below.

These changes will convert many, probably most bank deposit and deposit-like liabilities now owed to depositors and other "near-depositors" into bank liabilities owed to the central bank through its discount window or to the finance ministry through a similar facility, as depositors and near-depositors transfer funds, first gradually and then at a likely accelerating rate, from one set of accounts to the other.[48] It will of course correspondingly grow the central bank's or the finance ministry's asset portfolio, for these new discount window loans will be public assets.[49] I will have more to say about this new class of publicly held asset—especially its money-modulatory and credit-allocative potential—below.

The asset sides of private bank balance sheets need not immediately change all that much in response to the opening of digital Citizen and Resident Wallets—at least not if we do not wish for them to change either too much or too rapidly. Current portfolios can be left to wind-down in due course, per the maturities of the assets that are already held. All that will change quickly is the identity of the creditor on a newly large portion of the banks' liabilities that replaces a correspondingly diminishing portion of banks' liabilities.

That new creditor will be the central bank or finance ministry, pursuant to the discount window or like lending just mentioned.[50] This affords a benefit to banking institutions: neither the central bank nor the finance ministry is subject to the depositor collective action problem—nor, therefore, apt to "run" on the banks that will now owe it, meaning in turn that banks' required reserve and paid deposit insurance obligations will in aggregate be significantly lightened if not eliminated.[51]

Indeed, deposit insurance will become a significantly less prominent, if not indeed unnecessary, part of our bank-regulatory toolkit, meaning in turn that agencies like the U.S.'s Federal Deposit Insurance Corporation ("FDIC") will diminish in importance relative to the central bank and/or finance ministry if nations retain them at all. This in turn will mean that the task of capital regulation, which historically has fallen primarily to FDIC-like agencies on the theory that it must protect the public insurance fund, continue and complete their already ongoing migration to central bank administration in the name of enhanced macroprudential regulation—as, for example, under Title I of the Dodd-Frank Act in the U.S.[52]

In effect, as more fully described in Sect. 3, all private sector lending not funded by central bank or finance ministry discount window lending will be subject to a 100% capital requirement—that is, it will be bona fide credit-intermediation rather than credit-multiplication or -generation.[53] It will be, that's to say, "narrow banking" of various kinds.[54] As this transition proceeds, no administrative difficulties of any great significance need be posed; capital-regulatory staff now at agencies like the U.S. FDIC will simply become de facto or *de jure* staff at the central bank or finance ministry and will transition from imposing traditional "capital buffers" to developing and administering discount window lending conditionality, as I shall describe next.

If and insofar as we permit private sector banks to continue to lend in ways that find expression in the form of newly opened deposits, the latter will have to be deposited into Citizen and Resident Wallets, meaning in turn that the banks will have to borrow through the central bank's discount window or a finance ministry equivalent—for example, the U.S.'s Federal Financing Bank (again, "FFB")—going forward.[55] This presents a welcome opportunity to the public for purposes of money modulation and credit allocation—an opportunity that lies at the core and is indeed part of the object, of digitized Citizen Ledger Finance. For the U.S. Fed and other central banks already condition discount window lending upon the possession of socially desirable attributes on the part of that which it lends against—a practice that used to be more robust and can be made so again, as I'll demonstrate—such that converting all levered private sector lending to discount window lending will be to convert all such lending to explicitly publicly evaluated and approved lending.[56]

The central bank or finance ministry will in other words now *add* conditions that *further* their evolving credit-modulatory and -allocative missions—much as the U.S. Federal Housing Administration ("FHA") and associated GSEs, for example, have historically limited their insurance provision and secondary market-making activities, respectively, to so-called "conforming" loans whose criteria evolve over time.[57] Among such investment attributes that seem incontestably desirable will be those associated with the financing of small and start-up businesses, bona fide small family farms, employee-owned firms, non-outsourcing firms, renewable energy and other eco-friendly firms, and the like—all of the things that collective action challenges and other market failures of the kind discussed earlier in Chapter 5 prevent our adequately financing now.

As noted above and further discussed below, classic collective action challenges now prevent adequate capital flows from reaching such enterprises and enabling them to scale-up. Digitized Citizen Ledger Finance is all about changing that, and the central bank's or finance ministry's asset portfolio will be the site of that action. This form of financial republicanization and democratization will be the asset-side counterpart to that liability side republicanization and democratization which is the system of digital Citizen and Resident Wallets. In effect, then, the central bank discount window or a finance ministry equivalent will become the forthrightly public sector "gatekeeper's"—that is, credit-allocator's—"gate," and thus the focal point at which limiting private sector lending activity solely to healthy forms of productive primary market, not speculative secondary and tertiary market, credit-extension takes place.

It will, in other words, become the site of a new U.S. Glass-Steagall style regime far more fine-tuned and effective than the first, to say nothing of weaker Glass-Steagall successors like the Volcker Rule or EU Liikanen style "ring-fencing."[58] For now, instead of simply imposing one vaguely contoured categorical proscription ("no investment banking," or "no proprietary trading") and saying "have at it" for all else, we shall be laying down specific affirmative criteria and saying "nothing apart from this." Changing the presumption in this way, and thus in effect conditioning public credit extension on "conformity" of the "conforming loan" type that the U.S. requires for FHA mortgage insurance, for example, will convert the entirety of the public portions of our financial systems into engines of simultaneous primary market growth and secondary/tertiary market reduction, as I shall systematically indicate below.[59] And that is to say it will reverse and undo the past 50 years' course of developed world "financialization."[60]

In sum, then, most deposit insurance administrators now employed administering present-day capital-regulatory regimes, and many bank-chartering authorities now employed administering bank portfolio-regulatory regimes, will accordingly be transitioned to administering newly enhanced discount window conditionality regimes. By conditioning their own asset purchases in this way, crucially, the central bank or finance ministry will be governing bank *asset*-creation as well. And in so doing they will be publicly assuming the task of principled credit allocation upon which both credit modulation and sustainable economic growth depend. This takes us to a more careful look at the central bank's or finance ministry's asset portfolio changes under my proposal.

6.2 Asset-Side Reform: Digitized CB, NIC, PSF, and Other Public Issuances

The asset side of the public sector balance sheet, in some contrast to those of private bank balance sheets, will undergo significant changes over time with the offering of Citizen and Resident Wallets. Once again, I will use the U.S. Fed and Treasury as illustrative examples, first saying a bit about what they do now, then turning to what should and will change in a regime of full Citizen Ledger Finance.

6.2.1 What We Do Now: Finance Ministry Debt, Agency Debt, and (Sometimes) Other

Prior to the troubles of 2008, the U.S. Federal Reserve System's principal asset holdings consisted of Treasury securities of varying maturities, agency securities also of varying maturities, and miscellaneous other assets with dollar values that paled in comparison to those of the first two categories.[61] Among the latter were gold certificates, SDRs with the IMF, and various small loans and similar assets acquired in the course of affording liquidity to financial institutions in need of it.[62] Matters are similar post-2008, save that the two prior categories have grown much in magnitude, while several new categories also have been added.[63]

The prior categories that have expanded since 2008 include (a) longer-term Treasury instruments, taken on both to accommodate fiscal stimulus spending and, pursuant to QE1 and QE2, to afford "forward guidance" on future interest rates and (b) mortgage-related agency and non-agency securities, purchased pursuant to QE3 as noted earlier.[64] These categories continue to represent by far the greater part of Fed asset holdings, with the only changes from pre-2008 being first, the absolute quantities held, which are much larger than before, and second, the greater portion of mortgage instruments now represented by private issuances.[65]

A more qualitative than quantitative change to the Fed's asset portfolio since 2008 has come with the addition of new classes of asset corresponding to emergency measures the Fed took from 2008 onward to address domestic and foreign liquidity and solvency dangers associated with the 2008 crash and its aftermath.[66] These include, among other things, (a) swap lines provided to other central banks worldwide and (b) a number of discount window lending programs and other ad hoc facilities to prop up banking, insurance, money market funds, and other financial institutions, including "shadow banks," imperiled after 2008.[67]

The quantitative growth of and qualitative changes to the Fed's asset portfolio were not worthy of the term "radical," at least in any pejorative sense, even if they were admittedly important and, if what I propose is adopted, precedent-setting.[68] They were straightforward extensions of familiar Fed operations into new magnitudes or domains, undertaken to prevent a complete collapse of the U.S. and global financial systems.[69] Though controversial in some cases, they came over time to be accepted as necessary, even if only as necessary evils by some, tolerated on the understanding that they would be temporary.[70] This is why Americans continue, at regular intervals, to hear talk of winding-down the Fed's balance sheet.[71] Thus far, however, the winding-down has yet to occur in any serious sense, with each move in that direction quickly met by "taper tantrums" in the financial markets and obliging Fed postponement of the offload.[72]

This is of course to say nothing of the far greater expansion of the Fed's balance sheet in response to the Covid pandemic of 2020. Not only are multiple trillions of dollars' worth of new Treasury issuances now held but so are corporate bonds, paycheck-protection loans, other business loans, repos, swaps, munis, and a host of additional investments now totaling at approximately \$6.5 trillion and headed for upwards of \$9 trillion. Figure 6.3 summarizes in pictorial form the U.S. Fed's portfolio as of early 2022.[73]

In my view, the U.S. Fed's and counterpart institutions' inability to shrink their portfolios since 2008, like the U.S. federal government's now fourteen-year-long receivership of the mortgage entity Fannie Mae,[74] signals a "new normal" where public maintenance of financial and, with it, macroeconomic stability are concerned.[75] The fact of the matter is that at least unless and until certain underlying structural conditions of our decentralized exchange economies can change—in particular, any such economy's subjection to recursive collective action challenges and cognate market failures of the kind discussed above in Chapter 5—public asset portfolios will have not only to remain as large as they have become since 2008 but indeed even to grow *further* in proportion to GDP.[76] They might indeed ultimately have to constitute at least two-thirds of full national portfolios, as I noted Keynes to have predicted above.

What will change first in the coming years, then, is the portfolios' compositions, as we transition from ad hoc emergency measures to longer-term public investment and price stability maintenance measures.[77] And what will change subsequently is the portfolios' sizes. To the rough details of these changes I now turn.

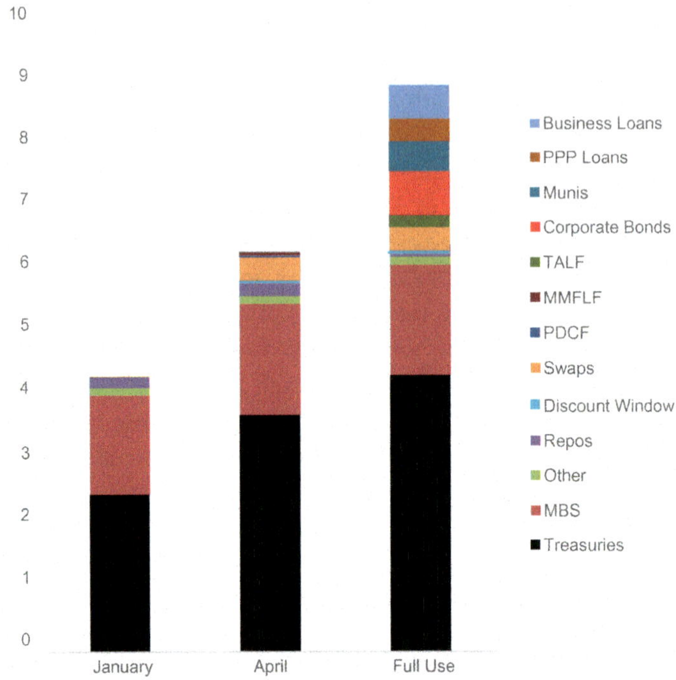

Fig. 6.3 U.S. Fed portfolio, measured in $ trillions, as of Spring 2020

6.2.2 What We Must Add: Digitized CB-Discounted Paper, NIC Issuances, PSF Holdings, and Other

Changes to the digitized asset side of central bank or finance ministry balance sheet under my proposal will emanate from two sources. The first source will be some of the liability side changes described above. The second will be certain structural changes that developed polities must make to their infrastructural and other productive finance arrangements in order to address the concerns I have laid out above and in prior work.[78]

There are two liability-side sources of likely change to central bank or finance ministry asset portfolios. Both will stem from the addition of Citizen and Resident Wallets to that side of the balance sheet.

First, the assets corresponding to many present-day *shadow* bank liabilities—in effect, short-term loans—that the central bank or finance ministry will effectively take over in paying IOR are at present substantially, if not indeed almost exclusively, speculative in character.[79] The institutions that now issue short-term shadow bank-like liabilities do so specifically to secure cheap funding to gamble on price movements among favored longer-term assets, and succeed in so doing by offering low returns to "cash managers" that at least exceed rates on bank deposits.

The central bank and finance ministry have no interest—pun ratified if not quite intended—in gambling on price changes among these assets with the short-term borrowings that their offering Citizen and Resident Wallets will equate to.[80] Indeed, they have every reason to edge-out and end such gambling much as U.S. Treasury Greenbacks edged out private sector bank monies in the late nineteenth century as described above, by affording interest-bearing Wallet deposits of the kind sought by the cash-management departments of shadow-bank lenders without using the proceeds of that short-term borrowing to gamble.

Central banks or finance ministries are accordingly apt, as in fact we should all require, to pair new deposit liabilities that it takes over from the shadow-banking sector with safer assets associated with productive primary market activity and the infrastructures on which such activity depends rather than speculative secondary and tertiary market assets of the kind shadow bank borrowing funds now.[81] Prominent among these will be NIC, SBA, and public bank style issuances, as well as what I call "systemically significant" issuances, of the kinds I discuss below.

In this sense, the central bank's or finance ministry's replacement of the banking and shadow banking sectors where deposit-taking and account-managing are concerned—their bringing these currently outsourced franchisee functions back "in-house"—will be a critical component of that reassertion of the public franchisor's role in our republics' money modulation and credit allocation tasks which I have been describing and prescribing both in the present book and in earlier work. And it will essentially complement that discount window conditionality I mentioned above.

The second liability-side reason that central banks' or finance ministries' digitized asset portfolios will change over time dovetails with the first. It is that, over a yet longer period of time, a growing portion of central bank or finance ministry deposit liabilities will not simply be transferred from current private sector bank and shadow bank balance sheets, but will be sovereign liabilities from the get-go as citizens, residents, and firms (a) borrow from institutions that credit their Citizen or Resident Wallets with loan proceeds, and (b) move to directly depositing, or directing the direct depositing of, funds from other persons and entities that transfer money to them, be those transfers payments or benefits, into their Citizen and Resident Wallets.

The central bank or finance ministry will presumably retain some discretion to determine what new assets to set off against some of these growing deposit liabilities—the ones to which no discount window loans to private lending institutions correspond. But this discretion must be legislatively guided in significant part toward investment in assets associated with the enhanced modulatory and allocative tasks that I have advocated in Chapters 4 and 5. This means that many of the new assets will be issuances of NIC type agencies, more on which below, while others will be acquired pursuant to central bank engagement in what I call "SIPI Stabilization," again both in prior work and below.[82]

It will be helpful here briefly to say a bit more about these NIC and PSF proposals, mentioned in passing in Chapter 5, since they will afford ideal assets to add to central bank or finance ministry digitized asset portfolios as liabilities associated with Citizen and Resident Wallets grow.

Starting with the NIC proposal, the idea here, again, is quite simple. On the one hand, much needed public infrastructure and even industrial investment is in the nature of an orthodox public good—it offers returns that are not capturable by individual investors thanks to their comparatively brief lifespans and lack of taxing authority. This in turn renders it individually rational to over-invest in speculative bets on short-term price movements in secondary and tertiary markets, and correspondingly to under-invest in long-term improvements in infrastructure and primary market productivity improvements.[83]

Since this is in turn collectively irrational inasmuch as it depresses long-term productivity improvement and associated benefits that everyone would choose could they control the macro environment and capture benefits commensurate to desired investment, we are faced with a classic collective action problem much like those that prompted the U.S. to establish the WIB and WFC in 1917 and the WPB and RFC in the 1930s as noted above.[84]

Constituted by the heads of national departments with jurisdiction over national infrastructures and heavy industries as noted above—in the U.S., e.g., the Department of Energy, the Federal Communications Commission, the Department of Transportation, etc.—the NIC will coordinate in developing coherent national infrastructure and industrial policy across sectors, regions, and the public and private sectors much as the U.S. Financial Stability Oversight Council ("FSOC") does in developing and implementing finance-regulatory policy across subsectors of our complex and hybrid financial sector.[85]

Most importantly for present purposes, the U.S. NIC will, in collaboration with the Fed and Treasury or their consolidated successor, issue multiple classes of digitized financial instrument in connection with specific infrastructure projects.[86] It will thereby offer investment outlets to "patient capital" now unable to find yields in productive as distinguished from speculative investments, counteract inflationary pressures otherwise generated by public infrastructure spending, and capitalize on markets' "price discovery" functions in determining the likely successes and public benefits thrown off by sundry prospective investments.[87]

A complementary role that the NIC will play is to coordinate with, and provide support for, certain other instrumentalities at all levels of government that themselves work to assist in capitalizing small businesses, small family farms, start-up firms, and the like. Prominent among these in the U.S. are the Small Business Administration ("SBA") and certain state and local development institutions.

The U.S.'s SBA is particularly interesting in the present context because it both (a) has specialized in aiding small businesses for decades, and (b) was in fact a subsidiary of the U.S.'s RFC itself until the latter was wound down in the late 1940s.[88] Depending on what form the NIC ultimately takes, it will likely make sense to bring the SBA "back" into its "family," along with such other still-functioning former RFC-subsidiaries as aforementioned Fannie Mae and the Export–Import Bank.[89]

Similarly, if and as subnational governments develop infrastructure plans and local business support institutions, including public banks patterned after the German Sparkassen or the U.S.'s Bank of North Dakota model,[90] the NIC will serve in both a coordinating and a supporting role. Importantly for present purposes, that can mean either or both (a) direct investment in such efforts themselves through the purchase of state government, local government, public bank, and small business issuances, and (b) "screening" of the latter on behalf of the central bank or finance ministry, which then can purchase such issuances directly for the asset side of the balance sheet.[91]

Unlike Germany, whose domestic development banking history is better known, the U.S., whose Fed was originally designed along German lines,[92] has a much richer past and even present with these forms of public sector capital allocation in support of socially desirable sectors of the economy than most people seem to realize. That is perhaps because large, dominant firms draw most of our attention but require no aid in attracting capital, while smaller firms, start-up firms, and other firms with desirable attributes—e.g., employee-owned firms, "green" eco-friendly firms, urban and rural "enterprise zone" firms, non-"outsourcing" firms, and the like—that escape our attention do often require, and receive, such assistance.[93]

The NIC and counterpart institutions can significantly expand, systematize, and publicly report on such operations for the cause of making a grand, democratically determined *national project* of inclusive republican investment and capital allocation. They will, in short, serve as primary agents of our republics' meaningful democratization of the financing of genuinely productive and socially desirable enterprise and infrastructure.[94]

The Price Stabilization Fund ("PSF"), or what I also call the "People's Portfolio," will complement the efforts just rehearsed as a secondary market complement to the NIC, U.S. SBA, and public investment institutions' primary market roles—rather as the U.S.'s Fannie Mae was originally founded in 1938 as a secondary market complement to the 1934 FHA's primary market role in democratizing home-ownership.[95] But it will also have a significance all its own.[96]

The idea here, too, is once again simple and straightforward. It is that more than just interest rates and housing prices are systemically important and thus in need of public "open market operations" conducted with a view to keeping them within reasonably narrow bands over time to assure overall macroeconomic stability and predictable investment horizons.[97] Many food, fuel, and other commodity prices are similarly influential on economic activity across the board.[98] Indeed, so are prevailing wages and salaries.[99] That is why our public instrumentalities have frequently made use not only of New York Fed Treasury purchases and sales but also of the Strategic Petroleum Reserve, the Department of Agriculture, and other agencies to stabilize critical prices in the past.[100]

A PSF, administered by the central bank, finance ministry, or NIC style authority, will accordingly conduct open market operations in the markets in question with a view to "collaring" their swings just as we collar borrowing ("interest") and mortgage rate swings now and have collared other swings in the past.[101] In effect, it will amount to a public fund counterpart to the market portfolio, through which the public will modulate price-swings within certain systemically important markets that are every bit as significant as are the "systemically important financial institutions," or "SIFIs," that Americans have recognized to be in need of "enhanced prudential regulation" since the passage of Dodd-Frank.[102]

The key point for present purposes is that digitized NIC and PSF issuances will be ideal candidates for new assets that the central bank or finance ministry will have to hold on the asset side of the balance sheet to associate with some of the new liabilities, in the form of new digital Citizen and Resident Wallet deposits, that will be tracked on the liability side of the balance sheet.[103] In effect, the central bank or finance ministry will then stand as the intermediating link between republics' savers and investors (liability side) on the one hand, and their stable and steady wealth and productivity growth (asset side) on the other hand, all while the liability side of the public balance sheet serves also as a single public payments ledger on which all payment transactions, commercial and financial, take place.

This will be fully digitally integrated, fully public, and purely productive and stable, as distinguished from speculative and volatile (secondary and tertiary price-gambling) finance.[104] It will amount to full public recognition, and counterpart action on the basis of that recognition, that (a) in a "commercial society" or "exchange economy" such as our own, a payments platform and associated system of digital wallets and digital currency is an essential public infrastructure and (b) that finance being rooted in money in any such society, with money in turn being no more and no less than "that which pays" and "that which counts" in a system of payments and value-accounting, any such *platform* will be the core of the nation's *financial* system as well—as indeed today's banking and payments system constitutes the core of *its* financial system.[105]

As noted earlier, private sector finance will continue under the digitized Citizen Ledger Finance reform I here advocate, but it will no longer be readily fueled by or supplied with our republics' public full faith and credit. The public credit prerequisite for endogenous private sector "money creation" will no longer be liberally "outsourced" to private sector gatekeepers, credit-checkers, and project-evaluators, but instead limited to strict public sector discount window conditionality. Private sector finance will, for its part, in effect be made to conform to its own oft-repeated false claims of itself—namely, that it is all a matter of intermediating between private suppliers and end-users of "scarce capital." Private lending and other forms of finance will, in other words, be made to conform to the intermediated scarce private capital story, channeling antecedently accumulated finance capital from accumulators to users in "one-to-one," rather than "one-to-many" or "none-to-many" fashion as described in Chapter 3.

Private sector banking will thus become much more like narrow banking, funded by actual private sector deposits that are not themselves bank loans.[106] Credit-generative banking—dependent as it is upon the monetized full faith and credit of us, the sovereign public that constitutes our republic—will for its part be reserved to (a) public instrumentalities, and (b) private banks able to secure central bank or finance ministry discount window lending, through strict conformity with the earlier mentioned conditionality, in connection with any loans they originate.[107]

The less proximate, more distant ramifications of these changes will be much more far-reaching than might at first meet the eye. For one thing, the entirety of the nominally private sector sides of our financial systems will change as public sectors by and large withdraw from them, converting them to being *truly private* sector rather than *mixed* public–private—that is, franchised—finance.

For another thing, the public sector sides of our financial systems will change as well. For many commonly drawn distinctions to which we have grown accustomed over the past 200 years but have not recognized to be outgrowths of franchising itself—distinctions, e.g., between central bank functions and finance ministry functions, between monetary policy and fiscal policy, and in the U.S. even between dollar bills (Fed Notes), sovereign securities (Treasury paper), and metallic coins (Mint tokens), diminish to near the vanishing point. To those I now turn.

6.3 Systemic Ramifications: Private Sector Transformation and Public Sector Consolidation

As just noted, the transition to full digitized Citizen Ledger Finance will bear farther-reaching consequences that might not be immediately appreciated. It will accordingly be helpful briefly to catalogue the more important among them, starting with the nominally private sector side of things, then turning to the forthrightly public sector side.

6.3.1 Private Money Capital: From Credit-Generation and -Multiplication to Honest Intermediation

In other work I have traced the flow of monetized public full faith and credit throughout the financial system—from the central bank, the finance ministry, and the commercial banking core to the farthest reaches of our capital, money, and shadow banking markets.[108] That is what mapping the franchise consists in.

Since what I propose here is meant to replace that hybrid financial system with a system in which digitized public credit-money originates from and flows primarily if not exclusively through public institutions while only genuinely pre-accumulated, "private money" flows through private sector institutions, the best way to trace the impact of digitized Citizen Ledger Finance on "private" sector finance might be to proceed in the same order that I follow in that earlier franchise-expository work. I shall do that now, systematically indicating what private sector finance will come to look like as the finance franchisors—that is, our republics—withdraw from the franchise and bring our republics' own public credit-money operations back "in house."

Beginning with the banking core, then, the central bank or finance ministry—whichever administers the digital Wallets saving and payments architecture and holds assets offsetting those liabilities—will now channel digitally monetized public full faith and credit primarily through the public sector NIC and PSF as described above. It will channel any such "public money" through private sector banking institutions only insofar as the latter originate productive primary market, not speculative secondary or tertiary meta-market loans that conform to strict discount window lending criteria. Earnings—privatized seignorage—on such lending will thus essentially be simply the spreads between interest charged on private sector bank-originated loans and interest paid on discount window loans.

Because demonstrably productive planned projects will be eligible for CB, NIC, and other forms of direct digitized public financing, private rates on bank-originated loans meeting the discount window criteria are unlikely to become usurious—there will, in effect, be "public options" with which private sector lenders will be competing. But it is also always possible to regulate spreads, and of course to lower both discount rates and the rates paid on Wallet savings, in the event that private sector rates do come to seem to be discouraging productive investment.

Private sector bank lending that *doesn't conform* to discount window conditionality, for its part, will have to be fully funded by private sector loans stemming from pre-accumulated private sector money—be these loans short-term "deposits," medium-term certificates of deposit ("CDs"), or the like—that the banks are able to attract. They will be, in other words, "narrow bank" loans of the kind advocated by "100% money" and, to a lesser extent, "40% money advocates of the stripe that I noted in introducing this article and discuss more fully below in Chapter 9. The banks that extend credit on this (pre-accumulated) basis—that is, on the basis of so-called "base money"—will in that sense at long last conform to the one-to-one intermediation tale that they tell of themselves, and hence effectively function as today's lending companies or money market funds function.[109]

Turning from the banking core to the capital market near-periphery as Chapter 3 above and my earlier work does,[110] commercial bank lending for the purpose of purchasing firm-issued equities or other securities, and investment bank margin lending for the same, will no longer be possible.[111] For these loans, used as they are to fund secondary or tertiary market purchases, will not be eligible for discount window lending and, therefore, public sector credit allocation outsourced to private sector franchisee institutions.[112] Rather, they will have to be funded, "one-to-one," again as any narrow bank, mutual fund, or lending company's investments are funded.[113] That is, again, with antecedently accumulated private sector "loanable funds."[114]

The same now will hold true of securitization and repo markets as well, at least in their capacities as recipients of monetized public full faith and credit.[115] Banks will not be able to offload loans "originated to distribute" onto securitization trusts in order to amplify lending and thereby disseminate ever more public credit.[116] For again, all lending now will be either fully privately funded lending or discount window-conforming lending. And, the latter will be almost exclusively "buy and hold" lending since the usual justifications for "originate to distribute" lending—viz., liquidity needs and associated "cost of capital" minimization—will, as I now will explain, no longer be applicable.[117]

On the latter justification for origination to distribute, it cannot be emphasized enough that the usual benign-sounding justifications given for allowing loan sales on secondary markets and the "origination to distribute" into which that always degenerates—the need for liquidity and the capacity thereby to "lower the cost of credit"—simply will no longer be applicable. For liquidity availability and the "cost of capital" are, crucially, *public policy variables*, variables that must be democratically determined in any democratic commercial republic such as our own. And they are variables that, under the reforms mapped above, now will be directly and transparently—hence again, democratically—controlled by the public's own central bank or finance ministry, rather than merely indirectly, opaquely, and ineffectively "influenced" through (seemingly always lax) liquidity and capital regulation of private sector financial institutions.[118]

This is just one, albeit very important, sense in which arguments commonly made in order to justify either tightening or loosening regulatory requirements will simply no longer be pertinent under the digitized republican Citizen Ledger Finance arrangements I am proposing. For all such justifications stem from our current system of hybrid public–private franchise finance. That is, they stem from the fact that credit-money availability is on the one hand a commercial republican policy variable, while the means of *varying* that variable presently make use of private sector institutions—that is, are "franchised out."[119]

End the franchise and bring digitized public credit-money modulation and allocation fully back "in house," and you remove the indispensable factual predicate of literally all such discussions. "Financial regulation" then divides and reduces to public finance policy on the one hand, corresponding to public sector credit-money generation, modulation, and allocation, and anti-fraud/consumer protection law on the other hand, corresponding to regulated private sector intermediation.[120]

Turning now to private sector repo, this will become smaller scale and reduce to "one-to-one" intermediation as well.[121] For returns on digital Citizen and Resident Wallets will eliminate most if not all incentive for cash managers to lend in the repo markets.[122] And the practice of rehypothecating repo collateral, which presently renders repo market practice something akin to credit-multiplying fractional reserve banking, will be prohibited per the "one-to-one" credit-intermediation principle to which all private sector financial institutions now will be required to conform.[123]

Once again the usual justifications given for what we do now—putative liquidity and short-term funding needs, the satisfaction of which "lowers the cost of capital"—simply will not be applicable. For again, liquidity and the cost of capital are policy variables that now will be handled directly by the public, not indirectly through "incentives" offered by the public sector franchisor to private sector franchisees. Repo will accordingly return to being what it was when the U.S. Fed invented it in 1917—a convenient form of bona fide short-term credit-intermediation, instead of indefinitely extended private sector credit-amplification.[124]

Turning next to derivatives markets and clearinghouses, the primary source of public credit here has in the past been the *ex post* rescue of failing such markets when they have grown "systemically important," and now includes additional *ex ante* assurances (and some accompanying regulation) in the U.S., at least, pursuant to Dodd-Frank style reforms.[125] There are two reasons that this outlet of public support will largely if not fully close under the digitized Citizen Ledger Finance proposals outlined above.

First, public credit use is the primary enabler of private sector financial institutions' and markets' growing systemically important in the first place. Cutting off that public credit channel as my proposals do in the ways just described—viz., prohibiting bank lending with public credit-money to secondary and tertiary market speculators—accordingly cuts off the source of systemic importance itself. The only "SIFIs" left under my reforms, in other words, are our republics' public sector FIs that preside over the "[financial] system" itself—our republics' *franchisor* institutions.

Second, should this somehow not suffice to derivatives markets from becoming systemically important, simply reinstating the "insurable interest doctrine" in derivatives markets will eliminate any remaining vestige of pure gambling in derivatives just as ending the rehypothecation of repo collateral as described above does in repo.[126] For these are the modes by which "one-to-one" credit-intermediation balloons into "one-to-many" credit-multiplication in these two spheres.[127]

Finally, coming full circle back to commercial paper ("CP") and money market funds ("MMFs") as my "franchise"-tracing work elsewhere does,[128] eliminating the practice of margin lending to funds that *purchase* paper in the commercial paper markets, along the lines described just above in connection with the *capital* markets, will immediately leave public credit only one channel into CP markets. Again, that will be discount window lending, which as noted above amounts simply to the public's directly determining the conditions of its own credit-extending and associated monetization, i.e., swapping of public IOUs for private IOUs.

6.3.2 Public Investment Capital: From Central Bank and Finance Ministry, Fiscal and Monetary, and "T-Bill," "Fed Note," and "Mint Coin" Separation to Digital Consolidation

Perhaps most surprising of all to those who do not often think of these matters will be the implications of digitized Citizen Ledger Finance for traditional distinctions familiar to public finance. We are accustomed to most modern commercial republics' having both treasuries or fiscal authorities on the one hand, and central banks or monetary authorities on the other hand. We are also accustomed to characterizing instrumentalities of the first kind as being engaged in forthrightly allocative "fiscal" policy on the one hand, and instrumentalities of the second kind as being engaged in putatively separable "monetary" policy on the other hand. And finally, some also are used to thinking of fiscal policy's making use of interest-bearing treasury or exchequer paper (sovereign bonds, bills, etc.), on the one hand, and of monetary policy's being concerned more with non-interest-bearing central banknotes (currency), on the other hand.

What we do not tend to think about, I suspect, is how all of these distinctions are rooted in finance-franchising itself, such that to back away from the franchise is to diminish the distinctions. The reason for, and nature of, the link are quite clear when one thinks on the matter: the whole *point* of the franchise arrangement is to delegate credit allocation primarily to private sector financial institutions, while consigning whatever public allocation we wish to engage in to our democratically accountable fiscal authorities. We then confer what we mistakenly think to be separable modulatory functions on monetary authorities, and expressly insulate them from democratic decision-making precisely in order to preserve what Chapter 4 called a "temporal uniformity" on the part of the value of public currencies.

But this means that once we grow skeptical of (a) modulation's practical separability from allocation, (b) private sector institutions' superiority as allocators to public sector institutions, and thus (c) the utility of attempting to distinguish between "neutral" monetary policy and forthrightly "winner" and "loser-picking" fiscal policy at all, we effectively grow skeptical of the ultimate rationale for franchising itself, as well as for separating central banking from treasury operations and currency from sovereign debt. Something we might have begun to suspect once, say, U.S. Fed Reserve accounts began paying IOR and thus became functional equivalents of Treasury securities[129]—namely, that the U.S.'s Fed and Treasury might not be necessarily different at all—then begins looking to be possibly confirmed. Likewise suspicions that grow when we notice the U.S.'s Fed, for example, is prohibited from *directly* purchasing Treasurys from Treasury on the one hand, while *routinely* purchasing Treasurys from "dealer banks" that are effectively required to purchase whatever the Treasury issues on the other hand.[130]

The whole business of allocation/modulation, fiscal/monetary, and Treasury/Fed separation then begins to look like an odd sort of sham—a "Noble Lie," perhaps, that we commercial republican citizens all tell ourselves so as to dodge the responsibility of deciding, together and democratically, how we shall spend our own money.

This "Noble Lie" is the foundation of finance-franchising.

It's why we do it. Yet the litany of dysfunctions with which I introduced this book and which I diagnosed in the prior chapters indicates that this lie might not be all that noble. It might be no more than a destructive and opportunity-squandering self-deception once justified but now obsolete.

As the foregoing chapters of this book indicate, there is no reason to think fragmented private sector institutions, unable to capture the benefits of public goods provision, unable to control macroeconomic variables, and unable even to plan, let alone coordinate across, vast stretches of national geographical space or of time, are the best allocators of public investment capital to productive primary market or infrastructural uses.[131] To the contrary, agents who act in the name of our spatially and temporally extended commercial republics as wholes are the only ones suited to that task, while spatially fragmented and temporally ephemeral private sector agents will nearly always find there is more to be gained by gambling on short-term price-swings in bubble-inflating secondary and tertiary financial and derivative markets—Chapter 2's "meta-markets"—than by investing "patiently" in productive primary and infrastructural markets.[132]

That is precisely the secret of, and the reason behind, the malady known as "financialization," which I defined above as the growth of secondary and tertiary market transaction volume, or "churn," relative to primary market capitalization.[133] Hence it is also the key to the steady erosion of the industrial and infrastructural bases of our productive economies, of our middle classes, and hence of our commercial republics themselves.[134]

It is time, then, to work a separation—private money for private uses, public money for public uses. And this *separation* is in effect the *consolidation* of traditional fiscal and monetary policy, of traditional fiscal and monetary instruments, and of traditional finance ministry and central bank operations. This is one of the reasons that I have repeatedly used the locution "central bank or finance ministry" above, and continue to use it below. It is because I do not believe that our franchise arrangements either can or will endure for much longer, or that any meaningful central bank/finance ministry distinction can long outlast it.

The consolidated digital Citizens' Ledger I laid out above, then, and the associated Democratic Digital Currency that I discuss in more detail below, amount in a way to the natural monetary outgrowth of this form of fiscal and monetary, central bank and finance ministry, sovereign debt and currency consolidation. Indeed, they are transparent accounting and institutional expression. They elide both the Fed Note and Treasury Paper distinction and its non-American counterparts as discussed above, and the present-day "token"/"account" distinction that I treat of in connection with digital currency technology below. They similarly elide the distinction between central-bank-issued "currency" and public mint—(hence finance ministry-) issued "coin."

What is going to matter in future is our productive commercial republics' digital value-storage, -transfer, and -accounting platforms—our republics' full digital ledgers—along with the Democratic Digital Currencies that will be their units of account. That Digital Currency and the interest-bearing Citizen and Resident Wallets that will be credited and debited "in" Digital Currency Units will be simultaneously currency and coin, token and account, monetary and fiscal policy instrument, … in short, central bank *or* finance ministry liability.

Against that digital backdrop, in which "all that [was once monetarily or fiscally] solid melts into air,"[135] what difference does it make whether we call our commercial and financial platform the finance ministry or the central bank? Let us just call it the Consolidated Citizens' Ledger, and its authority the Office of Public Finance ("OPF"). And that's it. Public and private finance separate, central bank and finance ministry consolidate, and public money flows only to bona fide publicly chosen, productive investments. To sum up diagrammatically, public money and our public money-modulators' and -allocators' financial relations to private sector persons and other entities under Citizen Ledger Finance will then come to look as depicted in Fig. 6.4.

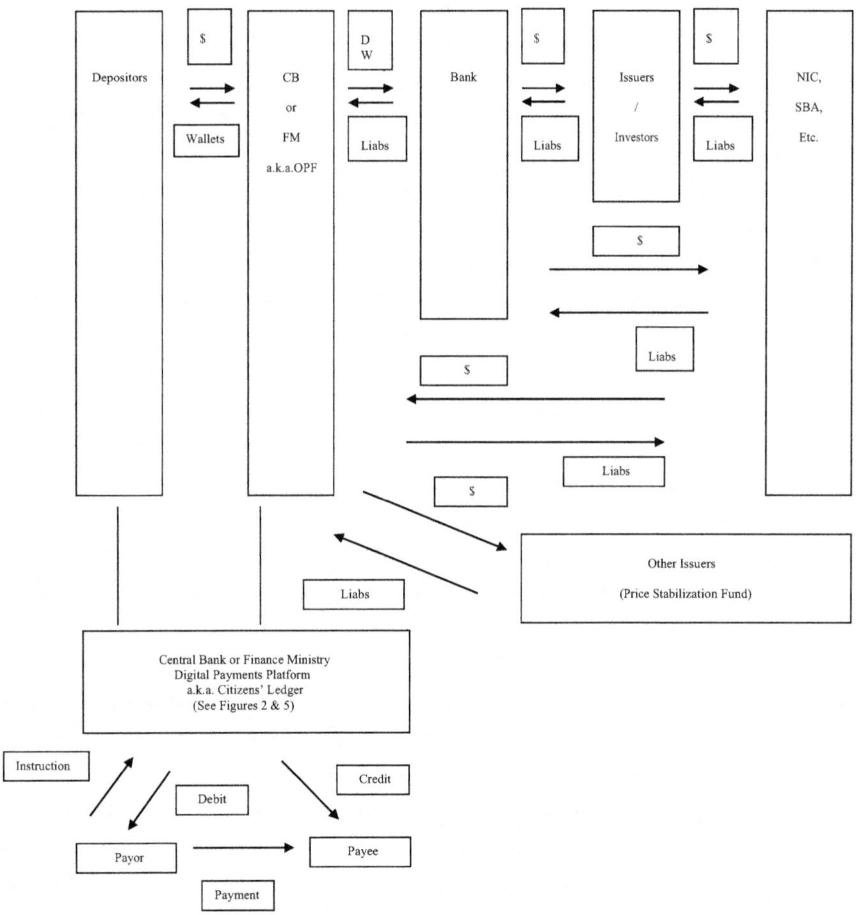

Fig. 6.4 Reformed bank/central bank/finance ministry/NIC w/ stabilization fund

Notes

1. *See* again Hockett, *Recursive Collective Action Problems, supra* note 110.
2. *See supra* notes 1, 4, and 67 (offering arguments in support of the preceding conclusion).
3. In particular, *infra* Chapter 6.
4. *See* again *supra,* Chapter 3, and my work cited there.
5. Again, for reasons discussed *infra,* Sect. 3. In brief, the reason is that ending the franchise means narrowing, if not indeed closing, the traditional gap between fiscal and monetary policy.
6. *See* 12 U.S.C. § 342 (2012) (authorizing federal reserve accounts for federal reserve member banks). A limited number of other categories of entities are authorized to hold Federal Reserve Accounts. *See, e.g.,* 12 U.S.C. § 391 (2012) (authorizing federal reserve accounts for the Treasury) 12 U.S.C. §§ 1435, 1452(d),1723a(g) (2012) (authorizing federal reserve accounts for mortgage GSEs); 12 U.S.C. §§ 347d, 358 (2012) (authorizing federal reserve accounts for foreign governments, banks, and central banks); 12 U.S.C. § 286d (authorizing federal reserve accounts for BIS, IBRD, IMF); 12 U.S.C. § 5465 (2012) (authorizing federal reserve accounts for designated financial market utilities).
7. *See Reserve Maintenance Manual,* Bd. of Governors of the Fed. Reserve Sys. (Nov. 19, 2018), https://www.federalreserve.gov/monetarypolicy/reserve-maintenance-manual-account-structure.htm [https://perma.cc/PCG4-NCD8] (explaining daily maintenance of account relationship between depository institution and Federal Reserve banks).
8. *See Credit and Liquidity Program and the Balance Sheet,* Bd. of Governors of the Fed. Reserve Sys. (Dec. 27, 2018), https://www.federalreserve.gov/monetarypolicy/bst_frliabilities.htm [https://perma.cc/73BZ-NM7Z] [hereinafter *Balance Sheet*] (explaining the system of federal reserve liabilities and institutional deposits).
9. *See How is the Federal Reserve System structured?* Bd. of Governors of the Fed. Reserve Sys. (Aug. 17, 2016), https://www.federalreserve.gov/faqs/about_12593.htm [https://perma.cc/S72Q-TGMS] (explaining the structure of the federal reserve system).
10. *See Why does the Federal Reserve lend money to banks?* Bd. of Governors of the Fed. Reserve Sys. (June 17, 2011), https://www.federalreserve.gov/faqs/banking_12841.htm [https://perma.cc/8249-CWUL] (explaining why the federal reserve lends money to banks).
11. Emergency Economic Stabilization Act of 2008, Pub. L. No. 110–343, § 128, 122 Stat. 3765, 3796 (2008) (authorizing the Federal Reserve to pay interest to depository institutions on the reserves they are required to hold against their deposit liability). IOR had been planned since 2006, to commence in 2011. The crash led Congress to bring up the target date in the name of emergency stabilization. *See* Peter N. Ireland, *Interest on*

Reserves: History and Rationale, Complications and Risks, 39 Cato J. 327, 328 (2019). The crash led Congress to bring up the target date in the name of emergency stabilization. *Id*.

12. This is a source of sheer rent-extraction by banks; they 'earn' a premium on their accounts with the Fed, only a fraction of which they pass on to those holding deposits with them. *See, e.g.*, *Is the Federal Reserve Giving Banks a $12 Billion Subsidy?* The Economist, March 18, 2017, at 70 (exploring income received by banks from interest on reserves).
13. The interest on reserves is equivalent to the coupon on a bill or bond. *See The Discount Rate*, Bd. of Governors of the Fed. Reserve Sys. (Oct. 15, 2019), https://www.federalreserve.gov/monetarypolicy/discountrate.htm [https://perma.cc/FLC3-Z5EY] (explaining how interest rates are applied by the Fed to depository institutions). More on this *infra*, Chapter 6, Sect. 3.
14. The discount window is the primary facility through which the Fed affords liquidity by directly or indirectly monetizing assets deemed both (a) worthy of monetization in the interest of maintaining systemic liquidity or encouraging specific industries or sectors of the national economy in need of solicitude, and (b) sufficiently safe as not to raise moral hazard concerns. *See* Federal Reserve Act, 12 U.S.C. §347b (authorizing the federal reserve to use discount rates); *see generally discount window Lending*, Bd. of Governors of the Fed. Reserve Sys. (Sep. 30, 2019), https://www.federalreserve.gov/regreform/discount-window.htm [https://perma.cc/T3BD-L4MF] [hereinafter *discount window Lending*]; Federal Reserve System Publication, The Federal Reserve System Purposes and Functions 35, 50, 104, (2016), https://www.federalreserve.gov/aboutthefed/files/pf_complete.pdf [https://perma.cc/YEH5-6NKY] (explaining how the federal reserve engages in monetary policymaking and monitors financial institutions).
15. The Fed actually *invented* the repo transaction, for example, over one hundred years ago as an incident of First World War finance. *See* Stephen Mihm, *The Repo Market is More than Mere Plumbing*, bloomberg (Oct. 9, 2019, 6:00 AM), https://www.bloomberg.com/opinion/articles/2019-10-09/the-repo-market-has-a-history-of-intrigue (exploring history of the repo market and repo transactions). 'Private' participants in financial markets began mimicking the arrangement decades later. *Id.* More recently, yield-curve-bending via quantitative easing, and swap line arrangements with counterpart central banks, have been pioneered to address the difficulties occasioned by the 2008 crash and its aftermath. *See Public Actors, supra* note 4, at 130–133 (examining the ways in which public actors intervene in private economics).

16. Federal Reserve System Publication, The Federal Reserve System Purposes and Functions 35, 50, 104 (2016), https://www.federalreserve.gov/aboutthefed/files/pf_complete.pdf [https://perma.cc/YEH5-6NKY] [hereinafter The Federal Reserve System Purposes and Functions] (explaining how the federal reserve engages in monetary policymaking and monitoring financial institutions).
17. *Id.* (explaining how the federal reserve engages in monetary policymaking and monitoring financial institutions).
18. John Kandrac and Bernd Schlusche, *Quantitative Easing and Bank Risk Taking: Evidence from Lending*, *in* Finance and Economics Discussion Series: 2017–125, at 16 (Oct. 27, 2017), https://www.federalreserve.gov/econres/feds/files/2017125pap.pdf [https://perma.cc/S86W-WST6] (discussing the QE3 program initiated in 2012).
19. The plan commenced in September, with a commitment to purchase $40 billion per month. *See Federal Reserve Issues FOMC Statement*, Bd. of Governors of the Fed. Reserve Sys. (Dec. 12, 2012), https://www.federalreserve.gov/newsevents/pressreleases/monetary20121212a.htm [https://perma.cc/8NU5-WAFR] (outlining economic recovery plan). The quantum was raised to $85 billion in December. *Id.*
20. *See Balance Sheet*, *supra* note 252 (explaining the system of federal reserve liabilities and institutional deposits).
21. *Id.* (explaining the other instruments).
22. The Federal Reserve System Purposes and Functions, *supra* note 260, at 21–22 (explaining the function and method of open market operations).
23. *See Balance Sheet*, *supra* note 252 (explaining the system of federal reserve liabilities and institutional deposits).
24. *Id.* (discussing the Federal Reserve's liabilities).
25. *International Summary Statistics: U.S. Reserve Assets (Table 3.12)*, Bd. of Governors of the Fed. Reserve Sys. (Oct. 25, 2019), https://www.federalreserve.gov/data/intlsumm/current.htm [https://perma.cc/RHJ8-J23Z] (showing U.S. reserve assets); *International Summary Statistics: Selected Foreign Official Assets Held at Federal Reserve Banks (Table 3.12)*, Bd. of Governors of the Fed. Reserve Sys. (Sep. 29, 2019), https://www.federalreserve.gov/data/intlsumm/forassets20190930.htm [https://perma.cc/GL4M-VX68] (showing selected foreign official assets held at federal reserve banks); *International Summary Statistics: Selected U.S. Liabilities to Foreign Official Institutions (Table 3.12)*, Bd. of Governors of the Fed. Reserve Sys. (Sep. 27, 2019), https://www.federalreserve.gov/data/intlsumm/usliabforinst20190930.htm [https://perma.cc/HBL9-T5HS] (showing selected U.S. liabilities to foreign official institutions).

26. *See generally* Robin Greenwood, Samuel G. Hanson & Jeremy C. Stein, *The Federal Reserve's Balance Sheet as a Financial-Stability Tool*, ECON. POL'Y SYMP. PROC. 335, 387 (2016) (indicating generally that the Fed has a large balance sheet: "[T]he Fed should keep a large balance sheet indefinitely going forward, even as rates rise well above the ZLB.").
27. *Id*. at 339 ("When the Fed maintains a larger balance sheet, it effectively takes over a part of the traditional debt management role from the Treasury, along with the associated fiscal risk.").
28. *See id.*
29. *See Balance Sheet*, *supra* note 252 (explaining the system of Federal Reserve liabilities and institutional deposits).
30. 12 U.S.C. § 461(b)(1)(A) (2019) (allowing only "depository institutions" to hold accounts at the reserve: excluding individuals, governments, companies, etc.).
31. Note that what makes this rent possible is citizens' need of transaction accounts irrespective of whether they be 'paid' by someone for the privilege of maintaining and using them. This need could readily be supplied by the public free of charge, as it is to large banking institutions not only free of charge, but with a 'bonus' in the form of IOR. *See Rousseauvian Money supra* note 67, at 33 ("Financial Institutions and markets now spring up as 'middle men' to enable these surplus and deficit units to find one another, overcoming 'search,' 'monitoring' and 'maturity-matching' costs in so doing. [Banks] broker (or contractually substitute for) contracts between parties for the use of 'scarce capital' at a price be that price 'interest,'"); *see also* Ann Saphir, *Yellen Draws Fire for Fed Policy to Pay Banks*, REUTERS (Feb. 10, 2016), https://www.reuters.com/article/usa-fed-yellen-politics/yellen-draws-fire-for-fed-policy-to-pay-banks-idU.S.L2N15P1Z7 [https://perma.cc/ZJV4-B3WX] (indicating that the Fed provides interest to banks).
32. *See* Catherine Martin Christopher, *Mobile Banking: The Answer for the Unbanked in America*, 65 CATH. U. L. REV. 221, 223 (2015) (stating that of the adult population of the United States, 10% are unbanked and 17% are underbanked).
33. *See* Christopher, *supra* note 276, at 224 (referring to the population of un- and underbanked Americans).
34. *See, e.g.*, *Money's Past*, *supra* note 17, at 11 ("In the midst of recession or liquidity trap, for example, our central bank will no longer need to supply cheap money to private banks and then hope they will lend it to ordinary citizens so as to prime the consumer spending pump.").
35. *See, e.g.*, Daniel Alpert, Robert C. Hockett, & Nouriel Roubini, *The Way Forward*, NEW AMERICA FOUNDATION (Oct. 10, 2011), https://www.newamerica.org/economic-growth/policy-papers/the-way-forward/ [https://perma.cc/279V-XLXT] (stating that the private sector "hoard[s] liquidity in the face of uncertainty over future investment prospects").

36. *See e.g.*, Robert C. Hockett & Richard Vague, *Debt, Deflation, and Debacle*, FEDERAL RESERVE BANK OF PHILADELPHIA (Apr. 9, 2013), https://www.interdependence.org/wp-content/uploads/2013/04/Debt-Deflation-and-Debacle-RV-and-RH1.pdf [https://perma.cc/9ZFH-V6VK] (discussing how consumers are in debt and the need, and implied absence, of, debt forgiveness for private debt); *see also National Investment Authority*, *supra* note 4, at 490 (indicating that speculative, secondary markets have abundant capital compared to primary markets).
37. Hockett & Vague, *supra* note 282 (indicating that student debt was the only type of debt to increase in the period after the Great Recession).
38. Alpert, Hockett, & Roubini, *supra* note 281 (arguing that supply-side solutions are inadequate). You can lead a horse to water, we might say, but you can't make him drink when he's not thirsty and will have, in any case, to pay the water back with interest.
39. *See* 12 U.S.C. § 461(b)(1)(A) (2019) (allowing only "depository institutions" to hold accounts at the reserve: excluding individuals, governments, companies, etc.). On why "central bank or finance ministry," *see infra*, Chapter 7.
40. See Robert Hockett, *Digital Greenbacks: A Sequenced TreasuryDirect and FedWallet Plan for the Democratic Digital Dollar*, 25 J. TECH. L. & POL'Y. 1 (2021), available at https://papers.ssrn.com/sol3/papers.cfm?abstract_id=3599419.
41. *See Money's Past*, *supra* note 17, at 10 (suggesting "[a]ll citizens will be able to maintain what I call 'Citizen Wallets' with the Fed"); *see also* Darylanda Bogle, *What Day of the Month Do I Get my Social Security Payment?*, SOCIAL SECURITY MATTERS, (June 6, 2019), https://blog.ssa.gov/what-day-of-the-month-do-i-get-my-social-security-payment/ [https://perma.cc/RG6T-KS23] (describing the systems through which Social Security benefits, based partially on birth dates but also including other considerations).
42. *See Alaska Permanent Fund*, INT'L FORUM OF SOVEREIGN WEALTH FUNDS, https://www.ifswf.org/members/usa [https://perma.cc/W24U-E3EV] (discussing the creation of Alaska Permanent Fund "as a way to save a portion of the state's oil revenues for the needs of future generations).
43. *See Reserve Maintenance Manual*, BD. OF GOVERNORS OF THE FED. RESERVE SYS., (Nov. 19, 2018) https://www.federalreserve.gov/monetarypolicy/reserve-maintenance-manual-account-structure.htm [https://perma.cc/3R9F-FR44] (stating inter alia that "[i]f an institution is not required to maintain balances to satisfy a reserve requirement, it may still establish a master account with a Reserve Bank and earn interest on reserve balances at the interest rate paid on excess balances, provided the institution is eligible to receive interest payments").

44. For more on "QE for the People" and "Helicopter Money' proposals" *see, e.g.*, Anatole Kaletsky, *How About Quantitative Easing for the People?*, REUTERS (Aug. 1, 2012), http://blogs.reuters.com/anatole-kaletsky/2012/08/01/how-about-quantitative-easing-for-the-people/ [https://perma.cc/3ERH-JPZ2] (suggesting that "[g]iving away free money may sound too good to be true or wildly irresponsible, but it is exactly what the Fed[eral Reserve] and the BoE [Bank of England] have been doing for bond traders and bankers since 2009. Directing QE to the general public would not only be much fairer but also much more effective"); Martin Wolf, *The Case for Helicopter Money*, FINANCIAL TIMES (Feb. 12, 2013), https://www.ft.com/content/9bcf0eea-6f98-11e2-b906-00144feab49a ("But the view that it is never right to respond to a financial crisis with monetary financing of a consciously expanded fiscal deficit—helicopter money, in brief— is wrong. It simply has to be in the tool kit."). The 'helicopter' colloquialism originates with Milton Friedman. Milton Friedman, *The Role of Monetary Policy*, 58 AM. ECON REV. 1 (1968). Keynes used the metaphor of burying money in bottles a bit over 30 years earlier. JOHN MAYNARD KEYNES, THE GENERAL THEORY OF EMPLOYMENT, INTEREST AND MONEY (1936).
45. *See* Kaletsky, *supra* note 291 (discussing "QE for the People").
46. *Cf. Balance Sheet*, *supra* note 252 (describing the Federal Reserve's Balance Sheets).
47. *Cf.* Jeff Cox, *Powell Says the Fed Will Start Expanding its Balance Sheet 'Soon' in Response to Funding Issues*, CNBC, (Oct. 8, 2019), https://www.cnbc.com/2019/10/08/powell-says-the-fed-will-start-expanding-its-balance-sheet-soon.html [https://perma.cc/D6EA-YMMQ].
48. By "near-depositors," I mean holders of "near-monies" pursuant to short-term lending arrangements of the kind constituting the so-called shadow-banking sector. This sector too is now part of our franchise arrangement.
49. *See Discount Window Lending*, *supra* note 258 (explaining the relationship between discount windows loans as credits to banks and as assets for the Fed).
50. *Id.* (emphasizing the Fed acting as a creditor when it issues loans through the discount window).
51. *See* again Hockett, *Recursive Collective Action Problems*, *supra* note 110.
52. *See* Hockett, *Macroprudential Turn*, *supra* note 4, at 246 (highlighting the historical and current position of the FDIC as the primary regulator).
53. See again *supra*, Chapter 3, and *infra*, Chapter 7 for more on these distinctions and their significance.
54. Id. Also infra, Chapter 9, on narrow banking.
55. *See* Richard A. Werner, *Can Banks Individually Create Money Out of Nothing?—The Theories and the Empirical Evidence*, 36 INT'L REV. FIN. ANALYSIS 1, 3 (2014) (explaining one-way banks lend credit is "in the form of what bankers call 'deposits' and this credit is money").

56. *See Discount Window Lending*, *supra* note 258 ("Primary credit is a lending program available to depository institutions in generally sound financial condition.").
57. *See* Hockett, *Republican Home-Owning*, *supra* note 29, at 15 ("FHA still operates today, guaranteeing and, in many cases, originating or refinancing mortgage loans that conform to the prudent standards that it maintains (so-called 'conforming' mortgage loans)."); Hockett, *Jeffersonian Republic, supra* note 29, at 148–152 (comparing the similarities between the FHA and the GSE, Sallie Mae, in terms of loan requirements and limitations).
58. For more on these regulatory segregation strategies and their significance, *see* Hockett, *Macroprudential Turn*, *supra* note 18.
59. See again *infra*, Chapter 6, Section C.
60. *Id.*
61. Fed. Res. Sys., 94TH Annual Report (2007), https://www.federalreserve.gov/boarddocs/rptcongress/annual07/sec6/c3.htm [https://perma.cc/23GB-QAC5] (listing U.S. government securities as $745,629 million out of the Federal Reserve Bank's total asset value of $915,129 million in 2007).
62. *See Id.* (reporting the Federal Reserve Banks' gold certificates and Special Drawing Rights making up 1.2 and 0.2% of total assets in 2007).
63. *See* Fed. Res. Sys., Federal Reserve Bank's Combined Financial Statements AS OF AND FOR THE Years Ended December 31, 2018 AND 2017 AND Independent Auditors' Report 1, 3 (2019), https://www.federalreserve.gov/aboutthefed/files/combinedfinstmt2018.pdf [https://perma.cc/SR49-ZFLZ] [hereinafter Fed. Res. Financial Statements] (reporting the Federal Reserve Banks' gold certificates and Special Drawing Rights being valued at $11,037 million and $5,200 million out of a total of $4,057,880 million assets in 2018).
64. *Id.* (valuing the 2018 mortgage-backed securities at $1,683,532 million, and the amount of long-term treasury securities lent before 2017 at $2,249,307 million, out of a total of $4,057,880 million assets).
65. *Id.* at 3 (reporting Fed's 2018 total assets as $4,057,880, including $2,302,462 in Treasury Securities and $1,683,532 in mortgage-backed securities).
66. *See* Michael J. Fleming & Nicholas Klagge, *The Federal Reserve's Foreign Exchange Swap Lines*, 16 Current Issues IN Econs. AND Fin. 4, at 1 (Apr. 2010), https://www.newyorkfed.org/medialibrary/media/research/current_issues/ci16-4.pdf [https://perma.cc/U522-CK8J] ("[T]he Fed[] … established the Term Auction Facility (TAF) to provide funding to U.S. banks … [and] swap lines … [to] reduc[e] funding pressures on [central banks] …").

67. Fed. Res. Financial Statements, *supra* note 306, at 10, 12, 18 (describing Fed's "liquidity swap lines," "discount window borrowing privileges," and "reverse repurchase agreements").
68. *See* Stephen D. Williamson, *The Balance Sheet and the Future of Fed Policy*, 25 Open Econ. Rev. 163, 163–64 (2014) ("The Fed's balance sheet has changed in important ways—both in size and composition—from what existed before the financial crisis.").
69. *See* Allen N. Berger et al., *Bank Loan Supply Responses to Federal Reserve Emergency Liquidity Facilities*, J. Fin. Intermediation, Oct. 2017, at 2–3 ("[T]o address the stigma associated with the discount window, the Fed[]… began the Term Auction Facility … [and] [c]ollateral eligibility and valuation procedures for the TAF were the same as for the discount window."). *See also* Fleming & Klagge, *supra* note 309, at 3 ("The Fed's establishment of swap lines with other central banks was not unprecedented.").
70. *See* James McBride & Andrew Chatzky, *The Role of the U.S. Federal Reserve*, Council ON Foreign Rel. (June 20, 2019), https://www.cfr.org/backgrounder/role-us-federal-reserve [https://perma.cc/N39R-8G7L] ("Though many economists argued that additional monetary easing doesn't help … many also considered QE to have been largely successful in staving off the worst effect of financial turmoil.").
71. *See* Trevor Hunnicutt, *Fed Announces Plan to End Balance Sheet Runoff in September*, Reuters (Mar. 20, 2019, 5:21 PM), https://www.reuters.com/article/us-usa-fed-balancesheet-idU.S.KCN1R12QA [https://perma.cc/2LPK-H3ZZ] ("[The Fed's] current practice … allow[s] up to $50 billion of Treasuries and mortgage-backed securities … to roll of its balance sheet each month").
72. *See id.* ("The Fed[]unveiled a long-awaited plan to stop scaling back the vast portfolio of bonds it built up."); McBride & Chatzky, *supra* note 313 ("While markets have remained strong, some analysts worry that the reversal of the Fed's expansionary policy could cause a repeat of the 2013 'taper tantrum'").
73. See Lev Menand, *Unappropriated Dollars* (2020) (working paper, on file with the author).
74. *See* Hockett, *Republican Home-Owning*, *supra* note 29 ("Ten years after failing and being rescued by our federal government … Fannie Maeremain[s] in federal receivership.").
75. *See* Williamson, *supra* note 311, at 166 ("There's a sense now in which, at the margin, the size of the balance sheet does not matter.").
76. *See* Andrew Foerster & Sylvain Leduc, *Why is the Fed's Balance Sheet Still So Big?*, Fed. Res. Bank OF S.F.: Economic Letters (June 3, 2019) ("The amount of currency in circulation has grown so much that it is not possible to shrink the balance sheet to its earlier size.").

77. *See* Loretta J. Mester, President & Chief Exec. Officer, Fed. Res. Bank of Cleveland, The Economic Outlook, Monetary Policy, and Normal Policymaking Now and in the Future, Address Before Money Marketeers of New York University, Inc. (Oct. 25, 2018), https://www.clevelandfed.org/newsroom-and-events/speeches/sp-20181025-economic-outlook-monetary-policy-and-normal-policymaking-now-and-in-the-future [https://perma.cc/4NQW-WJ8P] ("[A] relatively large balance sheet … mightgenerate requests for the Fed to aid other industries or use the balance sheet to fund government initiatives.").
78. *See supra* Chapter 4 (discussing circumstances causing public/private hybridity); *supra* nn. 1, 6, 61, 76 (suggesting structural changes now that functional reasons for private–public franchising have receded).
79. *See* Laura E. Kodres, *What is Shadow Banking?*, FIN. & DEV., June 2013, at 42–43 ("Shadow banks … raise … short-term funds in the money markets and use those funds to buy assets with longer-term maturities.").
80. *See* 12 U.S.C. § 225a (2012) (commanding the Fed to promote stable prices).
81. *See Lending to Depository Institutions*, FED. RES. BD. (Aug. 13, 2019), https://www.federalreserve.gov/monetarypolicy/bst_lendingdepository.htm [http://perma.cc/4P2S-VTGK] ("The Federal Reserve generally accepts as collateral for discount window loans any assets that meet regulatory standards for sound asset quality … includ[ing] most performing loans and most investment-grade securities.").
82. *See, e.g.*, Hockett, *Open Labor Operations, supra* note 29, at 1 ("The public agents in question work at the Federal Reserve Bank of New York in lower Manhattan. There they conduct familiar Fed open market operations—what I shall also call 'OMO.'"); Robert C. Hockett, *How to Make QE More Helpful—By Fed Shorting of Commodities,* BENZINGA (Oct. 14, 2011, 8:41 PM), https://www.benzinga.com/news/11/10/1988109/how-to-make-qe-more-helpful-by-fed-shorting-of-commodities [https://perma.cc/HC7G-XZGP] [hereinafter *How to Make QE More Helpful*] ("Monetary policy conducted by open market operations in Treasuries is meant to stabilize prices - usually consumer prices."); *see also Public Actors, supra* note 4, at 130 ("Perhaps the most familiar example of such routine market-moving in modern financial markets is that of the so-called open market operations (OMO) in which central banks or monetary authorities purchase or sell government debt securities.").
83. *See* FINANCING THE GREEN NEW DEAL, *supra*, note 18; Hockett, *Finance without Financiers*, *supra*, note 15.
84. *See* sources cited *id. See also* Hockett, *Recursive Collective Action Problems*, *supra*, note 110.

85. *See* Hockett, FINANCING THE GREEN NEW DEAL, *supra*, note 18; *Finance without Financiers, supra*, note 15; Hockett, *How to Make QE More Helpful, supra*, note 370. On a possible "consolidated successor" to the Fed and Treasury, *see infra*, Section C.
86. *See* sources cited *id.*
87. *Id.*
88. See sources cited supra, note 2. *See also* Hockett, FINANCING THE GREEN NEW DEAL, *supra*, note 18; Hockett, *Finance without Financiers, supra*, note 15.
89. *Id.*
90. *See* FINANCING THE GREEN NEW DEAL, *supra*, note 18; *Finance without Financiers, supra*, note 15.
91. *Id.*
92. See, e.g., Robert Hockett, *The Once and Future Fed—and Treasury*, 65 CHALLENGE 1 (2021); and Robert Hockett, *Building Banks Better* (2020), available at ....
93. *Id. See also* REPUBLIC OF OWNERS, supra note 1.
94. *See* sources cited *supra*, note 373.
95. *Cf. Republican Home-Owning*, *supra* note 43.
96. *See* FINANCING THE GREEN NEW DEAL, *supra*, note 18; *Finance without Financiers, supra*, note 15.
97. *Id.*
98. *See* FINANCING THE GREEN NEW DEAL, *supra*, note 18; *Finance without Financiers, supra*, note 15; *How to Make QE More Helpful, supra*, note 370.
99. *Id. See also Open Labor Market Operations, supra*, note 370.
100. *Id.*
101. *Id.*
102. *Id.*
103. FINANCING THE GREEN NEW DEAL, *supra*, note 18, at 35–37 (elaborating NIC issuances in greater detail); also Hockett, sources cited supra, note 52.
104. FINANCING THE GREEN NEW DEAL, *supra*, note 18, at 34–35 (elaborating NIC's capital-absorption functions in greater detail). also Hockett, sources cited supra, note 52.
105. FINANCING THE GREEN NEW DEAL, *supra*, note 18, at 37–39 (elaborating NIC's relations to Fed and Treasury in greater detail). also Hockett, sources cited supra, note 52.
106. *See infra* Chapter 8.
107. *Id.*
108. *See supra*, Chapter 3, and sources cited *supra*, note 15.
109. *See Finance without Financiers, supra* note 15, at 3–4, 5–6 (elaborating what the author calls the "(one-to-one) credit-intermediation" and "(one-to-many) credit- multiplication" models of financial flows, and the role played by "base money" in the latter).
110. *See, e.g., id.* at 12–17.

111. *Id.* (elaborating how bank-extended credit fuels purchases of firm-issued securities on the capital markets).
112. *Id.*
113. *See again Finance without Financiers, supra* note 15, at 3–4, 5–6 (elaborating what the author calls the "(one-to-one) credit-intermediation" and "(one-to-many) credit- multiplication" models of financial flows.
114. *Id.* at 9–10 (explaining the "loanable funds" misconception and its connection to the "(one-to-one) credit-intermediation" picture of financial flows.
115. *Id.* at 15–19 (describing the functions and operations of the securitization and repo markets, as well as the "originate to distribute" model of credit-extension that securitization encourages).
116. *Id.*
117. *Id.*
118. *See supra,* Chapter 3, rehearsing the nature of our public/private system of finance and the role of regulations as "franchise contract terms" therein.
119. *Id.*
120. *Id. See also Finance without Financiers, supra,* note 15 at 2–9 (laying out and comparing the credit-intermediation, -multiplication, and -generation models of financial flows).
121. *Finance without Financiers, supra,* note 15 at 17–19 (laying out the mechanics of repo transactions); and 2–9 (laying out and comparing the credit-intermediation, -multiplication, and -generation models of financial flows).
122. *Id.*
123. *Id.*
124. *Id. See also infra,* Chapter 9, for more on the history of the Fed-invented repo markets.
125. *Finance without Financiers, supra,* note 15 at 19–21 (describing the operations of the derivatives markets and clearing houses).
126. *Id.*
127. *Id.*
128. *Finance without Financiers, supra,* note 15 at 21–24 (describing the operations of the commercial paper markets and money market funds.
129. *See* again *supra,* Chapter 6.
130. By law, the Fed may not purchase Treasury paper directly from the Treasury, but only on "the open market." See 12 U.S.C.A. §14. The Fed accordingly simply purchases Treasurys from "primary dealer" banks that maintain "an established trading relationship" with the Federal Reserve Bank of New York on the one hand, the U.S. Treasury on the other hand. See Federal Reserve Board, "FAQ: Why Doesn't the Federal Reserve Just Buy Treasury Securities Directly from the U.S. Treasury," available at https://www.federalreserve.gov/faqs/money_12851.htm. The "established relationship" in each case is such that primary dealers step-in as counterparties when either central bank or finance ministry wish to purchase or sell newly issued or previously issued

Treasurys. In effect, the primary dealer banks serve as permanent funnels between Fed and Treasury.

131. *See, e.g., Finance without Financiers, supra* note 15; FINANCING THE GREEN NEW DEAL, *supra* note 18.
132. *Id.*
133. *Finance without Financiers, supra* note 15.
134. *Id.*
135. The allusion is the Marx & Engels' celebrated observation concerning capital's capacity to break down all previous legal, social, and cultural distinctions, in The COMMUNIST MANIFESTO (1848).

7

Digitized Citizen Ledger Finance: Logistics and Technics

Chapters 1–5 worked to motivate, and Chapter 6 worked to schematize, the proposal of full digitized Citizen Ledger Finance in broad outline, organizing discussion under the familiar balance sheet categories of assets and liabilities. I now turn to more detailed matters of implementation and logistics, by reference both to familiar and to now newly emergent finance and payment technologies.

7.1 From Abstract Accounting to Concrete Logistics: Making It Happen Now

I begin with some very basic questions that the digitized Citizen Ledger Finance proposal will implicate. For example, will there be central bank or finance ministry bank branches, teller windows, and ATMs? Will there be central bank or finance ministry online banking and mobile banking? Will the central bank or finance ministry lend to individuals, small businesses, and large firms as banks do? And what will credit-modulatory monetary policy look like?

Some of these queries are readily answered quite quickly, while others present optionalities that we should discuss. To begin with, because digital wallet and P2P payments technology, discussed briefly above and in detail below, are by definition device-associated and in that sense "online," public banking will indeed be online banking. The question accordingly is what role,

R. C. Hockett, *The Citizens' Ledger*,
https://doi.org/10.1007/978-3-030-99566-9_7

if any, we wish to retain for cash, perhaps for reasons sounding in privacy or familiarity, and how to accommodate this role in the event we decide to retain it for some time to come. That takes us to branches, tellers, ATMs, and the like.

Assuming we wish to allow for some cash continuance and ready convertibility of digital Citizen or Resident Wallet currency units to paper currency, one possibility is that private sector banking institutions, as they lose their traditional deposit-taking business to the central bank or the finance ministry, will want to downsize their workforces and physical plant.[1] These trained personnel and facilities then can be simply taken on by the central bank or finance ministry and continue, respectively, as public sector personnel and facilities.

Another possibility here would be simply to require, as a condition of bank licensure, that private sector bank branches offer necessary man hours and teller window face time to the conduct of digital Citizen and Resident Account deposit-taking, withdrawing, money-transferring, money-exchanging, check-ordering, cashiers' check franking, and so forth.[2] Banks can similarly be required to forgo charging fees on ATM and debit card transactions for Citizen and Resident Account users.[3] The appropriate regional central bank district offices—in the U.S., Federal Reserve District Banks—can then monitor compliance with these requirements.[4]

With respect to online banking and similar services, there is no reason the system of Citizen and Resident Wallets and associated P2P payments system cannot offer everything that private banking institutions do to their depositors with online access—save without exploitative rent-seeking fees and collateral services.[5] Indeed, the very large boost to its seigniorage revenues that the central bank or finance ministry will realize on a new system of digital Citizen and Resident Wallets should enable it to cover any new personnel and administrative costs occasioned by the new regime and then some.[6]

In time, most deposit, payment, online, and other services currently handled in person or via the web will likely migrate to mobile phones and other devices, as is of course already happening quickly in the U.S. and, even more quickly, in other jurisdictions today.[7] Indeed, if developments throughout Asia, Africa, and Northern Europe are any indication, we will achieve 100% financial inclusion through device-accessible digital banking long before we could build out any system of renewed postal or brick and mortar public banking.[8] The central bank or finance ministry will be well equipped both to benefit by and to shape this new revolution, as I detail below in Chapter 8 on the "Democratic Digital Currency." And I believe it a matter of urgent public interest that it does so now with all deliberate speed, for neither other jurisdictions nor the fintech industry is tarrying, as discussed below.

For purposes of the present discussion, however, the point to be noted is that logistical questions concerning bank facilities, spaces, and traditional services already are being addressed in new ways by private sector banking institutions themselves as new financial technology develops.[9] This means the digital Citizen and Resident Wallet regime will not so much "disrupt" today's retail banking and fintech development as take charge of, in the name of the citizenry, our republic, and our financial and payment systems, a disruption that is already well-underway.[10]

How about lending, and other "asset-side" activities in which private sector banks presently engage? Will banks no longer be lenders?[11] Well, this is in effect already answered at least partly above. Primary investment will be the primary function of the NIC style institutions referenced already, as well as of commercial banks whose loans will now have to conform to strict discount window conditionality as also described above.[12] In addition, commercial banks and other financial institutions—e.g., loan companies, money market funds, and even many shadow banking institutions—will continue to lend, but will simply have to do so with funds they are able to acquire from others, in one-to-one "narrow bank" fashion.

They will no longer be able to lend public credit-money save through the central bank discount window or some comparable facility established at the finance ministry.

In sum, then, I envisage private banks continuing to engage in safer renditions of their customary lending and retail investment functions, simply owing their liabilities now to the central bank or finance ministry rather than to borrower-depositors and thus required to conform to discount window conditionality. This will continue as the NIC and perhaps public banks of the German Sparkassen or U.S. Bank of North Dakota variety fill the plethora of small, large, and medium-sized gaps that relying solely on private sector franchisee institutions for credit-allocation now leaves unfilled.

It bears noting also that what I propose here is fully compatible and interoperable with other public option in lending proposals, including my own. The NIC itself, as described above, can lever the full faith and credit and superior risk-bearing capacities of the republic to assist public banks, local development banks, co-op banks, land banks, and all manner of other local development institution with their tasks.[13] Indeed, doing so can be interpreted as a form of fiscal-cum-monetary subsidiarity.[14]

What is true of the NIC here can be true of the central bank or finance ministry too as it develops its asset portfolio in tandem with its growing

Wallet liability ledger.[15] It will do so both in the form of NIC investments and perhaps in the form of portfolio-management under a PSF regime as mentioned above and elaborated in other work.[16] It can coordinate with the NIC in so doing, or act on its own, depending on public comfort at any given time with the central bank's or public fisc's being as forthrightly allocative in its asset-acquisition decisions as the NIC for its part is explicitly designed to be.[17]

The advantages offered by digitized Citizen Ledger Finance as I propose it here are many. The first are perhaps best grasped by reference to the three problems noted above to afflict present arrangements.

The problems of financial exclusion, the unbanked and underbanked, will be eliminated in a single stroke, as will the exploitative practices often engaged in by retail banks vis-à-vis less sophisticated depositors.[18] Additionally, the problem of rogue franchisee banks will be all but eliminated, as (1) the source of their cheapest funding—depositors—will significantly recede, while (2) the primary creditor to whom their liabilities are owed—the central bank or finance ministry—will now be better situated, and motivated, to monitor them and their compliance with discount window conditionality than are their scattered depositors.[19]

And finally, the pushing-on-a-string problem—and monetary policy leakage more generally—will be fully eliminated as well.[20] The central bank or finance ministry will be able to act directly to rein-in spending activity during booms and encourage or directly finance spending during busts, thereby affording us much more rapid and reliable macroeconomic growth. It can do this via changes in interest offered on Citizen and Resident Wallets, and via direct "helicopter drops"[21] in the unlikely event of any deep slump like that of 2008–2012—unlikely because solving the rogue franchisee problem as mentioned above will eliminate a primary source of the bubble inflation that culminates in busts in the first place.

Similarly, it could temporarily impound funds to slow "runaway inflation," after the manner suggested by Keynes in his *How to Pay for the War*.[22] But again this is virtually inconceivable during peacetime, for the source of inflation—public money disseminated by rogue speculative private sector franchisees—will simply be closed.

There are additional upshots to recommend what I propose here, but these are best handled under the heading of new financial technology, to which I turn next.

7.2 From Macro Logistics to Micro Technics: Why to Digitize Now

I have noted that the new financial and payments technologies now sparking hype and, sometimes, more sober attention are not strictly necessary to institute or implement digitized Citizen Ledger Finance.[23] We could probably have offered some lower tech rendition of what I propose just as early as we began doing it for private banking institutions with central bank Reserve Accounts over a century ago, and certainly by the time of Fedwire's and the WFC's introduction in the U.S. in 1918 or of the U.S.'s banking reforms of the New Deal era—by which time the U.S. and other republics even had full-on proto-NIC in the form of the RFC and its pre-war and post-war counterparts abroad.[24]

But the rapid spread and development of the new fintech modalities now underway present a particularly opportune time to move forward with alacrity. There are a number of reasons for saying this, some of which can be catalogued under what might be called the brighter, or more positive side of the ledger, and others of which belong under a darker, or more negative side of the same.[25] I will accordingly first say a bit about these two sides of the ledger. Then I'll discuss, in Chapter 8, more detailed options for what I shall call the "Democratic Digital Currency," or "2DC"—the currency counterpart of both the consolidated public ledger and the public payment platform that the system of digital Citizen and Resident Wallets will effectively constitute.

7.2.1 The Bright Side of the Ledger

As just noted, there are reasons that sound in affirmative benefit for going digital where Citizen Ledger Finance is concerned, and there are reasons that sound more in risk-preemption.[26] On the positive side, twenty or more central banks and monetary authorities worldwide, including the Bank of England (again, "BOE"), the European Central Bank (again, "ECB"), the People's Bank of China ("PBOC"), the Reserve Bank of India ("RBI"), the Bank of Japan (again, "BOJ"), and the U.S.'s Fed, are looking to upgrade their payments systems.[27] Indeed some are already doing so—or have already done so—as I recount more fully below in Chapter 8.[28]

Most seem to be considering some form of blockchain technology, partly for the replicability and associated indelibility properties these platforms offer where recording and tracking transactions is concerned, partly for the privacy and security optionality they offer, and partly for the simultaneity of clearing and settlement they afford as real prospects.[29] An added benefit is the ease of system interoperability they offer when it comes to linking up multiple national, subnational, and transnational payments infrastructures.[30]

There are at least three ways that these developments render the present an opportune time to move forward with implementing the new digital Citizen and Resident Wallets regime that I am here calling for, along with its associated Democratic Digital Currency—the monetary form that is counterpart to the payments system this regime will effectively constitute—which I sketch out below.

First, if central banks or finance ministries decide to upgrade national payments infrastructure in any event, as many are now planning to do, it will be comparatively easy to include an expansion to Citizen and Resident Wallets and an associated Democratic Digital Currency as part of that upgrade.[31] The change then can be characterized as simply an added benefit of that upgrade, much as new optionality accompanying phone, laptop, and other device operating system ("OS") upgrades typically are characterized.[32] And, crucially, this need not be marketing hype. It can be made true, inasmuch as the central bank or finance ministry, with the overwhelming bargaining power it will have in whatever partnership it might enter into in developing the new payment system architecture, can effectively bake optimal Citizen and Resident Account functionality in to whatever emerges.[33] I will say more about this below in Chapter 8, where I lay out the new payments system and Democratic Digital Currency that Citizen and Resident Wallets will effectively constitute.

Second, current fascination with cryptocurrencies and other forms of fintech offers both legislatures and central banks or finance ministries a rare public relations opportunity to "lean in" to what clearly is appealing to many people as an important new technological and associated social development, in making the transition to a system of digitized Citizen and Resident Wallets and an associated new payments infrastructure with a Democratic Digital Currency.[34] While the legislative change required to make such a transition is surprisingly simple—it can involve, if we wish, literally no more than the addition of one category to the eight or so categories of entity currently authorized to bank with the Fed[35]—popular buy-in could be more difficult until the benefits and absence of costs occasioned by the plan come to be more widely appreciated.[36]

Riding the current wave of enthusiasm for all things fintech would help the central bank or finance ministry sidestep that source of friction. So would riding the new wave of revulsion inspired by Facebook's Libra proposal—a proposal that enjoys the rare distinction of having alienated U.S. Congressional Democrats and Republicans alike.[37]

Finally, the new technologies do seem to offer many of the benefits noted above in connection with central banks' proffered reasons for taking interest in digital fiat currency and its associated platforms in the first place.[38] It is certainly true that the U.S. dollar, and most other sovereign currencies, already are digital in one sense of the word, and have been for as long as our banking and payments systems have been accommodating and employing electronic payments infrastructures—including Fedwire, which has been in operation since 1918.[39] It is also true, however, that some of the better-known crypto platforms warrant considerable skepticism where their putative speed and "frictionlessness" benefits are concerned.[40] But some of the new platforms now being developed and experimented with do seem to offer the prospect, in the not-too-distant future, of faster (even real time), safer, more private, and even user-friendly payment, clearing, and settlement than can presently be had, particularly among institutions not using Fedwire.[41]

One need not be a breathless fadster or deluded "cypherpunk" to believe that our payments systems are changing—and doing so, as I will elaborate in Chapter 8, in ways that we now both can and should capitalize on. One need to look only to the roughly forty-four jurisdictions that I will report on below, where central bank digital currency (again, "CBDC") development is already well-underway.[42] Or one can look, as I also will in Chapter 8, toward Europe, China, or Africa, where a large portion of transaction volume is now carried on via mobile phones and similar devices. Or one can look to the many largely rural countries in which citizens now do all banking by phone,[43] then remind oneself that digital wallets" can link just as readily to central bank or finance ministry Master Accounts as they can to anything else—another fact I highlight below in Chapter 8.

One can also, of course, look to China in connection with the darker side reasons for our central bank to get ahead of, rather than trailing or falling behind, the fintech revolution.[44] I turn to those reasons now.

7.2.2 The Dark Side of the Ledger

There are also risk-avoidance reasons for the central bank or finance ministry to associate digital Citizen and Resident Wallets with fintech developments. These reasons all complement the more opportunity-levering reasons just catalogued. The main one is the speed with which large private financial conglomerates and social media firms are now storming into this space, hoping to employ new financial technologies as means both to circumvent present-day finance-regulatory regimes and to exploit clientele.[45] Getting out front of fintech development will enable the central bank or finance ministry both to redirect wind from these sails and affirmatively to shape, indeed to determine, the course of fintech development itself.[46]

The wind in the sails to which I refer takes two forms, one of which amounts to hot air but operates insidiously nonetheless. First, profit-seeking private sector institutions appear to be beginning to use new fintech technologies to replicate, in not yet declaredly illegal ways, transactions that would themselves be illegal.[47] The most salient cases at the moment probably are (a) Facebook's ill-begotten Libra proposal, which amounts to a combined money market fund and forex platform that Facebook either naively or disingenuously proclaimed would be no more carefully regulated than PayPal[48]; and (b) various initial coin offerings, and exchange traded coin funds, all of which appear to be aimed at exploiting ambiguities both in the definitions of "securities" and "commodities" under the U.S.'s securities- and derivatives-regulatory regimes, and relatedly to exploit unclarity as to the boundary between the U.S. Securities and Exchange Commission and the U.S. Commodity Futures Trading Commission's jurisdictions.[49] But, there are many more cases of this sort now in gestation, and we can expect to see more of them proliferate at an accelerating rate in the near future.

Second, financial services industry personnel already are enjoying considerable success, as they have in the past, in convincing gullible or contribution-dependent public officials into believing that fintech is an exciting new field of only "upside" innovation, which legislatures must protect from innovation-stifling regulation with preemptive legislation.[50] The arguments offered on behalf of such urgings are in some cases difficult to articulate with a straight face, as they are literally the very same arguments offered in earlier times for insulating junk bonds, then financial conglomerates, then generic derivatives, then subprime mortgage loans and associated products, then credit default swaps, and then payday and auto loans against regulation.[51] It is always about consumer choice, synergies, and efficiency-producing innovation, we are told, when in fact it is about regulatory arbitrage, rule-evasion, and rents.[52]

This is all inadvertent false advertising or advertent propaganda, as the litany of innovations just cited should make plain.[53] But it is evidently persuasive propaganda in some quarters.[54] And one way to preempt its persuasive force at least among people who think and act in good faith is for citizen-owned instrumentalities like the central bank or finance ministry to embrace and commandeer the new technologies themselves, ensuring that they develop in salutary and public-benefitting rather than corrupt and public-exploiting directions.

This is not as fanciful as it might sound to those whose stereotyped impressions of public sector and private sector action have been conditioned by well-financed corporate and financial sector, not to mention privately financed think tank, public relations campaigns. As noted before, the U.S. Fed itself invented the repo transaction, which grew publicly salient only during the shadow-banking boom of the late 1990s and early 2000s, over a century ago.[55] And the U.S.'s federal home finance GSEs—Fannie Mae, Ginnie Mae, and Freddie Mac—invented securitization at least three and arguably six decades before securitization became publicly salient as yet another modality of shadow-banking in connection with private label subprime mortgage lending.[56] And in both cases, everything worked smoothly until, ironically, profit-seeking private sector entities were allowed into the act (not unlike what subsequently happened to formerly public entities in Eastern Europe after their handovers to private sector oligarchs).[57]

What distinguishes public sector franchisor from private sector franchisee finance, then, is not innovation. It is who and what the innovation is developed for, and how it is then deployed.

Public sector franchisor innovation, which remarkably (given private sector public relations campaigns) often seems to precede private sector franchisee innovation, is always developed and deployed for public purposes, and actually benefits the public in whose name it is developed.[58] Private sector franchisee innovation, by contrast, is seldom either innovative—copied as it is from public prototypes—or publicly beneficial. Unlike the internet, then, which the public sector invented and then relinquished to highly concentrated private platform companies, fintech, which looks poised to prove nearly as transformative as the internet promised to become two or three decades ago, should from the get-go be kept principally public.[59] The central bank's or finance ministry's taking charge of it in the cause of central banking and public payments infrastructure for all citizens and citizen-owned enterprises would be a most fitting way to ensure such a status.

It is worth noting in this connection, even if in closing this Chapter, that once we do this the messy array of coins, "stable coins," "coin funds," and cryptocurrencies on which too many ordinary Americans are now wasting their real money and attention will likely disappear.[60] These things are little more than crypto renditions of the nineteenth-century "wildcat" currencies discussed above, which died out in the U.S. when the Treasury, then the Fed, began issuing the Greenback that became today's U.S. dollar.[61] They will go the way of those currencies virtually the minute the central banks begin issuing Democratic Digital Currencies into new Citizen and Resident

Wallets via new digital payments platforms made possible by these Accounts themselves.[62] They will have no use but small in-group uses and criminal uses.[63]

Notes

1. *See* Thomas Heath, *Bank Tellers are the Next Blacksmiths*, WASHINGTON POST (February 8, 2017), https://www.washingtonpost.com/business/economy/bank-tellers-are-the-next-blacksmiths/2017/02/08/fdf78618-ee1c-11e6-9662-6eedf1627882_story.html (explaining Bank of America's reduction in bank tellers and expansion of robo-banking services).
2. *See generally What We Do*, OFFICE OF THE COMPTROLLER OF THE CURRENCY (last visited October 6, 2019), https://occ.treas.gov/about/what-we-do/index-what-we-do.html [https://perma.cc/RTN9-F4FA] (explaining the power of the OCC to issue rules and regulations over the banks it supervises). Also Robert Hockett, *What Is the Comptroller of the Currency—And Why Does It Matter?*, FORBES, January 19, 2021, at https://www.forbes.com/sites/rhockett/2021/01/19/what-is-the-comptroller-of-the-currency-and-why-does-it-matter/?sh=4ba66762717a.
3. *Id*. (explaining the power of the OCC to issue rules and regulations over the banks it supervises).
4. *See Consumer Compliance*, FED. RES. BOARD (last visited October 9, 2019), https://www.federalreserve.gov/supervisionreg/consumer-compliance.htm [https://perma.cc/NS2D-K5JM] ("A primary Federal Reserve responsibility is to ensure that the financial institutions under its jurisdiction comply with applicable laws and regulations established by Congress and the federal regulatory agencies.").
5. For more on these, *see, e.g.*, Robert C. Hockett, *Wells Fargo, Glass-Steagall, and "Do You Want Fries with That?" Banking,* THE HILL (Septemebr 22, 2016), https://thehill.com/blogs/pundits-blog/finance/297256-wells-fargo-glass-steagall-and-do-you-want-fries-with-that-banking [https://perma.cc/JF8Q-VAR8] [hereinafter, *Do You Want Fries With That?*] (discussing how Glass-Steagall would have prohibited banks from selling collateral services such as life insurance annuities, investment advisory services, and other financial products).
6. The Fed, for example, regularly earns a wide spread between the returns on its asset portfolio and the interest payments it makes. In recent years Fed seignorage has approached $100 billion annually. I anticipate that these revenues will rise substantially when the central bank or finance ministry grows its portfolio in tandem with new Citizen and Resident Account liabilities. For more on recent Fed seignorage revenues, *see Press Release: Federal*

Reserve Board Announces Reserve Bank Income and Expense Data and Transfers to the Treasury for 2017, BOARD OF GOVERNORS OF THE FEDERAL RESERVE SYSTEM (January 10, 2018, 11:00 AM), https://www.federalreserve.gov/newsevents/pressreleases/other20180110a.htm [https://perma.cc/ZL3K-TULM] (announcing Federal Reserve net income of $80.2B after payment of its interest expense).

7. In Kenya, for example, 90% of adults use the M-Pesa e-money phone app to transact, while in China the AliPay phone-based payment app accounts for nearly $19 trillion in transactions per annum. *See, e.g.*, Gillian Tett, *Facebook's "Stablecoin" Libra Raises Questions for Regulators*, FINANCIAL TIMES (June 13, 2019), https://www.ft.com/content/d4c1e00c-8dd6-11e9-a24d-b42f641eca37 (on central banks serious reaction to Facebook's introduction of Libra through nations' reaction to other nation's stablecoins). I will have much more to say about all of this *infra* Chapter 8.B.
8. Douglas W. Arner, Janos Barberis & Ross P. Buckley, *The Evolution of FinTech: A New Post-Crisis Paradigm*, 47 GEO. J. INT'L L. 1271, 1273–74, 1298 (2016). (discussing the rise in Asia and Africa of "recent FinTech developments" in the "pursuit of economic development").
9. World Economic Forum, *Beyond Fintech: A Pragmatic Assessment of Disruptive Potential in Financial Services*, at 90–94 (August 2017) (documenting traditional banks' methods of partnering with and developing fintech options to gain market share).
10. *Id.* at 84–88 (chronicling the changes among banks methods of payments and applications available to customers).
11. *See* Andrew F. Tuch, *The Remaking of Wall Street*, 7 HARV. BUS. L. REV. 315, 336–337 (2017) (arguing that banks' role as traditional lenders to consumers and businesses began to change after the financial crisis of 2007–2009).
12. David Schmidde, *Responding to the Subprime Mess: The New Regulatory Landscape*, 14 FORDHAM J. CORP. & FIN. L. 709, 715 (2009) (indicating "conforming loans" as loans meeting an amount limit and certain funding criteria established by government bodies); *National Investment Authority*, *supra* note 4, at 439 (suggesting the role of the NIC as a public partnership with greater influence with investors and lenders as an investment vehicle).
13. More on these matters, *see infra* Chapter 7 (discussing the implementation and logistics in finance and payment technologies for the Citizen Ledger Finance program). *See also*, *National Investment Authority, supra* note 4, at 439 (discussing the role of the National Investment Authority in supporting banking institutions and the abilities of collective banks). See also FINANCING THE GREEN NEW DEAL, *supra* note 18, which discusses these options at length.
14. Cf. Elizabeth J. Upton, *Chartering Fintech: The OCC's Newest Nonbank Proposal*, 86 GEO. WASH. L. REV. 1392, 1396 (2018) (arguing state level banks may act as a better "subsidiarity" in regulation as opposed to the federal government in light of their ability to govern "at the most local level").

15. *Assets of the Federal Reserve,* Classification under *Recent Balance Sheet Trends,* Fed. Reserve (October 2, 2019 7:35 PM), https://www.federalreserve.gov/monetarypolicy/bst_recenttrends.htm [https://perma.cc/9BWZ-GC8H] ("Total assets of the Federal Reserve have increased significantly from $870 billion on August 8, 2007, to $4.5 trillion on January 14, 2015"); *see also id.* at *Selected Liabilities of the Federal Reserve* ("On the liabilities side of the Federal Reserve's balance sheet, the amount of currency outstanding has continued to rise gradually, but reserve balances (deposits of depository institutions) have increased dramatically relative to prior to the financial crisis.").
16. *See generally*, Chapter 6 (arguing that certain changes to the balance of assets will stem from liability side sources, including from asset issuances from NIC, and addition of the Citizen and Resident Wallets); *Open Labor*, *supra* note 29, at 462 (documenting the Reconstruction Finance Corporation as a form of "OMO Plus" and its effects on the Federal Reserve's balance). Also, again, Financing The Green New Deal, *supra* note 18.
17. *See* again, Financing The Green New Deal, *supra* note 18. *See also* Hockett, sources cited *supra*, note 52.
18. For more on these, *see Do You Want Fries With That?*, *supra* note 352 (utilizing the need to insulate depository institutions from large financial firms as reason to update the Glass-Steagall Act).
19. Another collective action problem—that faced by depositors—will hereby be solved. *Id.* ("Another of Glass-Steagall's concerns was to limit the cheap funds that bank affiliates would make available to speculative non-bank investors whose activities in late asset price bubbles like those which burst in 1929 and 2008.").
20. *See* Alpert, Hockett & Roubini, *The Way Forward*, New AM. (October 2011), https://www.newamerica.org/economic-growth/policy-papers/the-way-forward/ [https://perma.cc/WWJ5-72LG]) (exemplifying the pushing on a string problem through the actions of the government in to affect supply and demand in 1932 and comparing it to actions to effectuate consumer demand in 2009 to 2013); Ashton S. Phillips, *Bank-Created Money, Monetary Sovereignty, and the Federal Deficit: Toward a New Paradigm in the Government-Spending Debate*, 36 W. New Eng. L. Rev. 221, 243 n.68 (2014) (citing *Aggregate Reserves of Depository Institutions and the Monetary Base-H.3,* Bd. Gov. Fed. Res. (February 20, 2014), http://www.federalreserve.gov/releases/h3/current/ [https://perma.cc/8JYT-Q8XU]) ("[B]anks, especially in the wake of the financial crisis... often retain 'excess reserves'... Economists refer to [this and] the reality that individuals sometimes prefer to hold their money in cash as 'leakages.'").
21. See *supra* note 291 and accompanying text (discussing the term 'Helicopter Drop' and its proposals).
22. J.M. Keynes, How To Pay for the War (1940) (proposing the preemption of inflation occasioned by war spending through a system of national

savings accounts which will be drawable on only in extremis during wartime, then opened up to fuel stimulus once demobilization begins and war spending ramps down.

23. *See Betting on Betacoin*, *supra* note 17 (discussing the concerns related to "buyers flocking to Bitcoin specifically").
24. On the history of Fedwire, *see, e.g.*, Adam Gilbert, Dara Hunt & Kenneth C. Winch, *Creating an Integrated Payment System: The Evolution of Fedwire*, 3 FED. RES. BANK N.Y. ECON. POL'Y REV. 1, 1–4 (1997) (describing the origins of the Fedwire system and its challenges). On the RFC, *see National Investment Authority*, *supra* note 4, at 458–463 (summarizing the development of the RFC).
25. *See* discussion *infra* Chapter 7 (discussing positive and negative aspects of the implementation of the Citizen and Resident Wallets regime).
26. *Id.* (observing benefits and risks associated with the Citizen and Resident Wallets regime).
27. *See* Agustin Carstens, *Guest View: Innovation Transforms Central Banking*, REUTERS (June 3, 2019, 6:20 AM), https://www.reuters.com/article/us-cen bank-technology-breakingviews/breakingviews-guest-view-innovation-transf orms-central-banking-idU.S.KCN1T41AB [https://perma.cc/WVK6-3FEA] (discussing how central banks are upgrading payment systems to work with fintech, mobile payments, and more).
28. When I began this project during late 2014, only a few digital currency enthusiasts seemed to be devoting substantial time and attention to this prospect. Since then the number of studies and proposals has burgeoned to seemingly no longer comprehensively citable proportions. A few early and notable examples are those cited *supra* note 21 (enumerating the proposals to offer central bank accounts to the public by different authors). Among the 20 or more central banks now issuing, or actively researching the prospect of issuing, digital fiat currencies on new fintech platforms are those of Brazil, Canada, China, Ecuador, the European Union, India, Indonesia, Japan, Malaysia, Norway, Singapore, Sweden, Turkey, Uruguay, the U.K., and the U.S., among others. A helpful recent survey of the now rapidly flowering terrain is COMM. ON PAYMENTS AND MKT. INFRASTRUCTURES & MKTS. COMM., BANK FOR INT'L SETTLEMENTS, CENTRAL BANK DIGITAL CURRENCIES (2018), https://www.bis.org/cpmi/publ/d174.pdf [https://perma.cc/4ZW5-KPV5] (explaining the concept of central bank digital currencies and their benefits and risks).
29. *See Money's Past*, *supra* note 17, at 9–11 (heralding "digital currency development" in the United States); *Betting on Betacoin*, *supra* note 17 (propounding that Bitcoin may be outcompeted by other cryptocurrencies); Robert C. Hockett, *Facebook's Proposed Crypto-Currency: More Pisces Than Libra For Now*, FORBES (June 20, 2019, 2:03 PM), https://www.forbes.com/sites/rhockett/2019/06/20/facebooks-proposed-crypto-currency-more-pisces-than-libra-for-now/#1d6ca7992be2 [https://perma.cc/4L8G-HWGD] [hereinafter *More Pisces Than Libra*] (asserting problems and vulnerabilities of Libra).

30. *See* Thomas Lammer, Jose Antonio Garcia & Sacha Polverini, *Establishing Payments Interoperability: Coordination is Key*, World Bank Blogs (September 26, 2016), https://blogs.worldbank.org/psd/establishing-payments-interoperability-coordination-key [https://perma.cc/B24P-EGDK] (discussing the benefits of worldwide interoperable payment systems).
31. *See Money's Past, supra* note 17, at 9–10 (predicting that the U.S. payment system "will be built upon something a lot like distributed ledgers" which will "render … 'Citizen Central Banking'" and that the "dollar will go digital").
32. *See id.* at 10 ("A Fed-issued and -administered digital dollar will be every bit as uniform and elastic as the Fed-issued and administered pre-digital dollar has been. Indeed it will likely be even more easily managed").
33. *See id.* (asserting that "[a] Fed-issued and-administered digital dollar will be every bit as uniform and elastic as the Fed-issued and administered pre-digital dollar has been").
34. *See More Pisces Than Libra, supra* note 377 (discussing the popularity of cryptocurrencies and central banks' plans to develop digital currencies based on cryptocurrencies and related financial technologies).
35. *See supra* note 147 and accompanying text (citing to 12 U.S.C. §§ 342, 391, 1435, 1452(d) & 1723a(g), 347d & 358, 286d, and 5465, which provide that, respectively, banks, the U.S. Treasury, government-sponsored enterprises providing mortgages, foreign governments, foreign banks, foreign central banks, and designated financial market utilities may hold accounts with the Federal Reserve).
36. *See* Bank for Int'l Settlements, Comm. on Payments & Mkt. Infrastructures, Central Bank Digital Currencies 1 (2018), https://www.bis.org/cpmi/publ/d174.pdf [https://perma.cc/LP2G-8Y55] [hereinafter BIS central bank digital currencies report] (suggesting that the provision of a digital currency by central banks "could bring substantial benefits" but the "benefits of a widely accessible [central bank digital currency] may be limited if fast (even instant) and efficient private retail payment products are already in place or in development").
37. *See More Pisces Than Libra, supra* note 377 (commenting that lawmakers have been very concerned about technology companies' use of consumers' personal data, and that "[a]dding money and payments to the mix only heightens the worry—as our already extensive regime of bank depositor privacy regulation, and as recent bipartisan Congressional hearings on fintech, abundantly attest").
38. *See* BIS Central Bank Digital Currencies Report , *supra* note 384, at 1 (commenting that some central banks are "analysing a [central bank digital currency] that could be made widely available to the general public and serve as an alternative safe, robust and convenient payment instrument" and that in places where cash is disappearing, "the provision of [central bank digital currencies] could bring substantial benefits").

39. Fedwire Funds Service, Assessment of Compliance with the Core Principles for Systemically Important Payment Systems 7 (2014) ("In the early 1900s, settlement of interbank payment obligations often involved the physical delivery of cash or gold to counterparties, which was both risky and costly. To mitigate these risks, in 1918, the Reserve Banks introduced a dedicated funds transfer network featuring a Morse code system that connected the 12 Reserve Banks, the Board, and the United States Department of the Treasury."). Retail payment networks in the United States are quite slow by global standards, as are wire transfers and credit card payments. Ironically, only interbank transfers, for which the Fed uses "real time gross settlement" (RTGS), are instantaneous. *See* Faster Payments Task Force, The U.S. Path to Faster Payments Final Report Chapter i: the Faster Payments Task Force Approach 52–54 (2017) (showing in a table how various types of payments in the United States are currently handled). While the Fed could presumably offer RTGS for all payments between Citizen Wallets and Resident Wallets using present technology, in particular Fedwire, currently developing payments platforms appear to be designed with precisely this optionality in mind. *See* Gilbert, Hunt, & Winch, *supra* note 197. For more on the history of RTGS, which dates to the 1970s, *see* Morton L. Bech & Bart Hobijn, *Technology Diffusion within Central Banking: The Case of Real-Time Gross Settlement* 1–3 (Fed. Reserve Bank of N.Y. Staff Reports, Staff Report No. 260, 2006) (discussing the history and development of real- time gross settlement systems and their use by banks).
40. *See, e.g.*, Alexander Kroeger & Asani Sarkar, *Is Bitcoin Really Frictionless?* Fed. Reserve Bank of N.Y.: Liberty St. Econ. (March 23, 2016), https://libertystreeteconomics.newyorkfed.org/2016/03/is-bitcoin-really-frictionless.html [https://perma.cc/4L7Y-QN54] (discussing the transactional friction that arises when Bitcoin is traded on exchanges).
41. *See* Fedwire Funds Service *supra*, note 388; Morton L. Bech & Bart Hobijn, *Technology Diffusion within Central Banking: The Case of Real-Time Gross Settlement* 1–3 (Fed. Reserve Bank of N.Y. Staff Reports, Staff Report No. 260, 2006) for a discussion about the development of real-time settlement and payment systems).
42. *See* Christian Barontini & Henry Holden, *Proceeding with Caution—A Survey on Central Bank Digital Currency* 7 (Bank for Int'L Settlements, BIS Paper No. 101, 2019) (presenting the results of a survey showing that 70% of sixty-three jurisdictions surveyed now have development of various central bank digital currencies underway). With regard to the ubiquity of mobile payments in African countries, *see generally* Mutsa Chironga, Hillary De Grandis, & Yassir Zouaoui, *Mobile Financial Services in Africa: Winning*

the Battle for the Customer, MCKINSEY & CO. (September 2017), https://www.mckinsey.com/industries/financial-services/our-insights/mobile-financial-services-in-africa-winning-the-battle-for-the-customer# [https://perma.cc/HS4Y-RQAU] (concluding that "Africa is the global leader in mobile money" and showing that the M-Pesa mobile payment platform is used by 90 percent of Kenyan adults). On the growth of mobile payments in Europe, *see generally* Sukriti Bansal et al., *Global Payments 2018: A Dynamic Industry Continues to Break New Ground*, MCKENZIE & CO. GLOBAL BANKING PRACTICE, October 2018, at 5 (presenting data showing that "individual European countries such as Sweden and Norway are executing no more than 20 percent of their transactions in cash"). On the growth of mobile payments in China, *see generally* Aaron Klein, *Is China's New Payment System the Future?*, ECON. STUD. BROOKINGS (Brookings Inst., Washington, D.C.), June 2019, at 8, https://www.brookings.edu/wp-content/uploads/2019/06/ES_20190620_Klein_ChinaPayments.pdf [https://perma.cc/VV9B-5JW7] ("Over 90 percent of people in China's largest cities use WeChat and Alipay as their primary payment method, with cash second, and card-based debit/credit a distant third.").

43. A few examples. China, Africa, South Asia. *See* Moses Mozart Dzawu, *Mobile Phones Are Replacing Bank Accounts in Africa*, BLOOMBERG (August 13, 2019, 12:00 AM), https://www.bloomberg.com/news/articles/2019-08-13/mobile-phones-are-replacing-bank-accounts-in-africa (discussing the rapid growth of digital mobile payments platforms in Africa, and concluding that "once people have phones there's no need for a bank account").
44. *See* Robert Hockett, *When Is "Social Credit" Orwellian?* FORBES (January 3, 2019), https://www.forbes.com/sites/rhockett/2019/01/03/when-is-social-credit-orwellian/ [https://perma.cc/NAL2-YUHA] [hereinafter, *When is "Social Credit" Orwellian?*] (discussing moral and policy concerns with China's electronically managed "social credit" system, which extensively surveys and assigns scores to citizens).
45. *See, e.g., More Pisces than Libra, supra* note 377.
46. *See generally* Jeff Galvin et al., *Synergy and Disruption: Ten Trends Shaping Fintech*, MCKENZIE & CO. GLOBAL BANKING PRACTICE, December 2018, at 3–4 (explaining that "[t]o successfully enter new markets, [fintech developers] must adapt to new sets of market dynamics and government regulations and select new markets based on a clear understanding of regional variations").
47. *See* Amy Castor, *Judge Applies Long-Established Securities Law to ICOs*, BITCOIN MAGAZINE (September 12, 2018), https://bitcoinmagazine.com/articles/federal-judge-applies-long-established-securities-law-icos/ [https://perma.cc/L5LA-AA42] (quoting former CFTC Chairman Gary Gensler as saying that many cryptocurrency exchanges "re basically operating outside of

U.S. law"); Frank Chaparro, *It Was True for Tulips*, BUS. INSIDER (June 23, 2018), https://www.businessinsider.com/ico-community-should-be-worried-about-a-coming-wave-2018-6 (highlighting the SEC's legal concerns about initial coin offerings); Aislinn Keely, *Facebook's Libra Could Meet Prying Regulatory Eyes from the U.S. and Beyond, Experts Say*, THE BLOCK (June 27, 2019, 7:52 PM), https://www.theblockcrypto.com/2019/06/27/facebooks-libra-could-meet-prying-regulatory-eyes-from-the-u-s-and-beyond-experts-say/ (explaining that regulatory bodies in the United States and Europe have voiced grave concerns about Facebook's proposed cryptocurrency project); Celia Wan, *Kik's Troubles Mount SEC Files Suit Claiming Securities Law Violations, Lawyers Say*, THE BLOCK (June 5, 2019, 12:00 PM), https://www.theblockcrypto.com/2019/06/05/kiks-troubles-mount-as-sec-files-suit-claiming-securities-law-violation-lawyers-say/ (highlighting attorneys' view and predictions about the SEC's allegations that Kik broke U.S. securities law with its initial coin offering).

48. *See More Pisces Than Libra*, *supra* note 377 (suggesting that it is not clear what value Facebook's Libra will add to the current financial ecosystem, "particularly in light of the regulatory burdens that they will inevitably and indeed necessarily face in connection with any such offering that isn't a mere glorified PayPal or Venmo").
49. *Id.* (explaining that Facebook's Libra will "likely have to register as and submit to exacting regulation both as a de facto money market fund and as a systemically important financial institution (SIFI) by the Securities and Exchange Commission (SEC) and the Financial Stability Oversight Council (FSOC), respectively"); Allen Kogan, Note, *Not All Virtual Currencies are Created Equal: Regulatory Guidance in the Aftermath of* CFTC v. McDonnell, 8 AM. U. BUS. L. REV. 199, 209–17 (2019) (explaining that currently, cryptocurrencies are regulated in part by the SEC and in part by the CFTC, and concluding that this regulatory regime is not satisfactory).
50. *See, e.g.*, Robert C. Hockett, *Let's Get Real About "Financial CHOICE,"* FORBES> (June 11, 2017), https://www.forbes.com/sites/rhockett/2017/06/11/lets-get-real-about-financial-choice/#55c3fe6e4c86 [https://perma.cc/TFT4-FCUG] (discussing dangers of the "F-CHOICE Act").
51. *Id.* ("It is that weaker or non-existent financial regulation somehow promotes —or even equates to—"innovation, growth, and jobs" in the broader economy.").
52. *Id.* ("What is the sophistical argument to which I refer? It is that weaker or non- existent financial regulation somehow promotes – or even equates to – "innovation, growth, and jobs" in the broader economy. Republicans and finance industry lobbyists are now routinely trafficking in this false equation, apparently hoping that we too will eventually come to associate the two things, Pavlov-style, if only we hear the words often enough. Take a look at what House Speaker Paul Ryan said on behalf of the F-CHOICE Act last week, for example ("a jobs bill for Main Street"). Or have a gander at what

House Financial Services Chair Jeb Hensarling had to say ("economic growth for all")...").

53. *Id.* ("Notwithstanding its Pravda-redolent repetition by partisan politicians and bank lobbying outfits, however, the putative 'growth' argument for gutting financial regulation is complete and intentional nonsense. It is not merely "flawed" or misleading. It literally lacks any basis in truth at all, and in fact stands the truth on its head.").
54. *Id.* ("Notwithstanding the Act's impending death on arrival in the Senate, however, it is urgent that we attend nonetheless to the would-be real-world effects of the F-CHOICE Act, along with what has emerged as the favored sophistical 'argument' that House Republicans and their clients now make on the F-CHOICE Act's behalf. For this phony pseudo-argument will be made in the Senate this week as it was in the House last week. And, as importantly, it will be made on behalf of much additional legislative mischief soon to be proffered by White House and Congressional Republicans in coming weeks.").
55. *See Finance without Financiers, supra* note 15, at 28 ("Turning from bank-replication to public accommodation and monetization, it is first worth noting, if only in passing, that the *Fed* actually *invented* repo, as a means of financing First World War expenditures, while the Federal Reserve Bank of New York ("FRBNY") now acts as the largest counterparty in repo markets.").
56. *See Jeffersonian Republic, supra* note 25, at 91 n.114. ("'Securitization' has grown rapidly in the last decade and has given rise to some of the largest and fastest growing securities markets. It is often overlooked that all of this began with, and continues to be largely driven by, the activities of erstwhile 'government sponsored enterprises' ('GSEs') like Fannie Mae.").
57. *Republican Home-Owning, supra* note 29, at 19 ("What changed after sixty odd years of republican home-spreading and price-maintaining success? In essence, the story is one of creeping privatization, deregulation, and attendant speculative profit-seeking, accompanied by classic asset price bubble dynamics that our principal money-modulator— the Fed—didn't see fit to tamp down till too late.").
58. Per Koch & Johan Hauknes, Innovation in the Public Sector 18 (2d ed. 2005) ("In the Public case studies we have found that idealism and the urge to develop a better society is an important driving force for public innovation.").
59. Public Banks Solution, *supra* note 10, at 3 (2013) ("Banking, money and credit are not market goods but are economic infrastructure, just as roads and bridges are physical infrastructure. Banking and credit need to be public utilities for a capitalist market economy to run properly.").
60. *Money's Past, supra* note 17, at 10 ("When we get there, what do you suppose happens? This too seems easy: The dollar will go digital. The Fed will issue 'Federal Reserve Coins" and their keystroke equivalents much as it issues

'Federal Reserve 'Notes' and their keystroke equivalents now. In this new world, there will be little more use for what I will call 'Wildcat Crypto' than there was for 'Wildcat Currency' after the Legal Tender, National Currency, and National Banking Acts of the 1860s. These 'assets' will simply fade out, retained only as curiosities on a par with Colonial Scrip and 'Confederate money' or as means of illicitly transacting in criminal activities until caught."); *Rousseauvian Money*, *supra* note 3.

61. *Id.*
62. *See Money's Past*, *supra* note 17, at 6 (concluding that the demise of bank-issued "wildcat" banknotes was inevitable when the Fed began issuing a centralized currency).
63. *See id.* at 10 (alluding to the fate of Colonial Scrip and Confederate dollars when these currencies were replaced and thus lost their value as cash).

8

From Digitized Citizen Ledger Finance to Citizen Fintech: Democratic Digitization and Its Possible Forms

As noted above, contemporary fintech is not strictly necessary for a set of proposals of the sort I make here, but it does make things simultaneously easier and more urgently necessary.[1] This Chapter accordingly situates the digitized Citizen Ledger Finance proposal within the contemporary fintech landscape and describes in greater detail a modern Democratic Digital Currency design that can be thought of as the technical, payments system face of the broader digital Citizen Ledger Finance proposal. It also takes stock of what central banks and monetary authorities—the U.S. Fed's and Treasury's counterparts—worldwide are now doing in this space.[2]

8.1 Moneys and Payment Systems

In view of the intimate linkages among finance, moneys, and payment systems, on the one hand,[3] and the way the central bank or finance ministry balance sheet under my plan will immediately constitute a potential payment platform, on the other hand, it will be both crucial and straightforward for the central bank or finance ministry to pair up my proposed system of Citizen and Resident Wallets with what I am calling a Democratic Digital Currency and associated savings and payments platform. While there are various forms that a Fed-administered digital dollar could take,[4] I think that one form in particular is both natural and clearly preferable in light both of the nature of Citizen and Resident Wallets and of the values that prompt my push for more

R. C. Hockett, *The Citizens' Ledger*,
https://doi.org/10.1007/978-3-030-99566-9_8

fully republican, Citizen Ledger Finance in the first place. I will accordingly first briefly note options that now figure in the literature, then describe the best option for present purposes, then report briefly on what other central banks and monetary authorities are already doing.

To begin with options, it might at first glance look as though there is a bewildering array of candidates to offer. Adequately assessing alternatives for digitizing Citizen and Resident Account money might accordingly look to require that one write a distinct essay devoted to that task alone. The existing literature is replete, for example, with centralized electronic "bank money" options like card, wire, and check-image services that build upon sovereign money claims.[5] It also features much on both centralized and decentralized electronic money, or "e-money," services like AliPay, Paxos, and M-Pesa.[6] And then there are variously centralized and decentralized currency substitutes that include CBDC; privately issued cryptocurrencies like Bitcoin, Etherium, and so-called "stable coins" with comforting names such as "Havven," "TrueCoin," or "TrueUSD," vaguely worrisome names such as "Tether," or groovy lyrical names such as Facebook's Libra.[7]

What, figuratively and literally, are we to make of all this? How should we choose among options in digitizing a central bank or finance ministry Citizen and Resident Account-associated e-Dollar?

As it happens, things are not nearly as complicated as at first they might seem. The system of digitized Citizen Ledger Finance I am advocating largely determines the form that a Democratic Digital Currency should take. It will be easiest to see why by proceeding sequentially through three contextualizing observations that bring policy-relevant order to the present-day chaos that is the digital currency literature—including the CBDC literature—now on offer. These observations make clear that we can bracket and sidestep, with confidence, all the confusion and unnecessary complication that vitiates most of the still-burgeoning literature on digital monies and payment platforms now on offer. Indeed we can render that thicket all but otiose.

The first contextualizing observation is that there is always a danger of internal tension, if not incoherence, within any discussion of money and payments, especially when conducted against the backdrop of our current, hybrid public–private franchise-finance system. We must take special care both to recognize and to avoid falling into these confusions.

There are two underlying sources of the confusion-potential to which I allude, which interact in a manner that gums-up much current "money-talk." One is that money is partly distinguishable from payment systems and thus independently addressable, up to a point, as a conceptual matter,[8] even while also in all cases being deeply embedded in and indeed constituted by payment systems as a practical matter.[9] The other source of confusion-potential is the fact that hybrid public–private financial systems like ours tend to produce multiple layers of money and near money within single hierarchies, each built on one publicly issued monetary base. These two facts tend to combine in a manner that breeds much confusion about money and payment systems that we must avoid—and that a Democratic Digital Currency and associated payment platform will render entirely superfluous.[10]

On the first point, money is, again, always "that which pays" within a given practice of paying or payments regime.[11] Payment is like a move in a game, we might say, and money is the score-keeping modality within any such game.[12] It is "that which counts" for purposes of accounting in any system involving reciprocal exchange, credits, debits, and associated "accountability."[13] On the second point, moneys that operate within different layers of a money hierarchy tend to count as payment-settling devices within different transactional settings, hence within different payment subsystems of the overall payments system, in confusion-causing ways I shall presently show and clear up.[14]

Against this backdrop, it can be tempting to think of distinct layers of a single monetary hierarchy as distinct moneys or forms of money, and then to explain the distinctions among them by reference to putatively distinct natural kinds such as, for example, tokens, claims, accounts, "b-moneys," or e-moneys, all treated as radically different phenomena.[15] How this gives rise to incoherence and confusion in the digital currency literature will become clear as I move through the next two contextualizing observations.

My second contextualizing observation is that the aforementioned danger of tension or incoherence *rises* as payment system complexity rises, with "complexity" here understood as the number of discrete nodes or steps, and associated institutions interposed between payors and payees, in any payment process. Indeed, in many cases, these distinct steps and associated institutions actually *constitute* the hierarchy of money layers just noted.[16] The more elements in a payment "value chain,"[17] in short, and hence the greater the degree of complexity that must enter into any comprehensive assessment of particular monetary and payment system possibilities, the more unavoidable it becomes to address multiple policy decision points and thus to draw distinctions like those just alluded to.

My third contextualizing observation is that the moment we bite the proverbial bullet and decide that all parties shall have central bank or public fisc digital wallets and be able to make payments to one another through them, we also eliminate all the layers and associated complexities that occasion all of the confusions that presently vitiate monetary and payment system discussion.[18] For the latter, again, all stem *entirely* from the presence of multiple steps and associated institutional interfaces in the processes of payment—steps and institutional roles that produce the aforementioned hierarchy of distinct moneys and near moneys in the first place. Put all accounts on liability side of the central bank or finance ministry balance sheet, then—the accounting sheet whose *unit* of account, whose *money*, is the sovereign issuance of the account-keeper itself—and you at once collapse money "*hierarchies*" into just *money*, then sidestep the bewildering and altogether unnecessary Ptolmeic distinctions pervading the literature that stem from those hierarchies.[19]

The upshot of these observations is that the Democratic Digital Currency that I propose will effectively moot most discussions of digital currencies and their associated technologies, including CBDC, that are now underway.[20] There simply will not be a "there" there anymore. In retiring this discourse my proposal will also, in consequence, dissipate that head-spinning and anxiety-prompting air of "*embarrass de choix*" that now hangs over most digital currency and digital fiat currency discussion.[21] There really are not all that many choices or options once money goes fully republican, for there are no longer multiple hierarchy layers to deal with.[22] My proposal will accordingly simplify monetary conversations in the same degree that it simplifies monetary and payment arrangements themselves.

It is easiest to show this by singling out two particularly oft-encountered, and putatively fundamental, distinctions that nearly all discussions of digital money now seem to assume as immutable background conditions.[23] My proposal, it will be seen, simply sidesteps both distinctions—and with them, therefore, most modern digital money proposals and associated discussions as well. It renders the laundry list of options that I rattled off in opening this Chapter instantly obsolete— something we need no longer waste valuable time on attempting to make sense of, let alone disentangle.

The first putatively fundamental distinction is the one often cited between so-called "account-based" and "token-based"—alternatively, "claim-based" and "object-based"—forms of money and payment.[24] Pursuant to this distinction, a payor can pay a payee either by directly remitting tokens or objects that are recognized as legal tender in all relevant settings—that is, cash—or can convey a claim to the payee that indirectly entitles her to some portion of cash or its equivalent in effect held by the payor in—or owed to the payer in the form of—some sort of account.[25] This distinction is important, we are told, because (a) payors or their account-administrators can prove to be insolvent before payments are settled and (b) cash, unlike accounts, allows for anonymity among transacting parties.[26]

In our current payments systems, this distinction does have some— dare one say it?—purchase, for it does highlight actual dangers that can afflict payment transactions over the course of the value chain—dangers the law must then mitigate.[27] Checks used to bounce, for example, and depository institutions could fail amidst multipart payment transactions such as those, for example, that letters of credit involve.[28] Much of commercial law, negotiable instruments law, and banking law accordingly prescribes to this day who has what rights to which things under what circumstances.[29]

Much current discussion of cryptocurrency and associated payment infrastructure options, be they central-bank-administered or otherwise, highlights and addresses these same sorts of dangers.[30] Likewise, many participants in current fintech discussions tout the preferability of "token" or "object" money over "account" or "claim" money owing to its cash-reminiscent anonymity properties.[31] These people accordingly speak of "digital cash" and "digital wallets" as things radically distinct from and preferable to "digital currency" and "digital accounts."[32]

It requires little acuity or imagination, however, to see that these distinctions and the dangers they highlight are entirely artifacts of a hybrid public–private payments system in which multiple steps and associated entities, nearly all of the latter being private sector institutions, stand between payors and payees in the payments process.[33] This means a move to a system of central-bank- or finance-ministry-administered Citizen and Resident Wallets and an associated Democratic Digital Currency like what I propose will, in collapsing the money hierarchy and removing its layers, immediately collapse the mentioned distinctions themselves and thus render discussions predicated upon them no longer interesting.

Physical currency tokens such as dollar, pound, or euro bills and coins, for example, are claims upon—liabilities of—sovereign instrumentalities just as demand deposits and associated transaction accounts are claims upon—liabilities of—the private sector banks and other financial institutions that offer and administer them. The aforementioned popular distinction between "token" and "account"—or "object" and "claim"—is thus less a distinction between kinds or types of money, in any natural kind sense of those words, than it is between layers in the same money hierarchy associated with public and private obligees—that is, between privately owned financial intermediaries and publicly run sovereign instrumentalities.

Since the system I am proposing simply dispenses with privately owned intermediary institutions where both banking and payments are concerned, these distinctions and the systemic vulnerabilities that render them salient simply collapse. "Token" and "account," "object" and "claim," become one and the same thing, just as they would be in a system in which all payments were made in sovereign issued coin and currency, and all bank accounts were publicly provided and guaranteed bailment services into which additional, lent money or "helicopter" money could be dropped.[34] In effect, what I propose is simply a digitized version of just that—a version that was technically unavailable in the eighteenth and nineteenth centuries but now can afford literally instantaneous clearing and settling in digital fiat currency between any two or more parties.

The one caveat to this observation is that physical cash does afford some privacy potentials that some systems of digital currency might not.[35] But this is a matter of system design that confronts any electronic issuance of anything, public or private, since electronic networks are, well, physical networks.[36] They are material infrastructures over which flows of electrons can in principle always be tracked or retraced.[37] This means that cash-simulating safeguards must be cryptographically built in—again, whether the system in question be publicly or privately administered.[38] I will come back to this shortly in describing the Democratic Digital Currency that is the monetary counterpart of the payment system that our central bank or finance ministry balance sheet will constitute in a system of Citizen Ledger Finance.

The second putatively fundamental distinction that is salient only under our current hybrid payments system arrangements is the difference between so-called "open loop" and "closed loop"—a.k.a. "peer to peer" or "P2P"—systems, a distinction that partly prompts interest in blockchain and other distributed ledger technologies among many enthusiasts in the first place.[39] Broadly speaking, in contemporary parlance, an open loop payments system is one in which intermediaries—typically, but not always, financial institutions—stand between transacting parties and whatever party manages the relevant payments platform or infrastructure.[40]

In a closed loop system, by contrast, only a single payment platform and system administrator stand between payors and payees.[41] The coexistence of open and closed loop systems is of course one case of that layering and complexifying via intermediating institutions that I noted above to be a confusion-sowing aspect of our present arrangements.[42] That is particularly true insofar as closed systems tend to integrate into and become subsystems of broader open loop systems over time.[43]

A stylized case of an open loop system would be one in which Jack pays Jill by in effect instructing his bank to pay Jill for him, whereupon his bank debits his account and pays the payment system administrator, which then pays Jill's bank, which then credits Jill's account. Most payment service providers with which most of us are familiar operate on some version of this model.[44] Credit and debit card payment systems, wire transfer systems, and even check image transfer systems are cases in point.[45] So is ACH—the Automated Clearing House Network—that has managed billions of payments for decades now.[46]

In a closed loop or P2P system, by contrast, payment takes the form of a payor instruction to the system administrator to credit the payee's account in the same system, which then occurs more or less simultaneously to the payor's account's being correspondingly debited within the system.[47] PayPal, Venmo, and Western Union are among the better-known payment service providers operating on this model in the U.S.[48]

While these systems are, by definition, "closed" relative to their immediate users, it is noteworthy that they typically also participate in wider "open" payments infrastructures in order to fund the interparty payments that they conduct.[49] Something like this happens, for example, when one uses a bank card to make her PayPal payment to a payee.[50] The open system/closed system distinction is thus a fuzzy or relative one even under present arrangements, and becomes ever fuzzier as closed systems integrate themselves into, and thus become subsystems of, broader open loop systems. This in turn tends to produce further payment system layering and associated money hierarchies of the kinds noted above—the kinds that then force a baroque system of distinct bodies of creditor/debtor, negotiable instrument, commercial, and banking law.[51]

The open/closed distinction can be salient in some circumstances under current arrangements notwithstanding its porousness, however, inasmuch as each sometimes offers distinct advantages and disadvantages.[52] For these apparent advantages and disadvantages positively and negatively motivate, respectively, much that now goes by the name of "innovation" in payment technologies.

One advantage of an open loop system, for example, is said to be that it can quickly be made to operate on a large scale because the intermediaries that act on behalf of payors and payees—typically commercial banks—already have large customer bases.[53] Even a small number of such institutions' joining a network accordingly brings millions of exploitable payor/payees into the payment system "value chain."[54]

The corresponding disadvantage of the open system is that operating rules must be established and then maintained across multiple layers of interfacing institutions, which then represent multiple "near-moneys" and associated sites of potential error and associated legal liability in the event something goes wrong.[55] Such error can of course pose systemic dangers and even occasion temporary payment system shut down—which, thanks to money's always being constituted by a payment system, can be the functional equivalent of a liquidity crisis that morphs into a depression- or recession-causing "credit crunch" in the financial system.[56]

Closed loop systems, by contrast to open systems, are comparatively simpler and present flatter money hierarchies and fewer sites of potential glitch and associated system-wide crash and liability.[57] Their corresponding disadvantage is that they ordinarily take more time and effort to scale-up than do open systems, because, unlike the latter, they do not always build upon already-large, ready-made client bases.[58]

This is one of the putative advantages that Facebook and other large firms and social media platforms tout in connection with proposals like Facebook's Libra. With nearly two and a half billion users worldwide, Facebook, in theory, could offer a closed loop system that boasts all the simplicity advantages of a closed loop while also enjoying the scaling advantages of an open loop system.[59] The same goes for WeChat Pay and AliPay in China, which are preparing to do there—save in collaboration with China's central bank—what Facebook proposes to do here.[60]

This in turn invites a thought: what better payments system could there possibly be than one that is both maximally open and maximally closed—i.e., one that cuts out all intermediating layers while also including all possible payors and payees, all citizens, residents, and businesses? The answer, as I will next show, is that no system could be better. And so that is what I will propose for central banks' or finance ministries' liability ledgers and associated Democratic Digital Currencies.

As suggested above, the same capacities to bridge open and closed loops that render a Libra or AliPay attractive to some people also account for some of the attraction of blockchain and other distributed ledger technologies, along with associated cryptocurrencies to the same people. In effect, these technologies can be seen as offering the prospect of a payments infrastructure bearing both the intimacy, quasi-anonymity, clearing-simultaneity, and middleman-minimization advantages of a closed loop system, and the scale advantages of an open loop system.[61] These reasons drive many of the more reasonable, less silly, contributions we sometimes find in the literature on crypto, blockchain, and other distributed ledger technologies.[62] This too, then, invites a thought: what need would there be for these technologies was our payments system already both maximally open and maximally closed? The answer, as again I shall indicate below, is "undeniably some, but not as much as cryptopians claim."

As in the case of the token/account or object/claim distinction discussed above, then, here too the salience of a popular distinction and a whole literature still growing around it is entirely an artifact of the roles played by multiple private sector entities in constituting multiple "near money" layers in our current hybrid, public–private payments infrastructure. Were literally everybody to hold Citizen or Resident Wallets with the central bank or finance ministry in a form that employs Democratic Digital Currencies as a unit of account, as I propose, there would be no need to develop a hub and spoke structures linking up various accounts already held at various institutions, as privately offered open loop payment infrastructures do.[63]

Nor would there be any need painstakingly to build user bases—or to piggyback upon private sector social media user bases—as privately run closed systems must do.[64] We would already have the whole possible user base—ourselves, in our shared capacity as citizens of a democratic commercial republic—available for inclusion.[65]

In such case everyone would immediately be on one ledger—a sort of Consolidated Digital Citizens' and Residents' Ledger like that imagined above in this book's Prologue—and payments would simply be simultaneous creditings and debitings on that single ledger.[66] There would be little need to distribute, even if some advantage in distributing, a ledger as a means of indelibly mimicking centralized clearing among disparate peers.[67] For there simply would be traceable centralized clearing among all paying and paid citizens and approved residents, via a democratically owned and operated digital payments system and associated Democratic Digital Currency platform.[68] Blockchain's sole use then would be less as a money-platform than as a useful "smart contract" and linked-transaction file folder, as I will explain presently.[69]

In effect, then, many putative benefits—at any rate, non-criminal benefits—said to be offered by new cryptocurrencies and associated tech architectures will be immediately rendered superfluous under my proposal.[70] They will have no more use in the future than have nineteenth century bank-issued "wildcat" currencies now.[71] We will have moved on from fintech to what might be called "Ourtech"—or perhaps even better, just plain old "tech."[72]

The same goes for all options mentioned in the opening paragraph of this Part. The only salient benefits that these technologies will offer will be (a) the privacy-maintenance prospects they promise and (b) certain book-keeping virtues they afford in connection with contracting apart from payment-consummation. The latter benefits are of some relevance for present purposes—indeed I am developing uses for them in other contexts such as mortgage registration and chain-of-title tracking[73]—but not as much as cryptopians claim. The former, or privacy, benefits, for their part, are easy to bake into a Democratic Digital Currency and associated payments architecture with cryptography.[74] I turn, then, to do just that.

8.2 From Payments to Moneys: Technical Options for the Democratic Digital Currency

What, then, should a Democratic Digital Currency look like? How should payments be made and transactions clear? The answer might initially look surprisingly simple. But the surprise should not be long-lasting in light of the foregoing observations. For those observations lead directly to the conclusion that most decision points commonly said to be implicated by digital currency proposals need not actually be decided upon at all. They can be mooted the moment we opt for central-bank- or finance-ministry-administered digital Citizen and Resident Wallets, for they rest on distinctions that are mere artifacts of our not having yet instituted such a system of public accounts.

My answer to the "what will a Democratic Digital Currency look like" question, then, is that all can proceed much as it appears on the surface—or, in industry parlance, at "the back end"—already, save without intermediating payment processors, banks, or other financial institutions calling shots under the surface—that is, at "the front end." The central bank or finance ministry will simply debit and credit transacting parties' Citizen or Resident Wallets, just as the U.S. Fed, for example, now does with bank Reserve Accounts. Payment instructions for their part can be made to the central bank or finance ministry much as they are presently made to banks or to closed loop payment service firms like PayPal—namely, via phones, laptops, chip cards, strip cards, wire, etc.— in short, all of the above and all that might emerge in the future.[75]

In this connection, the central bank or finance ministry can supply payment cards to those who prefer plastic with strips or with chips to smart phones or other devices, and will post freely downloadable "Wallet apps" for use on electronic devices. We should also, I think, continue to make cash and coin available, at either or both ATMs and teller windows as noted above, at least for the time being. And these forms should be freely interchangeable with all digital forms just as they are now via check-cashing and ATM withdrawals. Perhaps one day paper currency, coin, and other old money-media will die out, but I see no need publicly to force the issue, and see compelling reasons not to do so.[76]

How about privacy? Well, as noted above it is easy to bake this in to any digital system in a manner that replicates or simulates what we do now with cash and bank-administered transaction accounts.[77] Under this regime, transactions in cash or by transfer, when for values below certain threshold amounts, enjoy specific privacy protections. Transactions in amounts exceeding those threshold amounts, by contrast, must be reported.[78]

There is no reason we cannot import this regime into the system of Citizen and Resident Wallets, either with (a) cryptographic protections provided to transactions valued at amounts lower than the same thresholds, prepaid value cards whose amounts can be withdrawn at will, or (c) both (a) and (b). Digital Currency Units can thereby be made to constitute cryptographic currency or coin up to stipulated threshold amounts in connection with specific transactions, and something more like presently traceable bank money beyond those thresholds.[79]

Violations of such protections by public instrumentalities including the central bank or finance ministry itself, in turn, would of course constitute actionable violations of constitutional (in the U.S., for example, Fourth Amendment) rights.[80] And the regime will at all events always be, as it is now and as central banking systems more generally are in democratic republics, democratically determined—by statute.[81] This is far better for privacy than would be any system driven by the profit- or rent-seeking motives that could move privately owned banks and other financial institutions, not to mention Facebook and other social media firms whose business model just is data-"harvest" and -sale, to violate user privacy.[82]

As for blockchain and other distributed ledger technologies, these will be contingently useful even though not strictly necessary in a central-bank- or finance-ministry-administered Democratic Digital Currency payments system. One virtue of blockchain technology, for example, is the ease with which it enables associated transaction records to be in effect "stapled" together for purposes of tracking complex sets of transactions as clusters or wholes. Letter of credit transactions are obvious cases in point, as would be mortgage lending and transfer transactions and other species of negotiable instrument transaction.[83] In essence, any transaction type involving multiple component actions with documents associated with each component—e.g., the multiple documents used in documentary letter of credit transactions, or the documents linked in a chain-of-title—will of course lend themselves to tracking by suggestively named blockchain technology.[84]

Insofar as payments within such transaction clusters are made across central bank or finance ministry digital Citizen or Resident Wallets, it would presumably become convenient at some point for the central bank or finance ministry to make use of blockchain technology in effecting the relevant transactions.[85] It would be of obvious benefit to the parties, and probably also to the central bank or finance ministry itself. Hence one can deem it desirable. It would not be essential, however, hence the decision whether to do it will amount to a garden-variety cost–benefit decision we can leave to the central bank or finance ministry, or to the legislature.[86]

Similar remarks hold for all forms of distributed ledger technology.[87] On the one hand it will not be necessary to my proposal insofar as the tracking benefits that typically recommend it are already had on a centralized ledger such as the liability side of the central bank's balance sheet will be.[88] On the other hand, it offers other benefits that the central bank, finance ministry, or legislature might deem worth offering when upgrading our payments systems with the new features I am here proposing, particularly as they become less costly. At the very least, their replicability and associated indelibility properties lend them good back-up or potential that can afford payment system resilience once the new Democratic Digital Currency regime is in place.

And that is essentially it. There need be no further complication or layering. Nor, therefore, need there be any more "hierarchy" of moneys and "near moneys" associated with discrete privately managed subsystems of the full public payments system. There will simply be one payment system, run on the liability side of the central bank's or the finance ministry's balance sheet, and one associated digital payments platform and associated currency. And both will be democratically sovereign and citizen-owned.

Diagrammatically, then, the system I envisage is as depicted in Fig. 7 in Chapter 6 or Fig. 8.1 immediately below. Payment from any A to any B will take the form of a card or mobile device or other such instruction to the central bank or finance ministry Master Account administrator, which will then simultaneously debit A's and credit B's Citizen or Resident Wallet. Any person C, moreover, will be able to convert dollars she holds in some form

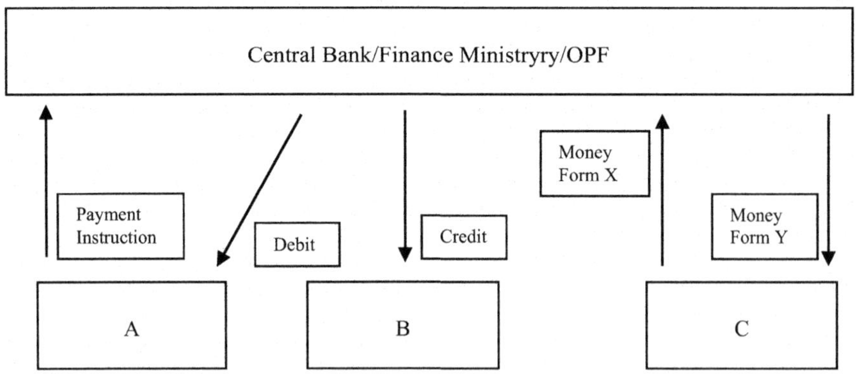

Fig. 8.1 Central-bank- or finance-ministry-administered democratic digital currency payments system

X—e.g., digital cash—into dollars she wishes to hold in some other form Y—e.g., paper notes or metallic coins.

How does this compare to what other jurisdictions are doing? As noted earlier, many central banks and monetary authorities worldwide—nearly twenty at this point—are now considering the adoption of some form of digital fiat currency.[89] News of Facebook's Libra proposal, moreover, appears since late 2019 to have instigated some acceleration along these lines.[90] Some central banks at present are merely studying the prospect of issuing digital currencies, others are actively conducting limited experiments with a view to determining in advance what opportunities to exploit and what pitfalls to avoid before actually instituting anything, and a few are now actively doing such instituting.[91] The farthest along at this point is Sweden's Riksbank, and I think it is no accident that the Swedish plan also is the one that most closely resembles my own.[92]

Plans now being actively considered or vetted fall into two broad categories, which I will call "citizen-benefitting" (or "retail") and "bank-benefitting" (or "wholesale").[93] The idea behind proposals being made and studies being conducted under the latter category is in essence simply to make improvements to existing payments infrastructures, not to upend or replace them.[94] The focus is on the wholesale central bank to private bank transfers and wholesale intra-bank transfers among private sector banking institutions themselves.[95] And the thought is that cryptographic distributed ledger technology might make safer, faster, and more cost-efficient real time gross settlement of large batches of payments possible.[96]

Central banks exploring this model are accordingly thinking simply in terms of incremental "system-upgrading" rather than far-reaching systemic transformation.[97] Prominent among central banks going this route thus far are those of Brazil, Canada, the Eurozone, India, Japan, Singapore, South Africa, and Thailand.[98] The consensus concerning the results of CBDC experiments conducted to date in these jurisdictions seems to be that distributed ledger technology does offer promise along the desired lines just enumerated, but that it is not quite ready for prime time yet.[99] Presumably the technology will grow more cost-effective in time, and thus we might well see wholesale CBDCs being adopted in some of the enumerated jurisdictions before long.[100] This prospect is not altogether interesting in connection with what prompts my proposal, however—apart, perhaps, from the system interoperability benefits it might ultimately afford people with central bank or finance ministry Citizen or Resident Wallets who wish to transact abroad.

More interesting are plans and proposals of the first category I mentioned—citizen-benefitting CBDC. These plans and proposals fall into two sub-categories, one of them well-suited to countries that already have well-developed payments infrastructures, the other well-suited to countries with less well-developed such infrastructures. The idea in the latter case is for the central bank or monetary authority simply to issue digital tokens on a distributed ledger platform instead of paper currencies and metallic coins.[101] These then could be held in and paid out of digital wallets. The central bank would not necessarily hand out or manage the wallets, but it would replace physical cash with digital cash that can interface with such wallets.[102]

The prompting considerations behind these plans and proposals seem to be to avoid having (a) to build extensive payments infrastructures from scratch, (b) to incur the printing and minting expenses that non-digital cash issuance occasions, and (c) to deal with the untraceable illicit financial flows that non-digital cash can enable.[103] Countries whose central banks are either implementing, experimenting with, or considering this model include China, Ecuador, Lithuania, the Marshall Islands, Senegal, Tunisia, Uruguay, and Venezuela.[104]

The other subcategory of citizen-benefitting CBDC now being implemented or considered makes use of already well-developed payments system capacity, but has the central bank opening and administering accounts like Citizen and Resident Wallets in which a digital rendition of the existing currency serves as the unit of account.[105] This is Phase 2 of the e-Krona project, now under study by the Riksbank of Sweden and its counterparts in Denmark and Norway.[106] Phase 1, which is further along, is more limited, resembling the pilot plans mentioned above underway in China, Ecuador, Lithuania, and several other jurisdictions.[107]

The prompting considerations behind e-Krona are essentially two.[108] The first is that Sweden has gone largely cashless by now, with many payees no longer accepting paper notes or metal coins.[109] The Riksbank is accordingly worried that system failure on the part of privately run e-payment services could bring down the Swedish financial system and broader economy.[110] A digital form of sovereign banknote is accordingly needed.[111] This is what prompts e-Krona Phase 1.[112]

The considerations prompting e-Krona Phase 2 are in sync with my own, though the Riksbank is less un-ambivalently committed to acting upon them than I am.[113] They include interest in a more inclusive electronic payments infrastructure that will facilitate much more effective monetary policy transmission.[114] Sweden plans also to enable at least some degree of anonymity as I have recommended above, by issuing e-Krona in the form of prepaid cards limited in value even after opening Riksbank accounts to the citizenry if such they do.[115] Phase 2 of the e-Krona has just moved, since the start of 2020, into a pilot program now operational "on the ground."[116]

At present, the e-Krona project eschews reliance on DLT, presumably because (a) the technology underlying the Swedish payments infrastructure is already apparently safe, fast, and cost-efficient, and (b) DLT is itself still developing along those lines, as noted above in connection with the first category of CBDC experiments that I noted.[117] Presumably the time will come when DLT proves itself worthy of deployment in a comprehensive payments system upgrade.[118] Fortunately in light of present purposes, however, Sweden and possibly Norway might have in place something like what I am proposing even before that, thereby affording a live experiment from which to learn by the time my proposal draws sufficient attention to invite movement.[119] Even before that, the State of New York, in which legislation I've drafted to institute what I call an "Inclusive Value Ledger" is now before the State Assembly and Senate, might offer our republic a live pilot in our largest metropolitan area and indeed the world's very financial center.[120]

Notes

1. *Id.* (concluding that "the speed, reliability, and tractability of distributed-ledger- tracked credits and debits" will help enable banking services directly between citizens and the Fed).
2. *See* Tommaso Mancini-Griffoli et al., Int'l Monetary Fund, Casting Light on Central Bank Digital Currency 27 (2018) (providing examples of nations "actively exploring" the use of centralized or decentralized digital currencies).
3. Conference Report, Eur. Cent. Bank-Bank of Eng., *Payments and Monetary and Fin. Stability* (November 12–13, 2007), https://www.ecb.europa.eu/pub/pdf/other/paymentsmonetaryfinancialstability200801en.pdf [https://perma.cc/M65N-27GK] ("In the most basic terms, the central bank seeks to ensure the ongoing ability of payment systems to support the monetary economy and, by extension, the desired path of economic growth.").
4. Chris Matthews, *Why the Coming Recession Could Force the Federal Reserve to Swap Greenbacks for Digital Dollars*, MarketWatch (September 21, 2019), https://www.marketwatch.com/story/why-the-coming-recession-could-force-the-federal-reserve-to-swap-greenbacks-for-digital-dollars-2019-09-06/print [https://perma.cc/GY33-JHJ8] ("'The debate isn't about whether we need [a digital currency],' Michael Bordo, an economist at Rutgers University and a fellow at the Hoover Institution, the public-policy think tank at Stanford University, told MarketWatch. 'It's about how you do it.'").

5. *See* Tobias Adrian & Tommaso Mancini-Griffoli, Int'l Monetary Fund, The Rise of Digital Money 4 (2019) (commenting that "The key distinguishing feature of [bank] money is that its redemption guarantee is backstopped by the government.").
6. *See id.* (distinguishing electronic money from bank money in that the former's "redemption guarantees are not backstopped by governments. They merely rest on prudent management and legal protection of assets available for redemption.").
7. *See id.* at 3 (providing a diagram of various types of digital currency).
8. We can talk for some purposes, for example, about money's functions as a 'unit of account,' 'medium of exchange,' and 'store of value,' as economists do, in abstraction from the mechanical details of any particular payments system, leaving 'exchange' as it figures into the second of those features unelaborated. This can then lead us to assume, mistakenly, that the mechanics of particular payments systems do not matter for purposes of theoretical discussions of money, even though such systems are always essential backdrops to and even constitutive of moneys. *See Rousseauvian Money, supra* note 67, at 44–46 (stating that while it has been argued that coins once held value outside of debt and obligations, they were in fact always intertwined); Robert C. Hockett, *Money's Constitutive Contexts* (2018) (working paper, on file with the authors) [hereinafter, *Money's Constitutive Contexts*].
9. *See Rousseauvian Money, supra* note 3, at 39 ("You temporarily transform narrowly accepted notes into widely accepted note, horizontal money into vertical money, private money into public money.").
10. *See Rousseauvian Money, supra* note 3, at 37–38 lamenting confusion about private and public capital).
11. *See Rousseauvian Money, supra* note 3, at 14 ("[O]ur money is just the general form of our shared mode of organizing distributive and hence productive activity in any 'decentralized exchange economy' such as our own.").
12. *See id.* at 17 ("[M]oney's rootedness in normativity, obligation, accountability and associated accounting, but also its elaboration into the notions of credit, asset, and liability that populate the familiar legal and financial 'universe'—or, if you prefer, 'environment' or 'game reserve.").
13. *See id.* (explaining that the system of accounting-credits and debits, depends on reciprocal arrangements).
14. *Id.* at 37–38 (illustrating how financial institutions can be used to give credit in the same way that private individuals can give credit to other individuals).
15. *See generally*, David S. Bieri, *Chapter 16: Regulatory Space and the Flow of Funds Across the Hierarchy of Money*, *in* Handbook of The Geographies of Money and Finance 377, 382 (Ron Martin & Jane Pollard eds., 2017) ("[T]he Löschian system as a spatial monetary order where money and credit are created by different financial institutions at separate levels of the hierarchy.").

16. *See* Jamie Toplin, *The Payments Industry Ecosystem: The trend towards digital payments and key players moving markets*, Bus. Insider (December 21, 2018 11:44 AM), https://www.businessinsider.com/payments-ecosystem-report (illustrating the corporate players in a digital payment value chain, as well as the hierarchy and layering effects present in the chain).
17. This is a term of art in the literature. *See, e.g.*, *Exploring the Payments System Value Chain,* First Data 1, 2–3 (2009), https://www.firstdata.com/downloads/thought-leadership/fd_insight_payments-value-chain_wp.pdf [https://perma.cc/2HR6-W224] (explaining the changes to the payments value chain post financial crisis); *Payments Value Chain*, Metasection (last visited April 2018), https://www.metasection.com/payments-value-chain/ [https://perma.cc/BV42-9XA5] (introducing what a payments value chain is and breaking down the hierarchy of said chain); Toplin, *supra* note 431 (illustrates the corporate players in a digital payment value chain, as well as the hierarchy and layering effects present in the chain).
18. *See Money's Past*, *supra* note 17, at 1 (arguing that once central banks start to upgrade their payment systems and the Fed moves towards a crypto currency, banking will become centralized monetary policy will become simplified).
19. *See Money's Past*, *supra* note 17, at 8 (arguing that once the distinctions between public and private distinctions are discarded, then money can be centralized and digitalized in the modern age).
20. *See* Ben S.C. Fung & Hanna Halaburda, *Central Bank Digital Currencies: A Framework for Assessing Why and How*, Bank of Canada, 1, 12 (Novomber, 2016), https://ssrn.com/abstract=2994052 (discussing the positives and negatives in implementing a central bank digital currency); Dong He, *Monetary Policy in the Digital Age: Crypto assets may one day reduce demand for central bank money*, Int'l Monetary Fund, 13, 15 (June, 2018), https://www.imf.org/external/pubs/ft/fandd/2018/06/pdf/fd0618.pdf [https://perma.cc/49NP-2JAK] (exploring the ramifications of not issuing a central bank digital currency).
21. Dan Lohrmann, *"Could a New Wave of Cryptocurrencies Be on the Horizon?"*, Government Technology (May 26, 2019), https://www.govtech.com/blogs/lohrmann-on-cybersecurity/is-a-new-wave-of-cryptocurrencies-coming-soon.html [https://perma.cc/5QJY-F35V] (showing the wide number of cryptocurrencies already in existence, as well as the many more that are planned and will be coming).
22. *See Money's Past*, *supra* note 17, at 1 (arguing that once central banks start to upgrade their payment systems and the Fed moves towards a crypto currency, banking will become centralized monetary policy will become simplified from the complex hierarchical layers that came before).
23. *See* Adrian & Mancini-Griffoli, *supra* note 417, at 2 ("The first attribute that defines a means of payment is type-either a claim or an object."); Open

Loop Card, *supra* note 241 ("An open loop card is a general-purpose charge card that can be used anywhere that brand of card is accepted.").

24. *See, e.g.*, Bank for Int'l Settlements, Comm. On Payments and Mkt. Infrastructures & Mkts. Comm., CENTRAL BANK DIGITAL CURRENCIES 4 (March 2018) ("Money is typically based on one of two basic technologies: *tokens of stored value* or *accounts*... Cash and many digital currencies are token-based, whereas balances in reserve accounts and most forms of commercial bank money are account-based."); *see also, e.g.*, ADRIAN & MANCINI-GRIFFOLI, *supra* 417, at 2 ("The first attribute that defines a means of payment is *type*—either a claim or an object."). Other work employs similar terminology in drawing what appears to be the same attempted distinction.
25. *See* BANK FOR INT'L SETTLEMENTS, *supra* note 230, at 6 (discussing the direct and indirect nature of transfer mechanisms where "[t]he transfer of cash is conducted on a peer- to-peer basis, while central bank deposits are transferred through the central bank, which acts as an intermediary").
26. *See* ADRIAN & MANCINI-GRIFFOLI, *supra* note 417, at 3 (discussing that central bank digital currency "could protect users' data from third parties" but unlike cash, it "would likely not be anonymous").
27. *See generally* BANK FOR INT'L SETTLEMENTS, *supra* note 441, at 9 (discussing legal considerations where some countries may not "have the authority to issue digital currencies" and "issuance may require legislative changes").
28. *See, e.g.*, Federal Deposit Ins. Corp. vs. Philadelphia Gear Corp., 476 U.S. 426 (1986) (involving a failed bank in the midst of a standby letter of credit transaction).
29. *See generally, e.g.*, Dodd-Frank Wall Street Reform and Consumer Protection Act of 2010, Pub. L. No. 111-203, 124 Stat. 1376 (stating pertinent law relating to the Durbin Amendment on debit card issuers); Credit Card Accountability Responsibility and Disclosure Act of 2009, Pub. L. No. 111-24, 123 Stat. 1734 (establishing "fair and transparent practices relating to the extension of credit under an open end consumer credit plan"); Check Clearing for the 21st Century Act of 2003, Pub. L. 108-100, 117 Stat. 1178; 12 C.F.R. § 210 (2017) ("Collection of Checks and Other Items by Federal Reserve Banks and Funds Transfers Through Fedwire (Regulation J)."); 12 C.F.R. § 229 (2018) ("Availability of Funds and Collection of Checks (Regulation CC)."); 12 C.F.R. § 235 (2012) ("Debit Card Interchange Fees and Routing (Regulation 3)."); 12 C.F.R. § 1005 (2017) ("Electronic Fund Transfers (Regulation E)."); U.C.C. §§ 3-101–3-605 (NAT'L CONF. OF COMM'RS on UNIFORM STATE LAWS 2009–2010) (stating pertinent law on negotiable instruments); U.C.C. §§ 4-101–4-504 (NAT'L CONF. OF COMM'RS on UNIFORM STATE LAWS 2009–2010) (stating pertinent law on bank deposits and collections); U.C.C.§§ 4A-101–4A-507 (NAT'L CONF. OF COMM'RS on UNIFORM STATE LAWS

2009–2010) (stating pertinent law on funds transfers). At the time of this writing, members of Congress recently proposed another piece of payment system legislation that would be rendered unnecessary by my proposal. *See* H.R. 3951, 116th Cong. (2019) ("Payments Modernization Act of 2019."); *see also* S. 2243, 116th Cong. (2019) ("Payments Modernization Act of 2019.").

30. *See, e.g., Republican Home-Owning*, *supra* note 339, at 2 ("[Systemically important prices and indices] render financial markets vulnerable to many of the same systemic dangers as do [systemically important financial institutions]"). Also Robert Hockett, *To Reverse Inflation Now and Prevent It Tomorrow, the Fed Must Short-Sell Commodities*, FORBES, January 30, 2022, at https://www.forbes.com/sites/rhockett/2022/01/30/to-reverse-inflation-today-and-prevent-it-tomorrow-the-fed-should-short-sell-commodities-now-as-we-speed-up-production-for-later/?sh=6ff03e8b5e49; and Robert Hockett, *Fine-Tuning Monetary Easing, Part 2: The Fed's New Chicago Trading Capacity*, FORBES, January 31, 2022, at https://www.forbes.com/sites/rhockett/2022/01/31/fine-tuning-monetary-easing-part-2-the-feds-new-chicago-trading-capacity/?sh=66624b76318d.
31. *See* BANK FOR INT'L SETTLEMENTS, *supra* note 230, at 17 (demonstrating the preferability of cash-like properties by arguing that "the more anonymous the instrument and the more decentralized the transfer mechanism was, the greater the opportunity for cross-border activity").
32. *See id.* at 4–6 (highlighting the key distinctions between token-based money and account-based money where token-based benefits from anonymity and peer-to-peer transfers while account-based does not).
33. *See, e.g.*, Toplin, *supra* note 432 (listing the various private institutions that play a variety of roles including issuers, card networks, and processors in the "payments ecosystem").
34. *See Money's Past*, *supra* note 17, at 3 (discussing generally what "sovereign-issued currency looks likewhen paid out" by banks).
35. *See generally*, Mauro Conti et al., *A Survey on Security and Privacy Issues of Bitcoin*, 20 IEEE COMM. SURV. & TUTORIALS 3416 (2018) (discussing Bitcoin and cryptocurrency security risks and possible solutions).
36. *See* Daniel DiMase et al., *Systems Engineering Framework for Cyber Physical Security and Resilience*, 35 ENV'T SYS. AND DECISIONS 291 (2015) (discussing cyber physical systems security and risk management).
37. *See id.* at 295 (stating that track and trace mechanisms provide "the internal and network-based process and tools for determining the current and past locations and logistics security controls" to perform their required duties).
38. *See, e.g., id.* at 298–298 (demonstrating that safeguards such as "resilience" must be "built into the framework").
39. *See, e.g.*, Troy Segal, *Open Loop Card*, INVESTOPEDIA, (July 16, 2019), https://www.investopedia.com/terms/o/open-loop-card.asp [https://perma.cc/RQT5-QDFL] (defining open loop systems); Julia Kagan, *Closed*

Loop Card, Investopedia, (April 11, 2019), https://www.investopedia.com/closed-loop-card-definition-4683996 [https://perma.cc/UN76-HGS6] (defining closed loop systems); *Finance without Financiers*, *supra* note 1 (discussing institutional integration of banking and capital markets).

40. Segal, *supra* note 457 (describing how "open loop" systems are for general use; cards may be used at a wide variety of places—credit cards and debits are good examples of "open loop").
41. Kagan, *supra* note 457 (describing "closed loop" systems, such as store-specific gift cards).
42. *Money's Constitutive Contexts*, *supra* note 421.
43. As discussed immediately below. *See generally Republican Home-Owning*, *supra* note 339 (developing a general account of systemically important prices and indices, and the market vulnerabilities to which they can give rise); *National Investment Authority*, *supra* note 4 (offering an account of "collective goods" as solutions to collection action problems in decentralized markets). Segal, *supra*, note 457 (describing commonly-used open loop cards from payment service providers like credit card companies, banks, and credit card unions).
44. Segal, *supra* note 457 ("Open loop cards can take a variety of forms… credit cards, debit cards…."); Fed. Res. Bd., Report to the Congress on the Use of the Ach System and Other Payment Mechanisms for Remittance Transfers to Foreign Countries (March 2013) ("Less commonly, consumers… use 'open-loop' payment systems such as wire-transfer systems, correspondent banking channels, and ACH networks.").
45. Fed. Res. Bd., *supra* note 463 (clarifying that ACH networks are a type of open loop system).
46. Kagan, *supra* note 457 (describing how closed loop systems allow card-holders (the payor) to purchase from one specific vendor (the payee)).
47. Brett King, *U.S.A—World's Largest Closed Loop Payment Systems?* Bank Innovation (October 1, 2013) https://bankinnovation.net/allposts/biz-lines/payments/usa-worlds-largest-closed-loop-payments-system/ [https://perma.cc/BZ8W-DPZJ] (discussing the presence of large closed loop payment systems, including Venmo and PayPal, in the United States.).
48. Kagan, *supra* note 457 (providing a brief overview of closed loop system payment infrastructures).
49. *Id*. (discussing card processing in closed loop systems).
50. *See generally Open Labor*, *supra* note 29 (offering a case for institutionalizing continuous public operations in labor markets analogous to continuous Fed operations in money markets); *How to Make QE More Helpful*, *supra* note 329 (suggesting innovations to monetary policy).
51. *See* Dan Kosir, Open vs. Closed Loop Mobile Payments, Clearbridge Mobile (May 21, 2014), https://clearbridgemobile.com/open-vs-closed-loop-mobile-payments/ [https://perma.cc/V842-MEHB] (laying out the

advantages and disadvantages of closed and open loop systems as well as some emerging hybrid systems).

52. Segal, *supra* note 457 (listing several large financial institutions, including banks and credit card companies that utilize open loop systems).
53. American Express Co., 2018 Annual Report i (2018) ("As our 2018 results show, we... added 12 million new Card Members").
54. *See generally*, *Finance without Financiers*, *supra* note 1 (discussing banking institutions' interactions with the public and banking liabilities).
55. Probably still the most infamous case in point is the brief global scare brought on by Bankhaus Herstatt in 1974—a scare which both occasioned the establishment of the Basel Committee so beloved by finance regulators and provided a name to a specific form of systemic risk routinely now noted to afflict financial markets: 'Herstatt Risk.' Opinion, *The Long Dark Shadow of Herstatt,* ECONOMIST, April 14, 2001, at 70–71 (discussing a new financial institution aimed at reducing the risk of a crisis in foreign-exchange payments post-Herstatt); Julia Kagan, *Settlement Risk*, Investopedia (January 9 2018), https://www.investopedia.com/terms/s/settlementrisk.asp [https://perma.cc/9CZV-J9QX] (describing settlement risk, also called "Herstatt Risk").
56. *See* Kagan, *supra* note 457; *see also* Segal, *supra* note 457 (juxtaposing the closed loop system with the open loop system).
57. *Id*. (discussing a specific disadvantage of a closed loop system that an open loop system does not have).
58. *See More Pisces Than Libra*, *supra* note 377 (arguing that because of Facebook's large user base they can offer a closed loop system, therefore precluding an issue of scaling).
59. *Id*. (stating that similarly to Facebook, WeChat and Alipay can offer a closed loop system because of their large user base).
60. *See* Kosir, *supra* note 470 (laying out the advantages and disadvantages of closed and open loop systems as well as some emerging hybrid systems).
61. *See id.* (discussing benefits of hybrid systems).
62. *See Money's Past*, *supra* note 3, at 10 (arguing that a Citizen Account will centralize banking and make it more efficient).
63. *See More Pisces Than Libra*, *supra* note 377 (juxtaposing the Citizen Account approach with the approach of social media giants like Facebook who rely on their user bases).
64. *Id.* (arguing that a user base would already be pre-built if a Citizen Account proposal was created because everyone would be on a "Citizens' Ledger").
65. *See Money's Past*, *supra* note 17, at 10 (predicting that the Fed will begin administering a Distributed Ledger Technology to more efficiently track transactions).
66. *Id.* (describing the benefits of a centralized distributed ledger).
67. *Id*. (describing the benefits of a centralized distributed ledger).

68. *Id.* (suggesting that blockchain technology's primary use would be to track transactions).
69. *See More Pisces Than Libra, supra* note 377 (noting that if Facebook makes the Libra "regulatorily tolerable" then it will result in the Libra being monetarily superfluous).
70. *See Money's Past, supra* note 17, at 10 (arguing that if the Fed adopts a digital dollar, the current cryptocurrencies would have no use).
71. *Id.* at 12 (arguing that even though technology is changing the way we use money, it will always be "our money" (the sovereign public's money) that is allowing these new technological changes; hence "ourtech").
72. *See, e.g.*, Robert C. Hockett & William Fry, T*HE* S*IMPLIFIED* M*ORTGAGE AND* R*ECORDED* T*ITLE* (SMART) A*CT OF 2019* 19-04 (Cornell Legal Studies Research Paper, Paper No. 19-04, 2018), https://papers.ssrn.com/sol3/papers.cfm?abstract_id=3298870 (providing an example of some of these uses in another context).
73. *See More Pisces Than Libra, supra* note 377 (analyzing privacy benefits of Facebook's Libra).
74. *See, e.g.*, Morgan Stanley, Payment Instructions, (last visited October 16, 2019) https://www.morganstanley.com/spc/amazon/docs/en/Payment_Instructions_Amazon.pdf [https://perma.cc/J65V-WR7J] (providing an example of payment instructions at Morgan Stanley).
75. I say this notwithstanding the warnings of Kenneth Rogoff, whose concerns are readily addressable by means that do not throw elderly people off of the payment technologies to which they are accustomed. *See generally* KENNETH ROGOFF, THE CURSE of CASH (2017). For more reasons not to dispense with contemporary cash forms too quickly, *see, e.g.*, Satyajit Das, *Think Twice about Going Cashless,* BLOOMBERG (May 21, 2017), https://www.bloomberg.com/opinion/articles/2017-05-21/world-should-think-twice- before-abolishing-cash.
76. *See More Pisces Than Libra, supra* note 377 (stating that digital currency utilizing distributive ledger technology affords consumers increased privacy).
77. Filing Obligations for Reports of Transactions in Currency, 31 C.F.R. § 1010.311 (2011) (requiring reporting of transactions over $10,000).
78. *Are Cryptocurrencies Anonymous?*, COINBASE (last visited Oct. 16, 2019), https://www.coinbase.com/learn/are-cryptocurrencies-anonymous [https://perma.cc/NQU3-T3X9] (stating that cryptocurrencies are generally traceable).
79. *See, e.g.*, Protection of Nonpublic Personal Information, 15 U.S.C. § 6801 (2012) (creating an obligation on financial institutions to protect the privacy and confidentiality of its customers).
80. *See, e.g., id.* (providing an example of a federal statute protecting against Fourth Amendment violations).
81. *See More Pisces Than Libra, supra* note 377 (describing major data breaches of personal data like that of Cambridge Analytica).

82. *See, e.g., Rousseauvian Money, supra* note 3, at 45 (providing an example of such mortgage-lending transactions).
83. *See* Sayuri Shirai, *Central Bank Digital Currency: Concepts and Trends*, VOX (March 6, 2019), https://voxeu.org/article/central-bank-digital-currency-concepts-and-trends [https://perma.cc/RRB7-8AAC] ("Blockchain is a type of distributed ledger where each transaction is verified using encryption keys and digital wallets; the numbers of the transactions are recorded on a new electronic distributed ledger, which is then connected through a chain (using hash functions) to previous, proven distributed ledgers using the proof-of-work process.").
84. As noted below, central bank experiments with DLT-based CBDCs thus far suggest that the technology is promising but not yet cost-effective. *See* Sayuri Shirai, *Central Bank Digital Currency: Concepts and Trends*, VOX, (March 6, 2019) https://voxeu.org/article/central-bank-digital-currency-concepts-and-trends [https://perma.cc/RRB7-8AAC] ("Most of the central banks concluded that their experiments successfully transferred digital tokens on a distributed ledger in real time and in reasonable volumes.").
85. *Id.* ("[N]o central banks have found strong advantages to issuing their own digital coins due to technical constraints.").
86. *Id.* ("The board of directors shall perform the duties usually appertaining to the office of directors of designated financial market utilities (as defined in 12 U.S.C § 5462[4]) and all such duties as are prescribed by law."); *see also* Simon Scorer, *Central Bank Digital Currency: DLT, or Not DLT? That is the Question*, Bank Underground (June 5, 2017), https://bankunderground.co.uk/2017/06/05/central-bank-digital-currency-dlt-or-not-dlt-that-is-the-question/ [https://perma.cc/49EX-2NAR] ("It's important for central banks to determine exactly what might motivate them to ever issue CBDC").
87. *See supra* Chapter 5 ("As early as the 1920s, foreign central bankers were noting how U.S. Fed open market operations had become the primary determinants, not only of the U.S., but also of the global money supply.").
88. *See, e.g.*, Mike Orcutt, *At Least 15 Central Banks Are Serious About Getting into Digital Currency*, Mit Tech. Rev. (December 15, 2018), https://www.technologyreview.com/s/612573/at-least-15-central-banks-are-serious-about- getting-into-digital-currency/ ("In fact, no fewer than 15 such central banks around the world are taking the idea seriously, and many others are at least exploring it, according to a recent report from the International Monetary Fund [IMF].").
89. *See, e.g.*, Ana Alexandre, *China's Central Bank Developing Own Digital Currency in Response to Libra*, Coin Telegraph (July 8, 2019), https://cointelegraph.com/news/chinas-central-bank-developing-own-digital-currency-in-response-to-libra [https://perma.cc/QEU2-KLCV] ("China's central bank is reportedly developing its own digital currency in response

to Facebook's Libra..."); Claire Jones, *Central Bank Plans to Create Digital Currencies Receive Backing*, FIN. TIMES (June 30, 2019), https://www.ft.com/content/428a0b20-99b0-11e9-9573-ee5cbb98ed36 ("Global central banks may have to issue their own digital currencies sooner than expected..."); Nicholas Megaw, *BIS Warns on Facebook Risk to Finance After Libra Plan Unveiled*, FIN. TIMES (June 23, 2019), https://www.ft.com/content/db37a29e-95a8-11e9-8cfb-30c211dcd229 ("The BIS, the central bank for central banks, said regulators worldwide may need to 'revamp' rules to deal with the structural changes being brought about by entrants that control 'key digital platforms' such as ecommerce sites and social networks.").

90. *See supra* notes 509–10.
91. *See* Gabriel Söderberg, *What is Money and What Type of Money Would an e-Krona Be?*, SVERIGES RIKSBANK ECON. REV. (2018) (discussing Sweden's central bank issued digital currencies and the e-krona).
92. A number of jurisdictions are still very much in "study and deliberation mode." These include the Bahamas, Curcao, the Czech Republic, the Eastern Caribbean Central Bank, Malaysia, Switzerland, Turkey, Ukraine, Uruguay, the UK, and the U.S., among others. *See infra* nn. 514, 518, 524 (summarizing the various states of different central banks concerning the institution of digital currency).
93. *See, e.g.*, Sayuri Shirai, *Central Bank Digital Currency: Concepts and Trends*, VOX (March 6, 2019), https://voxeu.org/article/central-bank-digital-currency-concepts-and-trends [https://perma.cc/B79M-DS5Z] ("This proposal is the most popular among central banks because of the potential to make existing wholesale financial systems faster, less expensive, and safer."); *see also* Michael Kumhof & Clare Noone, *Central Bank Digital Currencies—Design Principles and Balance Sheet Implications* 23 (Bank of England, Staff Working Paper No. 725, 2018) ("CBDC is therefore a substitute for bank deposits, with substitutability determined by relative functionality and convenience, and actual substitution determined by these in conjunction with relative returns.").
94. *See* Shirai, *supra* note 514 ("In contrast, reserve deposits are available only to designated financial institutions such as commercial banks (and are thus called 'wholesale central bank money'), and are used for managing the real-time interbank payments and settlements system. Wholesale central bank money is not necessarily available 24 h a day or 365 days a year, although central banks have been making efforts to improve systems to enable faster and more efficient transactions.").
95. *Id.* ("This proposal is the most popular among central banks because of the potential to make existing wholesale financial systems faster, less expensive, and safer.").

96. *See* Ashley Lannquist, *Central Banks and Distributed Ledger Technology: How are Central Banks Exploring Blockchain Today?*, World Econ. Forum (March 2019) (discussing central banks use of blockchain).
97. *Id.* ("Since 2016, experiments have been conducted or examined by the central banks of countries including Canada, Singapore, Japan, Brazil, South Africa, and Thailand, as well as the euro area."); *see also* Yves Mersch, Executive Board Member, European Central Bank, Fairwell Ceremony for Pentti Hakkarainen, Deputy Governor of Suomen Pankki—Finlands Bank (January 16, 2017) ("In some European countries, for instance in
98. Sweden and Denmark, electronic payments have started crowding out the use of cash."); Laura Shin, *Canada Has Been Experimenting with a Digital Fiat Currency Called CAD-COIN*, Forbes (June 16, 2016), https://www.forbes.com/sites/laurashin/2016/06/16/canada-has-been-experimenting-with-a-digital-fiat-currency-called-cad-coin/#7f84279046a4[https://perma.cc/9LPX-R6QF] ("A momentous development in digital currency was announced in a low-key way on Wednesday, at a Canadian payments conference."); Ministry of Finance, Government of India, *Medium Term Recommendations to Strengthen the Digital Payments Ecosystem* (2017), http://finance.du.ac.in/du-finance/uploads/pdf/Reports/watal_report271216.pdf [https://perma.cc/H4TV-2XQC] ("[Digital payments] offers an unprecedented opportunity to our people, most of whom live in rural India or are migrants in big cities.").
99. *See Exploring the Payments System Value Chain, supra* note 432, at 4 ("SEPA and other market pressures have opened the box on European payments with the result that the industry's value chain is being fundamentally changed.").
100. *See* Shirai, *supra* note 514 (discussing the CBDC trend).
101. *See* Toplin, *supra* note 432 ("As noncash payment volume accelerates, the power dynamics of the payments industry are shifting further in favor of digital and omnichannel providers.").
102. *See Payments Value Chain, supra* note 432 ("The payments value chain has become increasingly industrialised, with back office processes increasingly automated and centralised.").
103. Toplin, *supra* note 432 ("This is helping payments become seamless, allowing firms to boost adoption, build and strengthen relationships, offer more services, and increase usage. But payment ubiquity and invisibility also comes with challenges.").
104. *Shirai, supra* note 514 (explaining that this model benefits emerging economies "desire to take the lead in the fintech industry, to promote financial inclusion by accelerating the shift to a cashless society, and to reduce cash printing and handling costs"); *see also El BCU presentó un plan piloto para la emisión de billetes digitales,*

BANCO CENT. DEL URU. (November 3, 2017), https://www.bcu.gub.uy/Comunicaciones/Paginas/Billete_Digital_Piloto.aspx [https://perma.cc/PT6B-HWWL]; *Uruguayan Central Bank to Test Digital Currency*, AGENCIA EEE, (September 20, 2017) https://www.efe.com/efe/english/business/uruguayan-central-bank-to-test-digital-currency/50000265-3385232 (quoting the president of the Central Bank that digital currency "will be implemented in Uruguay").

105. *See, e.g.*, Cecilia Skingsley, Speech at FinTech Stockholm 2016, Should the Riksbank Issue e-Krona?, at 10 (November 16, 2016) ("[T]he Riksbank is not intending to abolish banknotes and coins, but is considering supplementing them with another service to the general public.").
106. *See, e.g., id.* at 9 (stating that the Riksbank plans to investigate the feasibility of digital currency in Sweden); Stefan Ingves, Governor of the Riksbank, Do We Need an E- Krona?, at 3 (December 8, 2017) (explaining that "Sweden and the other Nordic countries" are ahead of the trend toward technological solutions to the decline of cash use); Jon Nicolaisen, Deputy Governor, Speech at Nor. Acad. of Sci. and Letters, What Should the Future Form of Our Money Be?, at 11 (April 25, 2017) (addressing Norges Bank's future will involve electronic central bank money).
107. *See* Skingsley, *supra* note 525; *see also* SVERIGES RISKBANK, THE RIKSBANK'S E- KRONA PROJECT: REPORT 2 38 (2018) [hereinafter *Riksbank Report 2*] ("[T]he initial focus will be on an e-krona that constitutes a prepaid value (electronic money) without interest and with traceable transactions"); Sveriges Riksbank, *Special Issue on the e-Krona*, SVERIGES RIKSBANK ECON. REV. at 25 (2018) [hereinafter *Special Issue on the e-Krona*] (acknowledging that the Riksbank has "begun to investigate the possibility of introducing a digital form of the Krona").
108. *See Riksbank Report 2*, *supra* note 527, at 2 (stating that the decline of cash and the Riksbank's need to promote safety are two important issues behind the investigation into e- Krona).
109. *Id.* at 5 ("According to the Riksbank's survey from 2018, only 14 percent paid for their most recent purchase in cash. The corresponding figure for 2010 was 39%t").
110. *Id.* at 29 (discussing e-Krona's effect on financial stability in times of ease and distress).
111. *Id.* at 2–3 (explaining the ways e-Krona can contribute to the public welfare).
112. *Id.* (discussing the conditions that gave rise to the e-Krona).
113. *Id.* at 35 (stating that "technology need[s] to be further examined before the Riksbank can decide how a development project could be designed").
114. *See Riksbank Report 2*, *supra* note 527, at 3 (describing how a completely neutral digital infrastructure could affect efficiency and inclusiveness by increasing competition, reducing fees, and reaching those without access to payment instruments other than cash).

115. *Id.* at 16–17 (explaining that all e-Krona transactions will be traceable "with the exception of a prepaid e-krona card used as cash and handed over from one user to another," so long as the card is no more than EUR 250); *see also* Shirai, *supra* note 276 (describing the two proposed models for Riksbank's digital currency as "non-anonymous" and "traceable").
116. *See* Riksbank Announcement, "Riksbank to Test Technical Solution for the e- Krona," February 20, 2020, available at https://www.riksbank.se/en-gb/press-and-published/notices-and-press-releases/notices/2020/the-riksbank-to-test-technical-solution-for-the-e-krona/ (last visited March 10, 2020).
117. *See Riksbank Report 2*, *supra* note 527, at 34 (explaining that e-Krona must be designed flexibly so that it may be "integrated with other systems in the financial infrastructure" of Sweden); *see also* Shiari, *supra* note 276.
118. *See* Shiari, *supra* note 514 ("[Central banks] have not taken further steps towards implementation because the current technology is seen as not yet sufficiently advanced to cope with privacy protection issues.").
119. *See Riksbank Report 2*, *supra* note 527, at 8 ("The Riksbank and Nordic central banks have mainly been interested in a version [of CBDC] that is broadly available to the general public...").
120. *See, e.g.*, Jordana Rosenfeld, "New York is Proposing the Creation of a 'Public Venmo,'" *Vice*, January 7, 2020, available at https://www.vice.com/en_us/article/pked9v/new-york-is-proposing-the-creation-of-a-public-venmo (last visited March 7, 2020).

9

Digitized Citizen Ledger Finance: Cavils and Competitors

I noted in introducing this article that many proposals have been made in the wake of our hybrid finance franchise's failings in the lead-up to 2008 and thereafter.[1] I noted also that I expect some to object to or quibble with what I propose.[2] Here, I will briefly consider some of those other proposals along with anticipated objections to mine. I treat them roughly in the order in which I first referenced them in the Introduction.

One objection that I expect is that I have misidentified the culprit in our nation's no longer tenable finance franchise arrangement—that it is the public franchisor, not the private franchisees, whose role should be newly curtailed or eliminated. Some will follow Ron Paul in crying "end the Fed!"[3] Some will follow Murray Rothbard in crying "back to free banking!"[4] Others will follow Peter Schiff in crying "back to gold!," investing in the same while so crying.[5] And still others will follow John Taylor and sundry traditionalist European—especially Bundesbank— central bankers in crying "tie their hands!" —"rules, not discretion!"'[6]

These would amount less to objections to my proposal than to counter-proposals, and the discussion above in Chapter 3 reprises and references, makes clear why they are very bad ideas. A usable currency must be a stable currency—one that retains more or less constant value across jurisdictional, temporal, and geographical spans.[7] That in turn requires managed currency "elasticity," which in turn requires daily fine-tuning by a central bank or other monetary authority—a publicly instituted collective agent able

R. C. Hockett, *The Citizens' Ledger*,
https://doi.org/10.1007/978-3-030-99566-9_9

to address that system-wide collective action challenge with which all financial and money markets involving exchange, not just those in a democratic commercial republic like ours, are continually confronted.[8]

As Chapters 4 and 5 above indicated, it took the U.S. quite literally over a century to learn this, during which time it successively rejected, first, wildcat banknotes; second, "gold-backed" Greenbacks; and finally, "rules-based" monetary policy.[9] U.S. advocates of Fed-ending or Fed-binding proposals of this sort might never have learned this history, but the world's commercial republics are, happily, unlikely to forget it.[10] The problem with the U.S. Fed and other central banks is their *incomplete* citizen-ownership, not their citizen-ownership. Hence the advocacy here of what I am calling Citizen Ledger Finance and a Democratic Digital Currency.[11]

A second objection I expect works from the other side of the public/private divide, in effect crying, not "end [or limit] the Fed," but "end [or limit] banking." The idea here is that "ending" banking a la McMillan, "narrow banking" a la Cochrane, "limited purpose banking" a la Kotlikoff, "100% money" a la Fisher, or perhaps what I call "40% money" after Admati and Hellwig, would be preferable to the system of Citizen Ledger Finance that I here propose.[12]

This line of thinking, like "end the Fed" thinking, agrees that the fault in our republics' finance franchise arrangements stems from their hybridity, but in effect faults the franchisee side of the public/private divide more than the franchisor side.[13] It is the height of moral hazard, the argument in effect runs, to entrust profit-seeking private sector entities with the management of a public resource that is as systemically important as the monetized full faith and credit of the sovereign.[14] Advocates accordingly hold that simply removing the credit-generation authority from banks—or at least, say, some 40% of that authority—is the appropriate policy response.[15]

Banks would continue to manage accounts and offer payment services to depositors under these proposals, but would no longer operate as disseminators of monetized public full faith and credit by lending in excess of what has been antecedently deposited with them.[16] They would effectively become mutual funds, and regulation would accordingly *make* true the intermediated scarce private capital story that I have long argued, as noted above in Chapter 3, is *not* true.[17]

It should be clear from what I have argued both here and elsewhere that I do not think it necessary or desirable that private sector banks and other financial institutions continue to operate as the primary allocators of our republics' monetized full faith and credit. Both the digitized Citizen and Resident Wallet plan and the Democratic Digital Currency plans elaborated above, and the NIC and PSF proposals reprised above and detailed elsewhere, make plain what I think about that.[18] But simply ending private bank credit-generation, without simultaneously replacing it thoughtfully and pervasively with public credit-generation, would be as profoundly deflationary as "returning to gold" would be.[19] Before ending credit-generative private sector banking, then, we must put in place explicitly credit-generative public institutions and procedures. That is precisely what the Citizen Ledger Finance and its Democratic Digital Currency as elaborated above do.

The next set of proposals I referenced in introducing this book involve various forms of small-scale "public banking," understood as embracing either or both (a) deposit-taking and transaction-account-managing, and (b) retail credit-extending and -allocating.[20] As my remarks on "narrow banking" immediately above should make plain, I sympathize with many such proposals. Indeed, I am explicitly associated with and working on *several* of them.[21]

I do not, therefore, regard these as being in any fundamental tension with my proposals. I see them, rather, as proposed local or smaller scale complements to my more comprehensive and nationally applicable proposals—micro or half-complete counterparts, as it were, to my macro Wallet, Digital Dollar, NIC, and PSF plans. The "central banking for all" proposals of McMillan and Gruen in 2014, of Andolfatto and Niepelt in 2015, and of *The Economist* in 2018, for example, overlap with what I propose at least for one piece of the liability sides of central bank balance sheets.[22] So does the Swedish Riksbank's already well-underway e-Krona project discussed above.[23] The many "public bank," revived "postal bank," and "microfinance" proposals made over the last thirty years also aim to do something akin to what I would do with the Fed's or the Treasury's liability book, not to mention my earlier "Shoeboc Bank" started for homeless friends and "Occupy Bank" founded during the Wall Street "Occupation" of 2011, prompted as these all are by the value of greater financial inclusion.[24]

What these earlier proposals do not do, however, is engage seriously with the asset-side counterparts of their particular liability side recommendations.[25] Nor do most of them concern themselves with how to make use of, or even more generally what to do about, the rapidly unfolding revolution now underway in the realms of financial, commercial, and payments technology.[26] And that is because each of them seems to concern itself with but one or two perceived problems instead of the broader array of mutually reinforcing problems that afflict contemporary financial and macroeconomic policy thanks to our system of hybrid, public/private finance.[27]

That narrowness of focus need not be a bad thing—there is much to be said for addressing discrete challenges in discrete ways. I do not think it possible to deal *optimally* with any one of the problems discussed in this book, however, without dealing with all of them. For they are all in this case, as argued above, mutually reinforcing. And *whatever* one thinks of the comparative merits of piecemeal and comprehensive structural reform strategies, the important point for present purposes is that *these* proposals need not in any event be at crossed-purposes to mine. We can go "both/and" here instead of "either/or," and in consequence let a thousand flowers bloom.

Another objection that I anticipate would stem from a claim that there is something "Orwellian" or otherwise "dangerous" about what I propose here—that putting us all on one Consolidated Ledger denominated in Democratic Digital Currencies will render us vulnerable to system-wide tech failure or subject us to centralized scrutiny and thereby imperil our "freedom." Those who issue these warnings might also argue that the blemishes presently marring our finance franchise arrangements are better rectified simply through better regulation.[28] Cautious "incrementalists," wild-eyed crypto-anarchists, and any number of starry-eyed cryptopians will likely approve this response to my proposal, as will some older school self-styled libertarians, money-launderers, drug-dealers, terrorists, and other criminals.

The problem with the response, at least in its good faith guise, is that it is ill-informed both as to the present *sources* of systemic and Orwellian danger and, therefore, as to how that same danger is best addressed.[29] As for the source of the danger, the discussion above should make plain that our present patchwork payments system, which has developed ad hoc through the actions of profit-seeking private sector institutions, is itself vulnerable to glitches and associated panics at each node and connecting line segment in the "value chain."[30] Indeed it is more vulnerable than any unitary system without multiple layers and connecting nodes ever can be.

Moreover, as also noted above, it is easy to build indelibility into transaction records on the central bank or finance ministry balance sheet not only with backup computing power as is done now, but also with the new payments technologies I have just discussed.[31] And lest anyone doubt that our republics' central banks and finance ministries have this capacity, they need only look at the comprehensive flow-of-funds data the U.S. Fed and Treasury, for example, and their counterparts compile, process, and publicly report every quarter.[32] Or, they can look at how each of the six mega-banks that now dominate the U.S.'s hybrid financial system handle clearing and settlement of transactions among the literal scores of millions of citizens and counterparties who transact on their books every hour.[33]

As for Orwellian danger, the discussion above also makes plain that Orwellian intrusion and invasion of privacy—indeed, even illicit mining,

"harvesting," and selling of private financial and other data—right now does not emanate from our citizen-owned, public sector, republican institutions. It emanates from gargantuan elite-owned private sector monopoles and oligopolies.[34] The threat comes, that is, from the huge platform and social media firms—Amazon, Facebook, Google, and so on— that now harvest individual data they both use and sell on in an ever-greater commoditizing of our general public for private gain.[35] Moreover, as noted above, large private sector banking and other financial institutions are now actively partnering with these same platforms and social media firms, precisely in order to circumvent banking and finance-regulatory privacy laws and extract further value from all of us.[36]

Reclaiming commercial and financial access and public investment as republican citizen functions, as my plan aims to do, is accordingly to be understood as a measure aimed at *recovering and safeguarding* citizens' access, privacy, and critical public infrastructures, not undermining or ending them. We cannot take away what we have already given away. We can only reclaim it. This is, again, precisely what the project of Citizen Ledger Finance laid out here is meant to do.

These same observations carry over to the suggestion that "regulation's enough." Obviously, regulation *is not* enough. That was the thrust of Chapters 1 through 5 and my prior work cited there. Financial privacy regulation is precisely what banks entering fintech right now are attempting to arbitrage out of.[37] And public money-modulatory and credit-allocative regulation is precisely what banks that successfully rolled back Glass-Steagall and cognate ringfencing regulation, derivatives regulation, mortgage loan regulation, consumer financial protection regulation, and now even U.S. Dodd-Frank macroprudential regulation are always and everywhere seeking to evade—and paying legislators to help them evade.[38]

Of course, they will try likewise to roll back a system of digitized Citizen Ledger Finance too once it is in place. But two things should be remembered here. First, it is much harder to take away popular public institutions than it is to roll back regulations, as the popularity and longevity of Social Security, Medicare, Medicaid, public education, the National Parks and National Monuments and a host of other civic institutions even in the comparatively libertarian-oriented U.S. attests.[39] And second, my proposal amounts also, especially in the long run, to a massive downsizing of precisely those industries whose enormous rent revenues and gigantic, "too big to fail," self-hostage-holding capacity have enabled them to strong-arm our legislators and other public officials in the first place. They will not be able to do that next time, for the plan here is precisely to shrink and disarm them, in addition to rendering us no longer dependent upon them.

Notes

1. *See supra* nn. 5–8 (describing events that prompt a reconsideration of our current economic system).
2. *See supra* p. 9 (suggesting the existence of objections or alternatives to the proposed new system).
3. *See* Paul, *supra* note 7, at 5 (suggesting ending the Federal Reserve "would be the single greatest step we could take to restoring American prosperity and freedom…").
4. *See, e.g.*, MRRAY N. ROTHBARD, THE MYSTERY OF BANKING 11 (1st ed. 1983) (popularizing a 'right wing libertarian' read of the 'Austrian' tradition of monetary economics).
5. *See, e.g.*, PETER D. SCHIFF, CRASH PROOF: HOW TO PROFIT FROM THE COMING ECONOMIC COLLAPSE 210 (2007) (describing the Federal Reserves' abandonment of the international gold standard in 1971 as bringing the United States dollar "to the brink of collapse").
6. *See generally, e.g.*, JOHN B. TAYLOR, GETTING OFF TRACK: HOW GOVERNMENT ACTIONS and INTERVENTIONS CAUSED, PROLONGED, AND WORSENED THE FINANCIAL CRISIS (2009) (popularizing a view developed in the academic literature over the 1970s).
7. *See Rousseauvian Money*, *supra* note 3, at 51 (describing how currency is not money, rather "represents money" in jurisdictions that recognize such representation); *Money's Past*, *supra* note 3, at 9 ("Nothing whose value is unstable can function for long as bona fide 'money'").
8. *See Money's Past*, *supra* note 3, at 9 ("A money whose supply can be 'modulated'… is essential if we're to avoid needlessly disrupting either transaction activity, investment activity, or currency value").
9. *See Rousseauvian Money*, *supra* note 3, at 3 ("Money figures as something that 'doesn't grow on trees,' must be 'backed up' by gold… and is 'debased' by 'the government' itself when the latter resorts to 'mere printing' of 'mere fiat' money."); *Money's Past*, *supra* note 17, at 6 (explaining how Greenbacks eventually brought an end to 'wildcat' banknotes).
10. *See Rousseauvian Money*, *supra* note 3, at 9 (characterizing our polity as our "joint emanation… our 'internal' means of selecting our shared destinations, not an 'outward' imposition of radically separate destinies").
11. *See supra* Chapters 6–8.
12. The "100% Money" plan originates with the remarkably fertile mind of Irving Fisher. *See* IRVING FISHER, 100% MONEY AND THE PUBLIC DEBT,

8–9 (2009) (arguing for a "plan to put and keep a 100% cash Reserve behind all Demand Deposits."). Variants were subsequently advocated by several Chicago economists, whereupon it began to be called 'The Chicago Plan.' Since the 2008 crash, revivals have been attempted by Cochrane, Kotlikoff, and several others, including my friends Jonathan McMillan. *See, e.g.,* LAWRENCE KOTLIKOFF, JIMMY STEWART IS DEAD, 157 (2010) (advocating a system that would require depository institutions to "transfer all their checking accounts into cash mutual funds and use their reserves to provide cash to back these shares"); McMillan, *supra* note 21, at 145–46 (advocating an expansion of the definition of solvency to include only "real assets" to prevent "a daisy chain of balance sheets" where "the solvency of one balance sheet... depends on the solvency of balance sheets further up the chain"); John H. Cochrane, *Toward a Run-Free Financial* System, *in* ACROSS THE GREAT DIVIDE: NEW PERSPECTIVES ON THE FINANCIAL CRISIS 197, 198 (Martin N. Baily & John B. Taylor eds., 2014) ("In this vision, demand deposits, fixed-value money-market funds, or overnight debt must be backed entirely by short-term Treasuries."). By '40% Money,' I refer, tongue- in-cheek fashion, to my friends Anat Admati and Martin Hellwig's recently proposed 40% capital requirement. *See* ANAT ADMATI & MARTIN HELLWIG, THE BANKER'S NEW CLOTHES 181–82 (2013) (postulating that there is no reason "why banks should *not* have equity levels between 20 and 30 percent of their total assets").

13. *See, e.g.*, McMillan, *supra* note 21, at 8 ("The banking system turned into a dysfunctional public-private project."); KOTLIKOFF, *supra* note 550, at 52 ("[T]he critical takeaways... are that power is extremely concentrated at the very top in modern American financial companies, that decisions are being made as much on emotion and ego as careful business planning, that the folks at the top are so rich as to face no real financial loss for themselves or their families if they role [sic] the wrong dice for their companies, that board after board of directors did nothing to oversee the decisions of their ultimate paymasters, and that the correlation between performance and compensation was negative.").
14. *See, e.g.*, MCMILLAN, *supra* note 21, at 43 ("[W]ith government guarantees in place, depositors now that their money is safe no matter what. They have no incentive to step in if their bank takes excessive risks. Knowing this, banks indeed take excessive risks.").
15. *See, e.g.*, ADMATI & HELLWIG, *supra* note 550, at 181–82 (arguing banks should be subject to somewhere between 20–30% capital requirements); FISHER, *supra* note 550, at 8–9 ("[P]ut and keep a 100% cash Reserve behind all Demand Deposits.").
16. *See, e.g.*, KOTLIKOFF, *supra* note 550, at 156–58 (describing the functioning of banks under his scheme).

17. Further elaboration on this point *see Finance without Financiers, supra* note 15 (characterizing financial institutions in this scheme as "effectively variations on the mutual fund form").
18. *See generally Finance without Financiers, supra* note 1; *Money's Past, supra* note 17; *supra,* Chapter 6 (expressing skepticism about the current banking system's stewardship of the people's full faith and credit).
19. This is precisely why Keynes politely declined to sign on to the first-ever proposal along these lines, when invited by Fisher to do so in 1934. See KEYNES, *supra* note 246, at 125 (critiquing the Fisher conception of appreciation and interest).
20. *See, e.g.,* BUILDING INCLUSIVE FINANCIAL SYSTEMS, *supra* note 10, at 92–94, 113. (discussing the new paradigm of commercial banks entering the micro-finance space); PARZEN & KIESCHNICK, *supra* note 10, at 78–85 (discussing the deposit and credit services that banks should provide under her system).
21. *Cf. Pre-Liberal Autonomy, supra* note 10 (citing and critiquing the small-scale models).
22. *See* Andolfatto, *supra* note 21 (describing a system of digital federal currency); Niepelt, *supra* note 21 ("Letting the general public hold reserves at the central bank and use them for electronic payments would lower the risk of bank runs and strengthen financial stability."); MCMILLAN, *supra* note 21, at 10, 164–65 (describing the effects of a system without banking: "[t]o spend more money than it earns, the government will have to gain trust from potential lenders, that is, from its citizens").
23. Riksbank *Report 2, supra* note 527, at 8 (discussing an electronic digital money widely available to the public).
24. *See, e.g.,* BUILDING INCLUSIVE FINANCIAL SYSTEMS, *supra* note 10, at 178–81.("Financial development could contribute directly to poverty alleviation by easing credit constraints on the poor and indirectly by fostering economic growth that benefits the poor.").
25. *See* PUBLIC BANKS SOLUTION, *supra* note 10, at 352–360 (discussing the various different proposals).
26. *See, e.g.,* PARZEN & KIESCHNICK, *supra* note 10; FISHER, *supra* note 550 (though perhaps this is merely the result of technology outpacing scholarship).
27. *See, e.g.,* Niepelt, *supra* note 21 (focusing on eliminating both "the zero lower bound on nominal interest rates" and "anonymous transaction[s] that may obstruct the fight against crime, money laundering, tax evasion, and the like").
28. *See When is "Social Credit" Orwellian?, supra* note 393 (discussing the perils of a widespread social credit system that extends beyond the purely financial).
29. *Id.* (drawing attention to the distinction between an algorithmic valuation of purely financial metrics and one of social ilk).
30. *See* MetaSection, *supra* note 432 (diagraming the complicated flow of payments systems); First Data, *supra* note 432 (highlighting the rapid change

in the industry and proclivity for the industry players themselves to drive that change).

31. *See Money's Past*, *supra* note 17, at 10 (praising the "superior tracking ability afforded by [distributed ledger technology]").
32. At the time of this writing, the most recent is FED. RESERVE SYS., *Financial Accounts of the Unites States, Quarter 1* (June 6, 2022), https://www.federalreserve.gov/releases/z1/20190606/z1.pdf [https://perma.cc/H6YT-6K7S].
33. *See* Steve Schaefer, *Five Biggest U.S. Banks Control Nearly Half Industry's $15 Trillion In Assets*, FORBES (December 3, 2014), https://www.forbes.com/sites/steveschaefer/2014/12/03/five-biggest-banks-trillion-jpmorgan-citi-bankamerica/#459c8976b539 [https://perma.cc/MG9F-WKMY] (reporting that the five biggest banks control nearly half of the assets held by banks in the United States).
34. *Id.* (highlighting large tech platforms' unauthorized use of personal data).
35. *Id*. at 7 (describing how tech companies can gain access to private financial, information and use it to influence consumers into buying what they want to sell).
36. *See, e.g.*, Kristina Russo, *Regulatory Oversight Uncertain Amid Growing Fintech Partnerships with Banks*, American Express (last visited November 9, 2019), https://www.americanexpress.com/us/foreign-exchange/articles/bank-fintech-partnership-regulatory-void/ [https://perma.cc/42P9-LVG3] (discussing the lack of regulation surrounding fintech and the partnering of banks with fintech to take advantage of this).
37. *See Money's Past*, *supra* note 17, at 2 (describing how fintech and cryptocurrencies create privacy "paradises").
38. Katy Milani, *Latest assault on Dodd-Frank has bank lobbyists beaming*, THE HILL (March 5, 2019) https://thehill.com/opinion/finance/376749-latest-assault-on-dodd-frank-has-bank-lobbyists-beaming [https://perma.cc/8VAE-Q44U] (describing lobbying efforts by banks to weaken and remove Dodd Frank regulations).
39. *See* Matthew Sherman, *A Short History of Financial Deregulation in the United States*, CENTER FOR ECON. AND POLICY RESEARCH (2009), http://cepr.net/documents/publications/dereg-timeline-2009-07.pdf [https://perma.cc/FYR6-V8G7] (describing the history of financial deregulation over the last three decades); *Historical Background and Development of Social Security*, SOCIAL SECURITY ADMIN., https://www.ssa.gov/history/briefhistory3.html [https://perma.cc/QDT4-SJF3] (last visited October 16, 2019) (detailing the long history of Social Security since its establishment in the 1930s and its history of perseverance since then).

Epilogue: From Fintech to Ourtech—And Our Finance

We have covered a fair bit of ground in this book, from characterizing our present public–private franchise systems of payment and finance, through explaining how they came to be and why they were destined never to be more than a way-station *en route* to full citizen-managed money and finance, to describing in detail that better and final destination. Along the way I have clarified the nature of money, credit, payment, and finance themselves—in particular, their continuing and yet still hidden character as public–private franchise operations—along with the new payments technologies that are now helpfully returning those natures to public attention.

The hidden character of our systems' hybridity, I believe, is responsible for many delusions and misapprehensions, which manifest themselves in the persistence of dysfunctional monetary and financial arrangements that prevent our all being as productive and prosperous as we could be, all while subjecting us to exploitative privately owned mega-firms that extract from us without giving back to us. These drive a bipolar financial treadmill that in

Edward Cornell Professor of Law, Cornell University; Adjunct Professor of Finance, Georgetown McDonough School of Business; Senior Counsel, Westwood Capital, LLC; Advisory Board, Stanford Digital Currency Lab. Advisory Board, Digital Fiat Currency Institute; Advisory Board, Public Banking Institute. Advisory Board, Berkshares Digital Currency Project. Warm thanks to Dan Alpert, David Andolfatto, Kaushik Basu, Mark Blyth, Sarah Bloom Raskin, Blanca Braun, Michael Casey, Amy Castor, Jeni Dho, Rana Faroohar, Aaron James, Ro Khanna, Ron Kim, Sandra Lee, Jamie McAndrew, Paul McCulley, Katharina Pistor, Julia Salazar, George Selgin, Robert Shiller, Dan Tarullo, Paul Tucker, and Christine Yuan.

R. C. Hockett, *The Citizens' Ledger*,
https://doi.org/10.1007/978-3-030-99566-9

turn trips us by rushing more quickly than we can run and then holds us back by not moving at all.

This ceaseless, manic-depressive oscillation between unstoppable bubble and unforgiving bust is the inevitable upshot of a finance franchise arrangement in which the franchisor routinely forgets its role, standing by idly as rogue franchisees dispense low-quality knockoffs of its product—effectively "counterfeiting" it—with abandon.[1] That is where regular over-emission and misallocation of our monetized public full faith and credit across all contemporary commercial republics originates.[2]

The solution is to bring to the surface what has been there all along and then to correct it. Our mutual credit and debit relations effectively constitute one Citizens' Ledger in each of the world's commercial republics. Our monetized public full faith and credit—our money—just is the set of relations that constitute that ledger in each such republic. It is accordingly both our prerogative and our responsibility both to put and to keep this ledger—*our* ledger—to rights. That is in effect what the world's polities did in the realm of political relations when they replaced dynastic monarchies with citizen-constituted and—constituting republics. What remains to be done is to do likewise in respect of our monetary—that is, our credit and debit—relations within our *commercial* republics.

The trajectory of contemporary commercial and financial development, I maintain, is such as to recommend doing this reclamation in one simple stroke. That is the stroke of making our central banks and public fiscs *our* central banks and public fiscs, our public investments *our* public investments, and our monies *our* monies. Those, in our contemporary commercial republics, will be Citizens' Central Banks or Finance Ministries, central-bank- or finance-ministry-administered public savings and payments platforms, and associated Democratic Digital Currencies. Those, in our democratically productive commercial republics, will amount to Citizen Ledger Finance.

Notes

1. *See Finance without Financiers*, *supra* note 15, at 3 (arguing that lack of quality control over franchisee performance leads to poor modulation and allocation of credit resulting in lower utilization of productive capacity).
2. *Id*. at 2 (describing public full faith and credit as prone to over-generation and misallocation).

Index

R. C. Hockett, *The Citizens' Ledger*,
https://doi.org/10.1007/978-3-030-99566-9

Printed by Printforce, United Kingdom